PLAN YOUR OWN ESTATE

PASSING ON YOUR ASSETS AND YOUR VALUES LEGALLY AND EFFICIENTLY

Deirdre R. Wheatley-Liss

Apress®

President and Publisher: Paul Manning
Acquisitions Editor: Jeff Olson
Editorial Board: Steve Anglin, Mark Beckner, Ewan Buckingham, Gary Cornell, Louise Corrigan, Morgan Ertel, Jonathan Gennick, Jonathan Hassell, Robert Hutchinson, Michelle Lowman, James Markham, Matthew Moodie, Jeff Olson, Jeffrey Pepper, Douglas Pundick, Ben Renow-Clarke, Dominic Shakeshaft, Gwenan Spearing, Matt Wade, Tom Welsh
Coordinating Editor: Rita Fernando
Copy Editor: Tiffany Taylor
Compositor: Bytheway Publishing Services
Indexer: SPi Global
Cover Designer: Anna Ishchenko

Distributed to the book trade worldwide by Springer Science+Business Media New York, 233 Spring Street, 6th Floor, New York, NY 10013. Phone 1-800-SPRINGER, fax (201) 348-4505, e-mail orders-ny@springer-sbm.com, or visit www.springeronline.com. Apress Media, LLC is a California LLC and the sole member (owner) is Springer Science + Business Media Finance Inc (SSBM Finance Inc). SSBM Finance Inc is a **Delaware** corporation.

For information on translations, please e-mail rights@apress.com, or visit www.apress.com.

Apress and friends of ED books may be purchased in bulk for academic, corporate, or promotional use. eBook versions and licenses are also available for most titles. For more information, reference our Special Bulk Sales–eBook Licensing web page at www.apress.com/bulk-sales.

Any source code or other supplementary materials referenced by the author in this text is available to readers at www.apress.com. For detailed information about how to locate your book's source code, go to www.apress.com/source-code/.

*I would never have had the confidence
to start this project, or the determination
to finish it, without the love, support, and
encouragement of my terrific husband, Dave, and
our wonderful son, Trevor. So my love and thanks
to my men. This book is dedicated to you.*

Contents

About the Author

Deirdre R. Wheatley-Liss, Esq., is a practicing trusts and estates attorney with over 15 years' experience. Her passion is educating the public about the law so they can be empowered to use it to their benefit. She graduated with honors from Johns Hopkins University, earned her law degree at Boston College Law School, and holds an advanced Masters of Law degree in taxation from New York University School of Law. Deirdre authors the award-winning *New Jersey Estate Planning and Elder Law Blog*, and she is a sought-after speaker and contributor to national publications such as the *New York Times*, *Consumer Digest*, and *Money* magazine. Deirdre often hears that she makes estate planning and tax law "fun" and that she is adept at breaking down complex topics into understandable, and actionable, elements. She resides in northern New Jersey with her husband and son.

Acknowledgments

Wow! Who ever thought that I would be writing a book? For anyone reading this who isn't surprised, "Thank You!"—because you are one of the people who helped me on my path of career and life.

I didn't know any lawyers growing up, and I considered law school because (1) what else do you do with a degree in international relations? And (2) I graduated in the middle of a recession.

I found that I love the law. My parents wisely told me when I went to college (and had just gotten my first less-than-inspiring grade in an advanced math class I felt compelled to take) that it's OK to enjoy your classes, and that you can choose to do things because you love them, not just because they are challenging. When I took my first tax law class, I was fascinated by the tax code. Here are all these rules about how the government tries to enforce policy and mold society by the way it interacts with your money, and here are all these exceptions (again coming from behavior we as a nation want to encourage or discourage). So, I followed my parent's excellent advice and created a career helping people use the tax code and the law to their advantage, and here we are. See mom, I do listen to you! Thank you for all the hugs, encouragement, listening, and "because I am your mom" advice throughout the years.

This book would not exist without my lead editor, Jeff Olson, who sent me an e-mail one day asking "Have you ever considered writing a book?" and the whole team at Apress Publishing. Thank you, Jeff, not only for giving me this opportunity, but also for all the cheerleading, prodding, patience, guidance, kudos, and suggestions. If you like the book, let Jeff know—I think I have some other ones in me! If Jeff is the "big-picture guy," then Rita Fernando, as the coordinating editor, is the "get it done gal." I had no idea what goes into publishing a book, and truth be told I still don't know all the details, because Rita has elegantly orchestrated all the moving pieces to produce this wonderful work that would not exist without her efforts, for which I am eternally grateful. I also need to acknowledge and thank my copy editor, Tiffany Taylor, whose talent at finding just the right word or turn of phrase polished my thoughts to a gleaming shine.

Acknowledgments

Hank Fein is my mentor and one of the finest attorneys I know. The best way for me to thank him for all the knowledge and opportunities he has shared with me throughout the years is to hope that he finds some of his thought process being shared with the world through this book.

Everything I am as an attorney comes from the team around me and the clients we serve. I must thank the Fein Such family, my partners, and my colleagues for the help they offer clients every day in solving their problems and reaching their goals. A law practice is nothing without its clients, and I greatly appreciate the trust they have put in us over the years. It has allowed me to develop the experiences that I am proud and excited to share with you in this book. Enjoy!

Introduction
Welcome to the Wonderful World of Estate Planning

I admit that I'm a bit of an odd duck: I find the law, and taxes in particular, just fascinating. I have spent 15 years talking to people just like you about how to take advantage of tax law. Usually, people find themselves on one side or the other of the law—the right side or (and I hope you avoid this) the wrong side.

Estate planning is different. Although estate planning laws create an outline of how you transfer your property, for the most part the law creates default answers to the question "What happens to my stuff when I die?" The great part is that you're free to change the answer to that question to what works best for you, your family, and your situation. That is what this book is all about—taking advantage of the law to make sure that, upon your demise, your assets and values are shared for the benefit of your family, and not for the government or people you don't know.

There are rules, of course—certain things you can and can't do. After all, this is the law we are talking about. And the lawmakers in your state capital and Washington, DC, spend lots of time coming up with rules that impact how, and how much of, your hard-earned assets can be transferred to your family. You can treat your kids differently, for example, but you can't leave out your spouse. And although you can minimize taxes, you might not be able to avoid them entirely. However, once you understand what the rules are, you, the person reading this book right now, have the power to change your estate plan to take advantage of some rules and reduce the impact of others.

Let's Face Some Facts

I'm going to be blunt here: Everyone dies. The old adage is that death and taxes are unavoidable (but with good estate planning, taxes can be a whole lot less!). Another truism is that you can't take it with you. The flip side of this, and the heart of this book, is that you *can* direct how it's left behind.

But if you don't create an estate plan—make out a will or trust—then there are certain things you just can't do. The biggest one has to do with minor beneficiaries. Without an estate plan, for example, you can't name guardians for your kids or have assets managed for a beneficiary older than 18 or 21. You also can't take advantage of rules to minimize estate taxes. Most important, if you don't make your own estate plan, you miss an opportunity to pass your values to your family along with your assets.

I understand that thinking about estate planning—death, taxes, disability—is about as much fun as thinking about a root canal, but it doesn't have to be. In this book, you and I are going to have a conversation about what questions you should be asking yourself, your family, and your advisors about your estate plan. The key is the word *conversation*. This book isn't a lecture, a diatribe, or even a do-it-yourself blueprint. Instead, this book is designed to guide you into making decisions about your estate plan that are right for you and your family, and then teach you how to implement them. This is the same conversation I have with families sitting in my conference room.

Only about 35 percent of Americans have created their own estate plan. That's mindboggling, considering 100 percent of us will die. Although there are many reasons for this, the top two that I see are lack of actionable information and plain old procrastination. You have worked hard for your money and your family, and in the Internet age there is no end to the sources telling you that you "have to do this" or you "have to do that" with your money. What these sources often don't get to is the *why* of what is being recommended. Why do you want a trust for your kids? Why is asset protection important? Why do you need to be worried about long-term care costs? In this book, we have a conversation about the *why* so you can determine what recommendations work for you and your family.

Benjamin Franklin said, "You may delay, but time will not." The fact of the matter is that if you die without creating an estate plan, it's too late to do anything about it. You'll have lost the opportunity to provide for your family in accordance with your values, to defuse disputes among your beneficiaries, or to stick it to the government by paying less estate tax. For parents of young kids, a failure to plan means you'll be giving a judge the right to decide who raises your children.

Over time, your family, your assets, your goals, and even the law will change. You have the power to make an estate plan that works for you now and to change the plan so it keeps working for you in the future. The time to start is now, and this book is the place to begin.

You Already Have an Estate Plan—But You May Not Like Its Terms

I'm guessing you didn't know that, but it's true. If you don't create your own estate plan, the state that you live in has been kind enough to create one for you, through something called *intestacy* laws. Now, when the state came up with its rules for who gets your property when you die, do you think it had you specifically in mind? Of course not. What the state had in mind when creating intestacy laws was rules for making sure the state could figure out who gets your property after any creditors have been paid. In some states, the intestacy rule is that half goes to your spouse and half to your children—not the way most married folks would set up their own estate plan.

The intestacy laws are also problematic because they're old—as in King Henry V of England old. We inherited the basis of intestacy laws, and all estate planning laws, from our colonial forefathers (England for most of us, but Spain and France for some). As a result, the intestacy laws don't always work well in the modern world. For example, the age of inheritance without a will or trust in place is 18. Anyone out there think that 18 is a good age to inherit money and make wise, long-term decisions about it? Didn't think so.

By creating your own estate plan, you have the power to totally avoid the intestacy laws, so I'm not going to talk about them in detail (see how it can be easier to make a plan than not?). But to get out of the dusty web of the intestacy laws, you need to understand the intersection of your goals and assets, educate yourself about what laws apply, and take action to make it happen. Then you can cross "update my will" off your New Year's resolution list!

How the Book Works

I've created this book as a resource for you. Your needs are different than those of any other person who is reading this. When I meet with families, I have a checklist of things to cover, but each conversation is unique. Some families want more of an education; others have a specific situation they need to address. A client's answers to questions I ask may lead to a new path of questions I didn't anticipate, or give rise to the need to circle back to more education on a specific point.

I kept this dynamic in mind in designing this book, so it would be of value to you, the reader, regardless of whether you're starting from scratch, looking to review and update an existing estate plan, just trying to educate yourself, or seeking a guide to how to get a complete estate plan in place as efficiently as possible. Although the book can be read cover to cover, it can also be used in a nonlinear fashion. You may go straight to "Planning Guide for Singles" (Chapter 15) but then want more information about gifting and flip back to "Resource Guide: Gifting—Give it Away Now" (Chapter 9) to find out whether a gifting strategy works for you. You could start at "Action Guide: Getting Started" (Chapter 22) to find out step-by-step how to put an estate plan in place, and then go back to "What Are Your Assets?" (Chapter 3) to prepare for a meeting with your attorney.

Parts of the Book

The book is divided into five parts. The progression is from overview, to education, to examples, to action steps, but you can move to and from the parts and the chapters to fit your needs. Having said that, I strongly recommend that you read the first three chapters before getting started, so you can create your own unique viewpoint for how the information in the book can be useful to you.

- *Getting Started.* This first part focuses on why estate planning is important, takes you through a process of identifying your goals, and gives you the tools to understand what your assets are from an estate planning perspective.

- *Resource Guides.* This is the part of the book intended to educate you about, and dare I say even interest you in, all the rules that impact your estate plan. I talk about types of property ownership, what makes up a will, methods to distribute money at death other than a will, the myriad ways to use a trust to your advantage, tax laws, gifting, selecting the right fiduciary, and the other documents to round out your estate plan. I promise you that the knowledge delivered will be far more exciting than this list conveys (the topics seem dry even to me).

- *Planning Guides.* These chapters go through some of the most common estate planning situations that I see—married couples, singles, parents, partners, second marriages, special needs, and business owners all come to mind. The planning guides review the most-asked questions and answers to those questions, and talk about the particular laws and practicalities that you need to be aware of in those situations.

- *Action Guides.* These chapters provide the step-by-step guidance to go from adding "make up estate plan" to your to-do list to checking if off. Here you find ideas about how to select and work with an attorney or use online services, as well as forms to complete so you have all the information to put your plan in place. I will "sit down" with you and go through the same process I use with every estate planning client in my office. I also talk about everything you need to do to make sure your plan is complete, and to check in on it from time to time to make sure it's up to date.

- *Rosetta Stone and Appendixes.* Let's face it: legalese isn't plain English. Terms of art are used in estate planning that come from Latin, old English, and the tax code, and the arcane vocabulary creates a barrier to making good decisions. This section tears down that wall by giving you a plain English translation guide to all those technical terms. Think of it as your personal translator.

Inside Each Chapter

In addition to all the thoughts I can get on a page, in each chapter you'll find overviews and tips to help you put your new-found knowledge into action:

- *Chapter Brief.* Each chapter starts with highlights of the chapter's key points. Use these to get a bird's-eye view of the chapter and determine whether you want to delve into it in more detail now or move on and save it for later. ("Chapter Brief"—get it? Lawyers write briefs, and this is a short summary. Sadly, these are the jokes we lawyers think are funny.)

- *Ask the Attorney.* These are frequently asked questions (FAQ) that often come up with clients when discussing certain topics. I've added them so you can start thinking about what you want your estate plan to say. I also use them to point out what issues I, as an attorney, am concerned about when helping a client design their estate plan.

- *Let's Get Real.* Although your estate plan can say almost anything, there is the practical aspect that somebody will have to carry out your wishes. These are comments that tell you it's time to take a deep breath and think about how your goals will realistically be met.

- *Real Stories from Around My Conference Table.* Sometimes, the best way to grasp a point is to read a real-life example. The names have been changed to protect the innocent, but these are real-life estate planning situations that I have dealt with that you can learn from.

Caveats and Disclaimers

Can you believe that an attorney is adding in a disclaimer? Shocking—I know. The truth of the matter is that this book can only be a guide. It can educate you, empower you to make good decisions, and highlight things to avoid, but it can't actually create your estate plan. This book is a tool and a resource, and you can come back to it over time to get the most out of your estate plan investment, but it can't answer every question.

To develop a truly personal estate plan that fits your family and goals, you need to sit down with an attorney in your state who focuses on estate planning. To be honest, working with an estate planning attorney requires an investment of both time and money. If that isn't an investment you find will give you value right now, there are online do-it-yourself resources that might be right for you. However, you need to take the time to educate yourself about whether an online solution is comprehensive enough for your family. Lucky for you, you're reading this book right now, so you have in your hands the tools to make that decision!

Location, Location, Location

In estate planning, where you live and where you have lived are important. This book speaks in generalities, but each state has its own specific laws about how property can be transferred from one person to another and who has rights in that property. In a community property state like California, any property obtained by a married couple is joint property, regardless of whose name is on it. In a common law state like Virginia, a married person can acquire property in their own name. To complicate matters, if you move from California to Virginia, the property you acquired while living in California is subject to community property rules, even if you're a Virginia resident when you die.

Each state's property laws govern the real property (real estate) located in that state. So if you live in Colorado but have a summer place in Texas, the law of Texas will govern the distribution of your summer place when you die, even though the laws of Colorado will govern the distribution of the rest of your assets.

I talk about all the different types of property ownership in "Will Alternatives and Probate Avoidance" (Chapter 5), so you can skip ahead to there if you want to find out more now. However, only an attorney licensed in your state(s) will have the in-depth knowledge of the laws that might apply to you.

The Shifting Sands of Tax Law

It would be nice if the government had fixed tax rules that you could rely on with some degree of certainty so you could actually make an estate "plan." Sadly, when it comes to tax law, this isn't the case. It seems that every two years the first thing the new Congress decides it needs to do is change the tax laws. Whether you're in favor of whatever tax change is being made or not, when it comes to estate tax laws, the existence or nonexistence of a tax is a key element of what your estate plan should look like.

Unfortunately, for the past ten+ years, we have been dealing with temporary federal estate tax laws. The current laws governing taxation of estates for deaths in 2012 are set to expire at the end of 2012, and a new, even more taxing regime is scheduled to be put in place for 2013 and forward. In the meantime, President Obama has proposed a "permanent" estate tax law starting in 2013 that is different from the current law and the scheduled forthcoming law. (I put "permanent" in quotes because when it comes to tax law, "permanent" means "until it is changed.") Lucky for you, I've thought ahead so this book will be relevant no matter what the tax law. I have a web site at www.deirdrewheatleyliss.com where I will update the information, so check it out to make sure you're up to date.

To add to the confusion, due to all the changes in federal estate tax law in the recent past, 22 states and the District of Columbia have imposed their own state estate or inheritance tax as a way to maintain revenue. You may live or own property in one of these states (there is a complete listing in Chapter 8), and thus your estate plan must possibly account for both federal and state estate taxes.

How do you know what tax laws might apply to you and, more important, how to minimize or avoid them? First, flip ahead in the book and check out "Taxes—The Government as Your Beneficiary" (Chapter 8). If you have a taxable estate, consider speaking to a local lawyer who is an experienced estate planner. I'm not knocking real-estate attorneys or litigators or any other type of attorney, but estate planning is a specialized practice area, and tax law even more so. If taxes are an issue for you, you should consult with someone who works with them day in and day out, who is on top of all the changes, and who is as jazzed about using them for your advantage as I am.

Estate Plans Get Stale

Even without the headaches of the ever-changing estate tax laws, the estate plan you design today will likely fit you less well in the future. You may move, have children, have grandchildren, get married, get divorced, start a business, become wealthier, or spend your children's inheritance. All of these changes are part of life, but if your estate plan doesn't keep up with them, it will start to look and fit like that jacket you bought 15 years ago—you'll wonder what you were thinking and realize what a different person you are today.

An estate plan should be reviewed every three to five years. A complete review includes an examination of your current family, goals, and assets, as well as rereading your documents. Your attorney should advise you about this and be up front about how the review process works in their office. (Questions to ask when you do the initial plan: Will they contact you on a periodic basis? Will there be a separate charge?) It's worth investing an hour or two a few times a decade to keep your plan fresh. After all, if you die and your estate plan doesn't fit your family any more, they will be stuck with the results or have to shell out a lot of money in legal fees to fix it.

Do-It-Yourself (DIY)

This isn't a DIY guide. This isn't because you can't create your own estate plan online; you can, and for many this is a good solution. The reason this book isn't a DIY guide is that I don't know if you have a situation that calls for a DIY plan. And neither will you until after you read the pertinent parts of this book. After going through the book, you may want to seek professional advice, or you may want go online. You'll have a good idea whether one or the other is called for. The goal of the book is for you to be able to examine the complexities of your own situation and decide for yourself what action you want to take to get your plan in place. Here I talk about the questions you should be asking, the laws that guide the estate plan design, and practical points based on my experience with hundreds of other families in situations similar to yours.

Because we lawyers have such bad reputations (unfortunately much of which is well deserved—and yes, I have heard every shark and snake joke out there), I do want to give a plug for your local estate planning attorney. The value they can bring to your family is immense. They're familiar with the laws of your state as well as the peculiarities of your particular jurisdiction (just because your state law may say things happen one way doesn't mean your county clerk carries it out that way). Even if you're going the DIY route, it may be worth paying for an hour of an estate planning attorney's time to get your questions answered.

Don't forget that while you may look at your estate plan once, twice, or ten times in your life, an estate planning attorney looks at estate plans that many times in a week. At the end of the day, all the decisions you make here will become irrevocable. So, when you've gotten what you want and need out of this book, considering reserving time to look at Chapter 22 to find out how to create a solid attorney relationship.

What Are Your Goals?

Sometimes It's About *Who* You Are, Not *What* You Have

You need to start with the end in mind. Who do you want to have your stuff if you get hit by a bus? When should they have it? In this chapter, I talk about the top-level questions you need to be asking yourself to either develop an estate plan or makes sure your existing plan is still working for you.

▓ **Chapter Brief**   Who can you leave assets to, and who must you leave assets to? What does *asset protection* mean, and why should it be your number-one goal? If estate planning is a long-term plan about things that might happen years in the future, why is short-term planning important? Can you pass along your life experience and philosophy with your assets?

Building an estate plan is a bit like building a house. Some things are necessary and must go in a logical place, like floors, walls, plumbing, and electricity. This is similar to how the law mandates certain elements of an estate plan—you need to identify your fiduciaries and beneficiaries, and follow a blueprint of how they are to share in your estate. What makes a house a home, however, is what you put into it—the colors, furniture, and decoration. Similarly, what makes an estate plan uniquely yours is how it reflects your goals.

Before you start thinking about questions to identify and prioritize those goals, there are some assumptions I'm making about your goals based on my years of experience. Among other things, you don't want to pay any more taxes than you have to or pay them earlier than you need to. You don't want to create something so complicated that it will cost a fortune to carry out. You want to understand what most people do in your situation so you aren't guessing about the best way to do something, even though you may choose a different way to go.

I've built these assumptions into the advice I'm about to give. Let's start with a deceptively simple question.

Who Is Your Family?

This may seem obvious, but the deeper point is this: Whom do you want to protect or benefit when you aren't here anymore? In today's America, the group of people you're looking to protect or benefit can grow far beyond the traditional nuclear family. Although your gut reaction may be "I want to protect my husband and kids," it's still valuable to go through a discussion about what other people might be part of your "family" for purposes of estate planning. In doing this, you may find that your world of beneficiaries has grown or that your gut reaction was right on target.

To make your time spent going through this list more valuable, I strongly suggest you make notes of the people you would like to benefit. (It's your book—hit the note button on your Kindle, or grab a pen and start writing in the margins!) Right now, you don't need to get to the point of *what* you would like to give people or *how* you want them to receive it; just note that this is a person you're considering including in your estate plan. And remember, there is no right or wrong—it's your stuff, and you worked hard for it. You can leave it to (almost) anyone you want:

- *Spouse.* Again, obvious. However, there are some finer points about your spouse as beneficiary. A spouse is one of the few people you can't eliminate as a beneficiary, which I'll talk about later. Also, if you have a same-sex marriage or civil union, be aware that it's only valid under the state law that created it, not federal law.

- *Partner.* More and more often, I encounter couples who are part of the same economic unit because they live together and share expenses, but they're not married. The intestacy laws don't provide at all for a partner, so you must create your own estate plan.

- *Children.* Different considerations must be given to how to leave assets to young children, who can't control their own wealth, and adult children, who may be better off having it left for them in a trust. Do you have stepchildren? Are they to be treated the same as your natural children? Are there people who are in a child-like relationship to you, even though they aren't your legal children?

- *Parents.* Have you seen the cost of long-term care these days? It's upward of $10,000 a month in places. Some children are concerned about their parents being able to provide for themselves in their senior years. Alternatively, your parents may be dependent on you. There are also situations where you might have joint economic interests with your parents that need be addressed separately from assets you're leaving to your spouse.

- *Grandchildren.* Perhaps you feel that your children have already done well for themselves, and your grandchildren are your priority. Are you providing for them equally? Maybe instead you want to make sure each of your grandchildren "gets something" upon your death. Are they old enough to manage the money, or does somebody else need to manage it for them?

- *Siblings.* If you choose to leave assets to your siblings, are you treating each of them the same, or do you want to leave more to some and less or none to others? Do you own any assets with siblings that you need to be sure go to that person?

- *Nieces and nephews.* If you include them, even as contingent beneficiaries, do you want to leave more to some and less to others, or perhaps a fixed amount, and leave the balance of the estate to somebody else? Are they old enough to be able to manage the assets by themselves, or would they benefit from a trust for any reason?

- *Sons-in-law and daughters-in-law.* To answer the question now forming in your mind, the vast majority of people provide only for their children and grandchildren and exclude sons-in-law and daughters-in-law (so much so that I often refer to them as "out-laws" in our planning discussions). The most common reason? If a person is still married to your son/daughter or parenting your grandchild, that person can receive an indirect benefit from the inheritance because there is more money in the family unit. However, if there's a divorce or that person is otherwise no longer part of the family, then they're excluded from receiving the benefit of any inheritance. Sometimes, though, you just may not like who your kids married, and that's fine.

- *Pets.* For many people, their pets are unquestionably members of their family. In some states you can leave assets in a trust for the benefit of your pet. Regardless, your estate plan should give direction (and funding) for how your pet is to be cared for if you're no longer here.

■ **Real Stories from Around My Conference Table**   Brandy and Vinny, a committed couple, didn't have children but had a menagerie (the usual dogs and cats, plus a parrot and a horse) that they loved as their family and wanted to make sure were cared for. I created a trust so that after the second of them died, all the assets would be held for the benefit of their pets to pay for their care, including caregivers, in the manner in which the pets had become accustomed to living (which was in a very nice manner, I must say), and that any balance after would go to animal charities. Although this may not be your plan, Brandy and Vinny created an estate plan to benefit those they truly loved.

- *Friends.* Not everybody wants to leave their assets to their family—in some cases your friends are more family than blood relatives are. In this situation, it's even more important to get professional advice about putting together your estate plan. I can't tell you how many times blood relatives that someone hadn't spoken to in years have hired an attorney because that person didn't provide for them in their will.

- *Charity.* Many people are consistent supporters of a charity, be it their house of worship, alma mater, or favorite nonprofit organization. If supporting a charity is important to you, you should think about how to provide for that organization upon your death. Some people give a small, fixed amount, and others, like Brandy and Vinny, make large gifts to charity upon their death under the theory that they're not using it anymore and the charity could benefit more than anybody else.

What Are Your Responsibilities?

You've gone through who you might want to be your beneficiaries—let's call them your *intended beneficiaries*. There are also certain people who must be beneficiaries—even if you don't want them to get a dime. And the kicker? The amounts that you're free to leave to your intended beneficiaries can only be calculated after payment has been made to your unintended ones.

You Can't Forget About Your Spouse

You aren't allowed to disinherit your spouse, even if you want to. All 50 states have laws that entitle your spouse to some part of your estate. Why? Because your state doesn't want you to impoverish your spouse in favor of your children, girlfriend, pool boy, or whomever. So even if your estate plan excludes your spouse, they can claim some part of your estate.

Ask the Attorney "Deirdre, I've heard that my senior citizen parents should leave everything to me and nothing to each other so they won't lose the house if they get sick. True?" First, please consider the source of that advice—I'm betting it wasn't an estate attorney. It's true that senior citizen couples often are very afraid that they will lose all their assets to the costs of long-term care, so they change their wills to leave their assets to their children. Although the fear is real, the problem is that the spouse's right to the assets is an asset itself, and failure of the spouse to exercise that right is considered a transfer of that asset to the children, which ironically could disqualify the spouse from the very benefits they need to provide for their long-term care. This is why you need legal advice from a lawyer—you don't get medical advice from your hairdresser, do you?

In most states, a spouse has something called an *elective share right*, which provides that even if the spouse is excluded from the will, they're entitled to approximately one third of the total amount of assets being transferred as a result of your death.

In other states, a husband has *dower rights* and a wife *curtesy rights*—think Jane Austen novels to get the historical background of these. Although only in force in a few states (Hawaii, Kentucky, Massachusetts, Michigan, Ohio, and Vermont), dower rights give a husband the right to one third of all of the wife's property, and curtesy rights give the wife a life estate (the right to live for life) in any of the husband's real estate. In a modern will where the spouses have provided for each other, these rights are waived.

In community property states (Arizona, California, Idaho, Louisiana, Nevada, New Mexico, Texas, Washington, and Wisconsin), each spouse is entitled to 50% of all property acquired during the marriage and thus already owns half of the first spouse's assets when he or she dies, so that half can't be left to anyone else.

Creditors Come First

I'm pretty sure that in your list of intended beneficiaries, you didn't name your mortgage company, a credit card company, the hospital, the funeral home, or even the lawyer or accountant working on your estate. However, all of these people and companies are entitled to get paid before your intended beneficiaries receive anything. Although mortgages might be able to continue (more on that in the next chapter), generally speaking, your debts are due when your time here on Earth expires.

Let's Get Real If you want to be sure your intended beneficiaries receive at least $X amount of dollars when you die, you may want to consider taking out a term life insurance policy to create those dollars at the time of your death.

Uncle Sam

What? You forgot to name dear ol' Uncle Sam on your list of intended beneficiaries? Don't worry. He can take care of himself through the beauty of tax laws. Although the most obvious tax in estate planning is the estate tax, whether on the federal or state level, Uncle Sam is a sly guy who's been around for years and knows there's more than one way to take a bite out of an apple. In the next chapter, "What Are Your Assets?" you'll see that retirement plans are particularly tasty because of all that yet-to-be-taxed accumulation.

The same as a creditor, if Uncle Sam is your beneficiary, his take will reduce the amount passing to your intended beneficiaries. I'll cover what Uncle Sam's share is, and how to minimize it, in Chapter 8, "Taxes—The Government as Your Beneficiary."

What Is Equal and Fair?

By now you have an idea of whom you want to provide for and whom you must provide for. The next question is, how do you prioritize among all of your intended beneficiaries? If you were to get hit by a bus tomorrow, who would get what? Don't think too hard—what you're looking for here is a visceral response of who you're concerned about. Maybe your kids are great, but your grandkids come to mind. Maybe it's really your dog you're worried about because everyone else can take care of themselves.

Who Comes First

Let's say your goal is to provide for your spouse and children. Does that mean you leave everything to your wife, and after that it's up to her? Are you concerned that she might get remarried and that your hard-earned assets might end up going to another spouse or other children? Instead, maybe you want your husband and kids, and just them, to all share the same pot of money.

Within your estate plan you have *primary beneficiaries*—the people who get whatever you leave them merely because they survived you. You also have *contingent beneficiaries*—the people who share in your estate only if a condition happens, such as someone (a spouse, in many cases) predeceasing you. Your contingent beneficiaries might also get what remains in a trust when the primary beneficiary dies (like leftovers).

Because it's your estate plan, the choice of how you prioritize is entirely up to you. Perhaps your reasoning is based on a person's relationship to you (you want to benefit your spouse before your children, or your partner and children equally), or their age (you're more concerned with a younger beneficiary than one who is already settled), or their needs (one niece is a doctor, the other a dance teacher), or who has been most involved in your life (a friend who has cared for you versus cousins you rarely see).

Go back to the list where you jotted down your beneficiaries, and put a number 1 by those who would be primary, a 2 by those who would be contingent, and a ? by those you aren't sure about.

Giving to Groups

What if your goal is to leave your money to a group of people, and you don't know right now who those people are? For example, if you say "children" or "grandchildren," you could have more of them between the time you write the will and the time you pass away. You need to be clear in your mind about whether the group you're leaving the money to is the group as it exists today (a *closed* group) or the group as it exists in the future (an *open* group).

You should also think about what happens if one of the members of that group passes away. Should their share go to the other members of the group, or should their children perhaps stand in their shoes?

Guess what's next? You got it. Update that list of intended beneficiaries. (Do you see now why I had you write them down?) Go back to your list, and note "closed" or "open" next to any group of beneficiaries. If your plan is that their children can take their place if they aren't living, put a + by the group to signify that it's open.

Specific Gifts

Most people put their beneficiaries into the categories of "I want these people to get something" and "I want these people to get most everything." For the "something" people, you should consider how you want them to be named in your plan, if at all. They could be remembered with a fixed amount of money or a thing—"$5,000 to each of my grandchildren," or "my lake house to my sister."

I talk about all the issues surrounding specific bequests (and yes, there is a whole host of issues) in Chapter 4, "What Goes into a Will?" Feel free to skip ahead if you want to know more now. If not, go back to your list of intended beneficiaries and jot down amounts of money or things that you might consider leaving the "something" beneficiaries.

Asset Protection—How Are Assets Given?

How will you give your assets to your intended beneficiaries? You're just going to hand them over, right? Wrong. In creating your estate plan, you can do something for your beneficiaries that you can't do for yourself. You have the power to create a vehicle in which the assets that you give your loved one can be available for their benefit, but not available to any of their creditors. If creditors aren't your concern—and after reading the next section, I'd lay odds that they will become your concern—what about beneficiaries who can't manage their own money because they're too young, they don't have the skills, or you're concerned about other influences in their lives (like friends and spouses you haven't yet met, or substance abuse problems)? Not convinced that asset protection planning should be your number-one estate planning goal? Read on.

Creditors and Predators

There is a world of people out there who are far more interested in getting their hands on your money than in working for their own. I put them in two categories: creditors and predators.

Creditors are the people your beneficiaries owe money to over their lifetimes, whether they intend to create a debt or not. The big example that comes to mind is the soon-to-be ex-spouse in a divorce. Having to pay half your assets over to someone you're ending a relationship with feels a lot like getting sued and losing. Generally speaking, inheritances are exempt from being distributed as part of a divorce. But in real life, a beneficiary often takes that inherited money and commingles it with the spouse (by buying a house in joint names or creating a joint account)—and now the inherited money has been converted into marital property, and the out-law may end up with half. I'm guessing that's probably not your plan. By leaving that same inheritance to your beneficiary in a way that protects it from marital claims, the beneficiary can use the money, but if the marriage ends, the spouse won't have a claim. Think this situation doesn't apply to you? Consider that about 45% of marriages end in divorce.

Not worried about anybody getting divorced? Well, are your intended beneficiaries successful—perhaps including a doctor, a lawyer, or a business owner? All these successful professionals have a higher risk profile for litigation than the average person. When someone becomes unhappy with the services they received, they may see your beneficiary as having deep pockets and start a lawsuit to get "their share" of those assets. Wouldn't it be nice if the inheritance was set up in such a manner that no lawsuit could touch it?

It could be that you internally snicker at the thought of your beneficiaries actually being successful. Maybe they never met a dime they weren't willing to spend as if it was a quarter, or they're trying to "find themselves," or they're too young, by age or attitude, to manage the type of money you're leaving to them. These are beneficiaries who might be facing bankruptcy, foreclosure, or the inability to support their lifestyle. What if instead of your inheritance going straight to their creditors, you could make it available to them but not to pay off any of those debts?

Predators are people who might influence your beneficiaries in the future. The good-for-nothing son-in-law, the boyfriend you haven't met yet, the spendthrift wife, the friend who knows that the end of the rainbow is "just around the corner," and the "insignificant other" all come to mind. Such people convince your son to buy the house he can't afford, your daughter to support their burning desire to run a restaurant, your spouse that "if you loved me" you'd put everything in joint names. I really don't have a poor opinion of human nature—people like this are the minority of the population. Unfortunately, they're attracted to money.

Scared you yet? Don't worry, there is a solution, and you'll read all about it in Chapter 6, "Trust in Trusts." My goal here is to get you to think not only of *who* you want to leave your assets to and *what* you want to leave to them, but *how* you leave your assets to your beneficiaries.

Minors

By law, minors can't inherit money directly. It must be put in a trust for their benefit or held in a custodial account. Or, if you have totally failed to plan, your local court will hold the money. That's right: if you don't create an estate plan, some judge you never met, or some person the judge appointed, will be managing your kids' money until they turn 18. Another point: the age of legal adulthood is 18 in most states. Raise your hand if *you* had great decision-making skills at 18. Yeah, didn't think so.

Also bear in mind that being a legal adult doesn't equate to having the skills to handle finances. You have created your wealth over years and years. You have made mistakes along the way. Much of your wealth is tied up in assets that you don't think of as being available to spend—your house, your retirement plan, that rainy-day fund. However, for your minor beneficiaries, everything is turned into cash.

We've all heard stories about lottery winners who were broke two years later. Is it because they were dumb or so much different from you? No, it's generally because they're under the influence of predators, have creditors, and simply never developed the financial skills to manage money. Managing money is a learned skill—it doesn't magically appear as a download in your brain at the age of 18, 28, or even 38. When leaving money for the benefit of younger people, you should consider how you can create a situation in which they get the benefit of the dollars and can gain the skills to manage and maintain the value of the inheritance you gave them. What's that word I'm looking for? *Trusts.*

Special Needs

Some people in your family may never be able to manage money. They may have a mental or physical disability, or they may even be potentially dependent on the state to provide assistance for them. Other times the disability is self-imposed—alcohol and drug abuse come to mind.

If you wouldn't turn money over to one of your beneficiaries outright right now to do with what they wish, but you might consider spending it on their behalf instead, then you need to think about how that goal can be mimicked in your estate plan. If your intended beneficiary is currently receiving financial assistance from the state, understand that any outright inheritance will make them ineligible for public benefits until the inheritance is entirely spent—thus leaving them with none of the security you planned for. Again, the answer you're looking for is *trusts.*

What about the Short Term?

Estate planning focuses on the long-term—when you die "at some point in future," and planning for the possible marriages, professional choices, or divorces of beneficiaries who might be 5 or not even born yet. But in putting together your estate plan, you also need to consider the short term. Just because you got hit by a bus doesn't mean the mortgage doesn't need to be paid, your bills aren't due, or your spouse doesn't need cash until she can go back to work.

What will your spouse, children, and partner need immediately to maintain their lifestyles? Is sufficient money available between your bank account and life insurance policies? Do they even know where your will is or have a list of all your financial assets? My recommendation: make sure you have immediately available liquid assets to cover three months of living expenses and that somebody in your family knows where all the important documents are in the event you pass away. And look at Chapter 5, "Will Alternatives and Probate Avoidance," to make sure some of the estate is immediately available.

What Are Your Values?

You now know who your intended beneficiaries are. You've thought about how you might want to prioritize among them and protect the inheritance from creditors and predators. But what part of *you* are you leaving to your beneficiaries? What have you accomplished in your life that's important to you and that you want to see carried on?

An estate plan can be a simple passing of property. Or it can be a reflection of how you came to be *you*. It doesn't have to be dry and boring and only something your lawyer comes up with. You can inject life (no pun intended) into your estate plan by taking the time to think about what you want to leave your beneficiaries other than your assets.

Establishing a Legacy

Let me be honest with you. Your will or trust, or anything else drafted by your attorney, doesn't normally reflect the heart of who you are. It talks in very dry terms about who gets what, when, and how. The old-fashioned style often buries in mounds of legalese the important goals you're trying to reach. So here are some ideas of things you might want to add to your estate plan to make it more *yours* and leave behind part of you along with your money:

- Set aside a fixed amount for your beneficiaries, and direct them to go on a trip with it—maybe somewhere you went as a family or somewhere they've always wanted to go.

- Leave money to your church, synagogue, or favorite charity with instructions to your beneficiary for how they can use it to honor you, so they become involved in the organization.

- Want to make sure your grandkids learn Greek? Set aside enough money every year for them to be able to take language lessons. And consider rewarding all that learning with a trip that lets them experience their heritage.

- Was your year abroad during college or your summer at camp a life-changing experience for you? Tell your trustees to make sure your children have the same opportunity.

- Want your child to have the honor of serving their country? Set aside money to supplement their living expenses while they're in the service.

Just as you decorate your house to reflect who you are, tell your attorney to make additions to your estate plan to reflect your values. This document is your legacy—it's part of your last communication with your family. Shouldn't it be something that makes them smile?

Disincentive

Sometimes I meet people who don't want to reward their beneficiaries for certain actions, or create incentives, but instead want to punish them for their perceived "bad behavior." First, some "if you do this / don't do this, then you get nothing" provisions are unenforceable as a matter of law. This includes, for example, mandating that somebody get divorced, or making the inheritance contingent on an heir marrying someone of a certain race or religion.

Second, why are you taking this stand in your will, of all places? If something is that important to you, why not communicate it to that person now? Give them a chance to see your point of view while you're still around to understand their point of view as well, and see if the situation changes. Remember, once a will goes into effect, you're dead—your words will live on forever, even if the people have changed.

■ **Let's Get Real**   This isn't *Dynasty*, *Dallas*, *Melrose Place*, or Wisteria Lane—this is real life, and your will shouldn't be a time for surprise. If you don't want to benefit someone, fine—leave them out. If you want to encourage action, structure incentives. If you want to "stick it to them" for doing you wrong, you need to make it simple. A Machiavellian scheme will be impossible to carry out, and let's face it; you won't be here to see it anyway. I encourage you to look at those you want to benefit and focus on them instead of those you don't—in the case of those people, you just don't add them as beneficiaries and move your energy and focus to others.

Wishes

Beyond what you're giving your beneficiaries, there's a world of things you hope your beneficiaries do with the money and in their lifetimes in general. You may want your spouse to take that second honeymoon you never got around to, or you may look at your 10-year-old niece and say to yourself, "I want her to have her dream of trying for Broadway." Some things you can't mandate, but just because wishes aren't legally enforceable doesn't mean you shouldn't make them for those you love.

I encourage you to write a letter to your fiduciaries and beneficiaries each year. In this letter, talk about what you think is important to be done in their lives. Use this letter to tell your fiduciary what you see your kids interested in now and what you would like to do to support that. You can tell your children what you hope they consider doing with their inheritance. Share with your spouse which advisors you think he should trust. The advice you give is entirely up to you. You can rip up last year's letter as you start each new one, or keep them as a family history.

I've handled hundreds of estates. I've seen families grieving, angry, and suing each other. I've also seen families celebrating their loved one's life instead of mourning their loss. Your best legacy is the people you leave behind, not the money. What do you want those people to know about you?

What Are Your Assets?
Sometimes It's About *What* You Have, Not *Who* You Are

It's not just how much you have but what you have that can drive your estate plan. This chapter discusses different categories of property, such as your "stuff," real estate, retirement accounts, and insurance, and how those assets coordinate with your goals. I also talk about your debts and liabilities, so you can calculate the total value of your estate. If you want to come up with the value while you're going through this chapter, flip back to the appendixes and fill in the form titled "Financial Questionnaire" as you go through this chapter.

Chapter Brief What amount of each asset belongs to you for purposes of estate planning? How do you add up all your assets in the world of estate planning? What makes real estate different from other assets? Why are retirement accounts so expensive to inherit? How do you value your estate today and in the future?

What's It All Worth?

Value is one of those gray areas. My piano, passed down from my grandmother, might be invaluable to me, but if you don't play, it might only be a dust magnet to you. What's that piano really worth?

The value of your assets for estate planning purposes can determine how much you have to pay in taxes or how expensive your probate or estate administration will be. Needless to say, there's a natural inclination on the part of families to show the value of assets as being as low as possible. The government is a bit smarter than that, however, and has a rule that the value of an asset in your estate is the *fair market value*: what a willing buyer and a willing seller, both in possession of all the facts, would decide is the transaction price of the asset. In my piano example, it's as if a dealer of pianos (without the emotional ties to my piano) was making a deal with a person who wanted a 65-year-old piano, and they both knew all the facts about the piano and arrived quickly at a price. That price is the fair market value. When valuing your assets to come up with a total estate value, try not to hedge on the low or high side, but look at what the asset is objectively worth to a hypothetical third-party buyer.[1]

How Much Is Yours?

How much do you actually own of what you consider to be yours? At its heart, estate planning is about passing property from one person to another. So, when you put together your estate plan, you need to know what property is yours to distribute. The way property is titled is key:

- *100% fee simple.* These assets are 100% yours—they're all in your name and nobody else's, and your estate plan will control who gets them upon your death.

- *Joint tenants with right of survivorship.* You own 50% of the asset (or a proportionate share if there are more than two owners). Upon your death, the other owner(s) will receive this property, regardless of what your estate plan says. If you aren't sure what kind of joint ownership you have, see if the title reads "A *or* B"; if so, it's likely joint tenants with right of survivorship.

- *Tenants by the entireties.* This form of property ownership applies only to a husband and wife who own an asset jointly, and generally only in the case of real property. Each spouse owns an undivided 100% of the property. Upon one spouse's death, the other takes ownership of the property, regardless of what your estate plan says.

---

[1] The value of some assets is obvious—you can look up the value of your bank account or investment accounts. Some asset values are a shot in the dark, like that of your business or inherited artwork. To get a handle on the value of those assets you need to get an appraisal from an expert. And yes, it will cost you some dollars.

- *Tenants in common.* You own 50% of the asset (or whatever other percentage is noted on the title of the asset). Upon your death, your estate plan will control the distribution of your percentage interest in this property. If you aren't sure what kind of joint ownership you have, see if it says "C *and* D"; if so, then it's tenants in common.

In Chapter 5, "Will Alternatives and Probate Avoidance," I give you some ideas of how you might use these different types of property ownership to your advantage.

If you're single, when calculating the value of your estate, add up your own assets even if you're in an economic relationship with someone else. If any are joint assets, make a note about them. If you're married, count all of your assets but put them into the categories Husband, Wife, and Joint.[2]

Personal Property

Personal property is your stuff: the things in your house that you wear, look at, sit on, or use as part of your everyday life. It's what goes into the moving van when you relocate and includes your jewelry, household items, pictures, decorations, family heirlooms, wardrobe, and furniture.

The funny thing about your personal property is that it may have little or no monetary value but can have unlimited sentimental value. In considering the value of your personal property, think about those items that you want to see preserved and those items that can be donated or recycled. You also need to identify items that truly do have value to a third party, such as jewelry, artwork, and collectible furniture. Put your best estimate of the value of all your stuff on the worksheet.

■ **Let's Get Real**   One of the most-litigated areas of an estate is who gets the personal property. This has nothing to do with the property's extrinsic value and everything to do with who is perceived to be more or less important in the family. One daughter may claim that you gave her your engagement ring before you died, or "promised it to her," and the others may not agree. One son may come in before you're even cold and clean out the entire house, refusing to allow anybody else to even see your stuff. I've seen situations in which a person can't let go of stuff and has to be evicted from the house so it can be sold. You need to consider practical ways to distribute personal property. If you have one engagement ring and two daughters, you might direct that the ring be

---

[2] There are financial worksheets in the appendixes (married and single) to help you put together a snapshot of the value of your estate.

sold. If you tell your executor to make scanned copies of all the family photos, everybody can share in them. You can have a "pick 'em" provision where all your beneficiaries draw numbers and pick which assets they want in numerical order. Or, if your beneficiaries can't agree, you can have a "sell 'em" provision that says if the kids can't agree on how to divide your stuff, your executor is to sell everything.

Real Estate

Real estate includes any interest you have in any piece of real property—house, condominium, commercial building, undeveloped parcel of land, and so on. Real estate, for the purposes of describing your assets, doesn't include any real estate owned by another entity such as a corporation, LLC, or trust. For now, make note of the fair market value of your share of the real estate.

In-State

Identify whether the real property is located in the state where you live or in another state. If the property is located in the state where you live, its distribution will be controlled by both your estate plan and the laws of that state.

In order to get a decent approximation of the value of any residential real estate, look at the website www.zillow.com. Another place to look for value is your real estate tax bill, but be aware that the assessed value for real estate tax purposes may not have a significant correlation to the fair market value of the real estate. For now, ignore any mortgages—I get into those later in the chapter.

Out-Of-State

Real estate located outside of the state where you live (or outside of the United States) warrants special consideration in your estate plan. Your estate plan will identify the beneficiaries of the real estate, but because the real estate is located in another jurisdiction, the laws of that jurisdiction will govern the distribution of the real estate. For example, suppose you live in Illinois and have a summer place in Wisconsin. Your executor opens a probate in Illinois upon your death. However, you may need a separate probate proceeding in Wisconsin (known as an *ancillary probate*) just to deal with the distribution of the summer home. Oh, and even if you don't have an estate tax in your state, there may be one in the state where the property is located.

▨ **Ask the Attorney** "Deirdre, How do I avoid a second probate if I own property in another state?" The easiest way is to hold title to the property in a vehicle that doesn't die when you do. I generally recommend using a limited liability company or revocable trust in this situation.

Cash Assets

Think of your cash assets as all your liquid assets. These might be held in money market accounts, bank accounts, or credit union accounts. They also include any significant cash that you maintain (like that lump under your mattress) and any certificates of deposit or CDs.

With all your cash accounts, you likely get a monthly statement telling you the exact end-of-the-month balance. Gather up copies of these statements and assign a current value to your cash assets.

▨ **Let's Get Real** Do you want to know the best feeling for an estate planning attorney? When a client comes in not with my financial worksheet filled out by hand, but with a printout of all their assets and liabilities. Ahh, nirvana. Seriously, the advice I give you is only as good as the information you give me. So, if you're looking at your estate plan, there is nothing wrong with doing a little financial housekeeping and seeing if Excel, Quicken, or Mint.com might work for you.

Investment Assets

Investment assets encompass your stocks, bonds, mutual funds, and other similar investments. These include any stocks or bonds that you have in physical form (that is, the stock certificate or actual bond is sitting in your safe deposit box) as well as those that are titled in an investment account held by your broker. Also add any dividend reinvestment (DRIP) accounts and investments in publicly traded real estate investment trusts (REITs). The goal is to capture the value of all assets that are publicly traded and have a readily available market.

For those investments that you hold in certificate form—you have physical possession of the actual stock certificate or bond—you'll have to do some research to find out their value. I suggest Google as a starting place. For the rest of your investments, you receive monthly or quarterly statements. Gather the most recent statements and add up the numbers to identify the current value of your investment assets.

▨ **Let's Get Real** It's a pain to have to deal with actual stock certificates in an estate administration. Sometimes the companies don't exist anymore, or there were stock splits, and so on, and you weren't issued additional certificates. Hours have to be spent researching this. Any transfer of the certificates needs to be *medallion guaranteed*, which means the fiduciary must take themselves and the stocks to a brokerage house to approve their signature before any transfers of the stock can be made. Do yourself and your beneficiaries a favor, and save yourself a ton of money—while you're still alive and kicking, take those certificates to your local discount broker house (such as Fidelity or E*TRADE) and put them into an investment account instead of keeping them in certificate format. Your beneficiaries (and their attorney) will thank you.

Retirement Accounts

Retirement accounts are very special creatures in the world of estate planning—and not necessarily because they're wonderful. Retirement accounts are terrific at the goal of making money available to you when you retire. In a typical retirement account (401(k), IRA, 403(b), SEP, pension plan, and so on—but not a Roth account) you set aside money for your retirement on a pretax basis. Because you didn't pay income tax on it when you put it into the account, income tax must be paid when it's withdrawn from the account.

When your beneficiaries inherit your retirement account, they then become responsible for paying income tax on any withdrawals from the account. To put this in context, say you name Renee as the beneficiary of your IRA, which has $100,000 in it when you die. Renee might only net around $70,000 after she pays all the federal and state income taxes on the withdrawals. If you instead gave Renee an investment account with $100,000, she would inherit the full amount.

In addition to paying income taxes on any withdrawals, a beneficiary of a retirement account, other than a spouse, must make withdrawals from the account starting at the time when they receive it—the beneficiary can't defer the withdrawals until their own retirement. The spouse has the option of doing a *rollover* of a retirement account into a new retirement account in their own name, which lets them defer making withdrawals until they reach age 70.5.

Oh, and even though retirement plans are subject to income tax, they're still part of your estate for calculating any estate tax. So, in my example, Renee may have to pay both income and estate tax on that IRA you left her, potentially bringing its value down to $50,000 or less. See why Uncle Sam loves IRAs so much?

Not all retirement accounts are the same—401(k)s and IRAs are both tax-deferred accounts, but the distribution rules can be different. A Roth IRA or 401(k) is funded with after-tax dollars, which are tax-free upon withdrawal. The world of investment options dealing with retirement planning is well beyond the scope of this book, but I encourage you (after you finish your estate plan!) to get a book on personal financial planning with retirement accounts.

You likely receive a monthly or quarterly statement giving the value of your retirement plans. Add those amounts together, and put them in the retirement plan section of your asset worksheet. Don't deduct the unpaid income taxes—they're not a deduction for purposes of determining any estate tax that might be due. If you're married, the retirement plan is an individual asset of the spouse who owns it. For those of you lucky enough to have a pension plan, speak to your HR department or go online to find out the pension plan's value at your death.

Life Insurance

Yes, life insurance is an asset of your estate. And yes, you value it based on the death benefit. Some people come to me convinced that life insurance isn't part of their estate, that it's somehow "different." Not true. If you own a life insurance policy on your own life, the death benefit of the policy is an asset of your estate.

When it comes to taxable estates, life insurance can be a particularly sneaky asset. Let's say Dan is a concerned father who took out a $1 million term life insurance policy when his first child was born. When Dan dies, $1 million is immediately added to his estate. If Dan lives in a jurisdiction with a low estate tax threshold (New Jersey at $675,000, for example), or the federal threshold is reduced to $1 million, the payment of the insurance itself can create an estate tax. Dan might have had $500,000 before he died, but because of the insurance, he has $1.5 million as of the moment of death. Instead of Dan's three kids getting 100% of the death benefit as Dan intended, they have to share it with Uncle Sam.

Life insurance is a very important tool in estate planning. I don't sell it, and I don't get paid when anybody buys it, but I recognize its value enough that an entire chapter of this book is devoted to life insurance: Chapter 10, "Insurance Trusts—Magic Tax-Reduction Trick."

For now, you need to identify each life insurance policy you have as well as the owner, the insured, the beneficiary, and the death benefit. Don't forget about life insurance policies you have through your employer—those count too.

Business Interests

Any ownership interest that you have in a company that isn't publicly traded should be listed as a business interest. This could be a corporation, a limited liability company, a partnership, a limited partnership, or an unincorporated business that you're operating under your own name or a trade name.

The first question in determining the value of your business interest is: Do you have an agreement with anybody to sell your business to them in the event of your death—such as a shareholders' agreement, partnership agreement, or operating agreement? If you do, the value set forth in the agreement is normally the value of your share of the business in the event of your death. If you don't have such an agreement, list the value for which you think somebody would purchase your share of the business, after taking into account any business liabilities that need to be paid.

■ **Real Stories from Around My Conference Table**   Mike and Kevin owned a successful software company that allowed both of them to make a very decent living. Kevin unexpectedly died, and his wife Danielle found herself having to deal with the business. At the same time, Mike found himself working twice as hard and needing to hire new staff to take over the roles Kevin played in the company. Danielle was concerned about her family and wanted her interest in the company to be liquidated as soon as possible at a high price. Mike was experiencing a cash crunch and wanted to pay a small amount for Kevin's interest, and only over a period of years. Long story short, Danielle ended up suing Mike. In the end, the company was liquidated, leaving them both with less than they would've gotten had they been able to work out a deal. The only people who made money were the lawyers. The moral? If you own a business with another person, you must have an agreement with them that deals with how the business will be sold to the surviving owner(s), how the price will be determined, and what the payout terms will be.

If you own your own business, look at Chapter 18, "Planning Guide for the Family Business," for strategies to work into your estate plan.

Trusts

You may already have an interest in a trust as a grantor, beneficiary, or trustee. In some cases, the assets in that trust are part of your estate. You need an attorney to tell you for sure, but here are some guidelines:

- *Grantor of revocable trust.* If you're the grantor (also known as the *settlor* or *trustor*) and the trust is revocable (sometimes called a *revocable trust* or a *living trust*), then all of the assets in the trust are 100% yours.

- *Grantor of irrevocable trust.* If you're the grantor of a trust that is irrevocable, and you can't change the terms of the trust or take the money back out, then you likely made a gift of the asset in that trust to the beneficiaries, and it's no longer an asset of your estate.

- *Beneficiary of revocable trust.* If you're the beneficiary of a revocable trust, and the grantor is still alive, then the assets of the trust aren't yours and won't become yours until the grantor dies.

- *Beneficiary of irrevocable trust.* Whether the assets of this trust are part of your estate depends on what the trust says and if you have certain powers over the trust. You need to see an attorney to determine if the assets in the trust are part of your estate.

- *Trustee of trust.* Generally speaking, the trustee of a trust isn't the owner of the trust's assets, unless the trustee is also the beneficiary. However, if you're the trustee of a trust, then you should have the attorney who is putting together your estate plan review the trust to make sure its assets won't be attributed to you and to discuss with you the liability issues associated with being a trustee.

Be aware that just because an asset in a trust is part of your estate for estate planning purposes, that doesn't mean you necessarily control how that asset is distributed upon your death. For example, one spouse can leave assets for the benefit of another spouse in a marital trust, but that marital trust could provide that upon the second spouse's death all the assets go to their children. Here, the asset is part of the spouse's estate, but they have no control over where it goes upon their death.

If assets are in a trust, they should be valued in accordance with the same methodology I've been discussing elsewhere in this chapter.

Loans Payable to You

I often talk to clients who have loaned money to other people, particularly members of their family—more so in the past four years or so than any other time. This might have been done to allow a child to purchase a house, to supplement their parents' income, or to help a sibling through a rough patch.

Many people are surprised to hear that the value of these loans is part of their estate—the loans don't just magically disappear at death.

The value of the loan is the amount currently due to you. If you have never gotten around to writing down the terms of the loan and having it signed by the borrower, consider this your kick to the rear end to do it now. There is no kind of litigation like the nasty type where, for example, Sam says the $100,000 was a gift from mom and dad, and Kristen says the $100,000 was a loan and should be paid back to the estate. The problem is that you, the person fully knowledgeable of whether it was indeed a gift or a loan, are no longer here on this Earth to clarify the situation. Write out a promissory note with the amount that's being (or was) loaned, the interest rate, the repayment schedule, and whether you plan to forgive the loan upon your death. The borrower must sign the note, and so should you. Keep a copy of the promissory note with your estate planning documents.

Two more things about family loans. First, if you forgive the loan at some point in the future, you're making a gift to that person in the amount of the loan you're forgiving. If that loan forgiveness takes place at your death, then that person is getting more of your estate than your other intended beneficiaries because the loan is an asset of yours that is going to that person alone and not being divided among the other beneficiaries. Second, if you intend to forgive the loan at death, make a clear statement of that fact in your estate plan to diffuse any dispute among your family.

Vehicles

Cars, trucks, airplanes, boats, quads, RVs—any vehicle that you own is part of your estate. To determine the value for these assets, I suggest you look at www.kellybluebook.com or a similar online site for other types of vehicles.

While you're doing this, I also urge you to verify who is on the title to each vehicle. Sometimes you forget that the truck was put in your wife's name, even though she drives the car. Or the title might be lost—something that is far easier for you to rectify than your executor. Oh, and make sure somebody knows where all the titles are.

Intangible Assets

Intangible assets are things that aren't financial assets and that lack physical "touch and feel," but that have value nonetheless. Such an asset might be a patent, copyright, or trademark that you hold. It could be a website or franchise that you own. Other intangible assets are designs you created, computer programs, contract rights, license agreements, and membership rights in organizations. Even though none of these things has a physical body, each is property of yours that will be transferred as part of your estate plan.

Sometimes it can be difficult to place a value on intangible assets—an asset might not have a lot of value today, but you hope the value will bloom in the future (think of that website you just created). The important thing is to put together a list of all your intangible assets. If something happens to you, such assets might be lost because nobody knew to look for them. If you can include an estimated value for each item, even better.

Digital Assets

In the digital age, there may be a lot of *you* out there on the Internet. Your Facebook page could represent years of family history, and the same could be said about your Flickr, Photo Bucket, Twitter, and Pinterest accounts (I could go on, but you get the point). Given how slowly (think of a tortoise walking in molasses) estate law is updated, the vast majority of jurisdictions are totally silent as to whether a digital asset is part of your estate. Does your executor or trustee have control of your digital assets when you die? Do you want them to? Or does your digital life belong to the company that owns the website (does that mean that Mark Zuckerberg owns us all?)

Although digital assets may not have any intrinsic value, they can be of great value to your family. You should consider creating a list of the sites on which you have content and each site's login credentials. Remember that the password list needs to be updated as frequently as you change a password.

If you don't want anybody to see your digital footprint, there are even web services that will delete your online existence in the event of your death. The law hasn't caught up to these assets yet, so you need to make sure your estate plan takes control of who gets your online life.

Debt: Liabilities and What You Owe

Unfortunately, your estate plan isn't just about your assets—you have to take your debts and liabilities into consideration as well. I mentioned this before, but it bears repeating: creditors get paid before your intended beneficiaries, and debts don't die at your death. Although there are some exceptions (retirement accounts being the most prominent, along with life insurance and the family home in some states), death is a collection event for many creditors.

Mortgages and Lines of Credit

Will your mortgage be called when you die? The answer depends on who gets your house. Let's say the mortgage can stay in place—do your intended beneficiaries have the ability to maintain the mortgage after you pass away? If the answer is "no," you should consider purchasing life insurance to cover the mortgage if your family would plan to remain in your home.

Generally speaking, any transfer of the underlying property securing a mortgage makes the mortgage immediately due and payable. However, if you own your home as (1) joint tenants with rights of survivorship or (2) tenants by the entirety, and one owner dies, then the survivor takes full ownership of the property by operation of law and the mortgage continues with no alteration to its terms. Alternatively, if you give the house to a person through your will or trust, and the person is a relative of yours, then the mortgage can continue after the property is transferred the other person.

■ **Ask an Attorney** "Deirdre, I want to leave my house to my same-sex partner. What about the mortgage?" Under current federal law, your partner isn't a "relative," regardless of your status under any state law—neither is a friend or business partner. If you leave the person the property in your will or trust, the mortgage can be called as being immediately due and payable and the house foreclosed. To avoid this result, you may want to consider owning the property as joint tenants with rights of survivorship, which doesn't require the surviving owner to be a relative in order for the mortgage to continue.

You should be receiving a monthly statement of the balance of your mortgage or any line of credit. That amount should be noted in the financial questionnaire. In the event that you have elected to receive your notices online, you may want to jot down who has your mortgage so that if anything happens to you, your family will know who the payments go to.

Student Loans

Other than buying a house, the second largest expense for most people is paying for an education, whether for themselves or for their children. While government loans are discharged at death, private education loans are based on the personal guarantee of the person borrowing the money, so if you pass away, the money is due in full.

Depending on the payment status, you may receive documentation about student loans anywhere from once a month to once a year. You should list the current balance and estimate what the future balance will be if you're still in the borrowing phase.

Revolving Debt

Got credit cards, anyone? I've read that the average consumer has four active credit cards. If you're not paying them off every month, then you need to list the average balance in the debt column of your sheet.

Quick aside: if you can't pay off your credit cards every month, you should be looking at a personal financial planning book to find a way to better finance your lifestyle or minimize it to live within your means. Credit cards are an expensive way to live and can leave your intended beneficiaries with zero dollars.

Private and Other Debt

On the asset side, recall that I asked if anybody owes you money. Here the question is, do you owe anybody money? Perhaps you owe your parents, your company, the government (taxes), your contractor, or the car loan that you personally guaranteed. What about a margin loan against your investment accounts or your retirement accounts? Gather up all the other stuff you might possibly owe (just estimate it), and put it in the liabilities column.

Bottom Line: What's It All Worth?

OK—the moment of truth is here. You've gone through and listed, categorized, and added up all your assets. You've similarly identified all your debts and liabilities. What's the value of your estate?

Assets − Liabilities = Value of Your Estate

Want to see where you'll be in 10 years? Try adding 2% a year to your assets and keeping your liabilities flat for a quick look.

So, how has this exercise been useful? First, the value of your estate will determine whether you have a taxable estate. If you do have a taxable estate or may have a taxable estate in the future, then you need to look at Chapter 8, "Resource Guide: Taxes—The Government as Your Beneficiary," to find out how to reduce the government's interest in your estate and maximize the amount of money flowing to your intended beneficiaries.

What if you don't have a taxable estate, or what if the value of your estate is negative right now? You *still* need to put an estate plan in place. Your focus should be on understanding what assets aren't available to satisfy your creditors, potentially increasing assets through the use of life insurance, and making sure assets are being left to your family in such a way that they can continue their lifestyle in the event you're no longer here.

4

What Goes into a Will?

The "Cans" and "Can'ts" of Your Last Wishes

What elements make up the anatomy of a *will*? After all, this is the document that will be here when you're gone, as a statement of your wishes and intent. In this chapter I talk about what a will can and can't do, what the boilerplate terms are, and why they're important. The goal of this chapter is to give you a blueprint to read your will and understand what it says.

Quick aside: You might live in a state like California or Florida, where a *revocable trust* or *living trust* is the customary document that controls what happens to your assets when you die. Or your attorney may have recommended a revocable or living trust as the centerpiece of your estate plan. Although I talk about these types of trusts in Chapter 5, "Will Alternatives and Avoiding Probate," this chapter is still important for you. The elements of a will or a revocable trust or living trust are essentially the same when it comes to answering the question "Who gets my stuff when I die, and how?" So, if this situation applies to you, think *trust* not *will* when learning how to decipher your documents.

■ **Chapter Brief**   Your will only controls certain assets when you die—it may not say where everything goes. How is your stuff distributed separately from your assets? What if you want to leave a specific something to someone? Who gets what if you leave your assets to a group of people? What does all that boilerplate mean, anyway? That's what this chapter covers.

What Does Your Will Control?

Remember that in Chapter 3, "What Are Your Assets?" I talked about how much of an asset is yours to distribute as part of your estate plan. Well, your will only controls certain property when you die:

- *Assets that are 100 percent yours.* They're all in your name and nobody else's: for example, a bank account in your name. A joint account passes to the joint owner, regardless of what your will says (unless it's tenants in common).

- *Assets without beneficiary designations.* An IRA or a life insurance policy has a named beneficiary. Your will does *not* control the distribution of those assets upon your death.

- *Assets that aren't payable on death (POD) or transfer on death (TOD).* Assets with these designations (usually bank account or bonds) go directly to the named payee, even if your will says something different.

Assets that are controlled by your will are referred to as *probate* assets. Assets that go to somebody regardless of what your will says are called *non-probate* assets.[1] Key point here? Your will only controls your probate assets, and details of ownership matter when planning your estate.

What if you only have non-probate assets? Maybe you're a married couple and everything you own is in joint names. Do you still need an estate plan? Absolutely! Your estate plan may focus on who gets the assets when the second spouse dies or on rearranging your estate to get tax savings. Look to the Planning Guides in Part 3 to learn the questions you should be asking about your estate plan, and then come back here to see how it all works.

■ **Real Stories from Around My Conference Table**   What can happen when you don't think about probate versus non-probate assets? Let's take Michael, who was 78 and worked with an attorney to carefully create an estate plan leaving all his assets equally to his three children. A few years later, Michael named his daughter Susan jointly on his largest bank account "so she can write checks," not realizing that his idea to be efficient meant that Susan would get the entire account when he died. Michael died, and Susan got the account *and* one-third of everything else, so she ended up with 60 percent of the estate. What happened? Confusion, anger, and litigation ensued. The family spent more on legal fees than each child got in the end, arguing over "what Michael really wanted." Estate planning is like safe driving—make your intentions clearly known.

---

[1] Non-probate assets are so important to your estate plan that they deserve a chapter of their own. Chapter 5 is all about assets that go to your beneficiaries without passing through your will.

Follow the Flow

A will is read, and an estate is distributed, in an orderly fashion. Some things always come first, others always second or third. This order of operation gives structure to how a will is laid out. The will has separate sections, each addressing a specific issue. Think of your will like a tower or high-rise building: you start at the top and work your way down, but you have to pass through each floor (and maybe take an action) before you can reach the next one. Each "floor" in this example represents a separate article of your will. Figure 4-1 provides a visual representation of how this works.

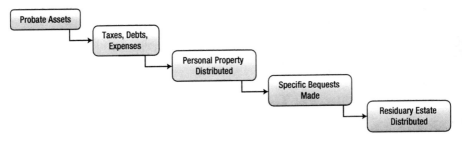

Figure 4-1. Blueprint of the structure of a will.

First Things First: This Is Your "Last" Will

It's called a Last Will and Testament for a reason: the first thing your will does is negate any prior wills. Why is this? Well, remember that by definition, when a will comes into play, you won't be here to say which version is really your last one, and great confusion (and potentially huge expenses) would be incurred trying to determine which one was genuine. We attorneys cut off that problem by saying that this most recent will is the real deal.

▓ **Ask the Attorney** "Deirdre, Should I mark up my will if I want to change something?" NO! BE CAREFUL WITH YOUR ORIGINAL WILL! Didn't mean to shout, but wills have very specific rules because they only come into effect when you're dead. If you mark up your original will (cross something out, add something), you may be deemed to have partially or completely invalidated that will, and a court will look to what your prior will said. Now, presumably you didn't want to use your prior will, or you wouldn't have created the most recent will. Remember, you aren't here to explain any mysterious inconsistencies in your will, so it must speak for itself. Marking up the will only creates confusion when you die, which is the opposite of the purpose of putting together an estate plan in the first place.

Moving On: Creditors Before Beneficiaries

I mentioned earlier that death is a collection event for creditors. In fact, the probate code of your state is set up to make sure your creditors are notified of your death and that they're paid before any property is distributed to your beneficiaries. Moving on to the next article of your will, you'll find it directs that all your debts and taxes be paid before your assets pass to your beneficiaries. And no, you can't avoid paying your debts or taxes by not having that provision in your will or by using a revocable trust or non-probate assets: creditors and the government are beneficiaries whether you provide for them or not.

Some creditors have priority over other creditors. Expenses related to your death and the administration of your estate (funeral bills, last medical expenses, attorney's fees, taxes, and so on) are paid in full before other creditors (such as Visa or your cable bill).

Personal Property: Your Stuff Goes Next

I spent time in Chapter 3 talking about how important it is to consider who gets your personal property or "stuff" and how to avoid problems. Because your stuff is different than your assets, which have extrinsic value, it generally has a separate article in your will. This article usually provides the following:

- A list of specific items to be given to specific people before a general gift of everything else ("my china to my granddaughter Christina"). In some states this specific list doesn't need to be in your will. Instead, you can use a *separate writing* to transfer your personal property at death. Look at the next section on specific bequests to learn what happens if the property no longer exists when you die.

- A general gift (or bequest) of the rest of your personal property to a person ("my husband") or a group of people ("my parents" or "my children"). If it's to a group of people, consider whether you need a mechanism for how the stuff will be divided. After all, you can't really divide your wedding ring into three parts.

- A statement about who gets the personal property if the first person isn't living ("to my wife, and if not living, equally to my children").

- Directions that anything going to a minor (person under 18) will be held by their guardian. After all, minors can't take legal title to property.

Specific Bequests: Person X Gets Thing Y

After giving away your stuff, you finally move to the floor (or article in the will) where you might be giving away specific assets or sums of money. Examples would be "my house to my sister, Theresa," "$5,000 to each of my grandchildren," or "forgive the balance of a loan owed by my son, Patrick." In each case, you're making either a *specific bequest* of a thing because it identifies (i) the person (or persons) receiving the item and (ii) what item is being given; or a *pecuniary bequest* of an amount of money, which identifies (i) the person (or persons) receiving or dividing some amount of money and (ii) what sum is being given.

The first thing to think about is what happens if the person to whom you're giving the gift isn't living when you die. Should the gift go to someone else or be forgotten about and the asset distributed along with the rest of your assets? You need to decide where you want the asset to go and make sure your will clearly provides those instructions. There is a huge difference between "my house to my sister, Theresa, and if she isn't living, to her children" and "my house to my sister, Theresa, and if she isn't living, this gift is void." In the first example, you direct the gift to stay in Theresa's family. In the second, you're redirecting who gets the house.

▊ **Let's Get Real**   Be aware that if the person you name as a beneficiary dies before you do, *your* will controls who gets the asset upon your death. If you gave an asset to a person and they die after you, *their* will controls who ultimately receives the asset. However, if you want to control who gets any remainder of the gift when the person you gave it to dies (for instance, you don't like your daughter-in-law and want anything you set aside for your son to go to his kids), you can do that using a trust. Find out more in Chapter 6, "Trust in Trusts."

Here's the second question: what happens if the thing you're giving away no longer exists? Suppose that after you made your will, you sold your house in Seattle, Washington and moved to Phoenix, Arizona. Does your sister Theresa now get your Arizona house, get nothing, or get an amount of money equal to what the Washington house was worth? There is no right or wrong answer, but to make sure your intentions are clear, you must provide direction to your executor and beneficiaries about who gets the house.

What happens if you make a specific bequest, and it turns out that upon your death either the person isn't living or the asset isn't there? Well, in that case, default state law takes over. Ready for the legalese? All states have something called an *anti-lapse* law to direct that a specific bequest goes to someone if the person you name to get it isn't living (you gave $20,000 to John, but he died before you did). If the gift was to a charity ($5,000 to Homes for Horses) and the charity no longer exists, the situation gets more confusing because there is an assumption under the law (the *cy-pres doctrine*) that you wanted the gift to go to some charity, and a charity with a similar mission must be found. Finally, if the asset subject to the gift (the house to Theresa) no longer exists, the *ademption* statutes take over to say, under the law of your state, whether the person gets nothing, or the value of the item in the will, or the successor items.

What should you take away from the legalese? There is no uniformity as to where the gift goes under the anti-lapse provision or ademption provisions, so you can't be sure what will happen if you don't direct where the property should go. And in the spirit of Murphy's Law, whatever your state statute says is probably not what your intention would be. The good news? All of this is totally avoidable. You just need to provide in your will what should happen to your gifts if the person or thing is no longer here.

Two final points. If you're giving a gift to a group of people (grandchildren), look in the next section at the considerations for how you leave the residue to a group. If some of the beneficiaries are minors, see Chapter 13, "Planning Guide for Kids," for some ideas about how to design an inheritance.

Residuary: Where the Rest of It Goes

We have finally moved to the heart of the will. Everyone else has gotten their piece, and now it's time to look at who gets the rest. (The rest, residuary ... see how they're similar?) You should already have in mind the *who* and the *how*. As mentioned earlier, it could be your spouse, kids, dog, partner, or whomever you like. This part of the will focuses on the mechanics of how your goals and intentions become reality.

It's All for Your One and Only

Maybe your plan is straightforward—you want your estate to pass to only one person, like your sister, your spouse, or your partner. In that case, you still have two questions to consider. First, should the residue pass to them outright or in trust?[2] Next, who gets the rest and residue if your one and only isn't living? This is your *contingent beneficiary*, the person(s) who gets the residue if your primary beneficiary isn't there. (I'll go over that in more detail in a bit.) You need to answer these questions in your will, because otherwise

---

[2] Consider a trust! You may find that it doesn't work for you, but trusts can be a powerful way to design an inheritance. I love them and want you to get to know them better, so I spend all of Chapter 6 on trusts.

the intestacy laws of the state you live in will say where all your hard earned wealth goes when you do.

Everything to a Group

It could be that your beneficiaries, either primary or contingent, are a group or class of people. Examples are your "children," your "nieces and nephews," your "grandchildren," or your "children and step-children." Typically, a group of beneficiaries is referred to by describing their relationship to you. This is done to allow the group to expand or contract over time as people are born or pass away. If you list the members of the group by name, you risk that if another person is born, that person won't be a beneficiary.[3]

■ **Real Stories from Around My Conference Table**   A single woman, let's call her Sally, left her entire estate to her five nieces and nephews, whom she listed by name. After she wrote her will, her youngest brother married for a second time and had a child, Kristine. Sally updated her will to change her executor before she died, but she didn't add Kristine to the list of beneficiaries. Did she intend to exclude her, or did Sally reasonably think that because she said "nieces and nephews" Kristine was included? What do you think? It is questions like these that lead to litigation. In this case, the family was close and all the beneficiaries agreed that Kristine should be part of the group. However, because there was ambiguity in the will, we lawyers had to seek an order interpreting the will to include Kristine, at significant expense to the estate (which was compounded by the fact that some of the nieces and nephews were under 18 and didn't have the legal capacity to sign off on the agreement). Because the agreement to include Kristine reduced the minor beneficiaries' share, a special guardian ad litem had to be appointed for them (an attorney acting to represent their interests) to sign off on the agreement. The moral? First, your will needs to be precise in wording. Second, you should consider adding language to describe your intent. If the will had read, "I leave my residuary estate to my nieces and nephews, Nancy, Rebecca, Peter, Stephanie, and Rebecca, and any after born nieces and nephews," then significant expense could have been avoided.

Contingent Beneficiaries: Your Plan B

It could be that the person you named as beneficiary isn't living at the time you die. It would be nice to think that everybody would review their will frequently and update it based on changing life circumstances, but that's not what happens. The reality is that most people make their estate plan and then

---

[3] Of course, it could be that you only want certain members of a group to benefit (only some of your children, for example). In that case, you should use the names of the people you want, instead of just their relationship to you.

promptly forget about it for years or decades to come. As a result, when you do pull out the will, it may very well be that a person you're leaving assets to is no longer here. Unless you come up with a Plan B in your will, the state you live in decides where your assets go upon your death. And as I've said, the state law default isn't likely to match your goals and intentions.

Contingent beneficiaries are people who become beneficiaries of your estate only when a certain condition has occurred, such as Person A predeceasing you. If the condition doesn't happen, the contingent beneficiaries get nothing. Contingent beneficiaries are important to your estate plan because you can predict foreseeable changes in circumstances in the future and give instructions about how you want them to be addressed. A common example: if one of your children predeceases you, do you want the share set aside for that child to go to their children or to be redistributed among your other children? Others conditions could be that a person has to reach a certain age, complete a level of education, or accomplish something else you think is important before they can have an interest in your estate.

Because the condition most often considered is, "What happens if Person A predeceases me?" let's look at some common solutions:

- *Lapse.* The gift lapses if the person isn't living. I talked about this earlier with reference to specific bequests.

- *Per stirpes.* Think of this as branches of a tree. Say you have three children, Jake, Katherine, and Liam. Katherine predeceases you and is survived by two children. Jake and Liam each receive one third of your residuary estate, and Katherine's children each receive one sixth of your residuary estate, because they divide the third you set aside for Katherine. This is by far the most common method of contingent beneficiary distribution.

- *Per capita.* Think of this as "he who lives, wins." In the previous example, Jake and Liam each receive half of your residuary estate, and Katherine's children get nothing. (This method is normally selected for groups of more remote beneficiaries, like "my grandchildren" or "my nieces and nephews," where your goal is to benefit the people you know, not necessarily their descendants who you have never met.)

- *Right of representation.* Think of this as going back to the drawing board. In the previous example, on Katherine's death the total number of possible beneficiaries changes from three (the three children) to four (one group consisting of the living children, and Katherine's children). Jake, Liam, and each of Katherine's children each receive one fourth of the residuary estate, which means Katherine's children receive more of their grandparents' estate—because their mom predeceased their grandparents—then they would have had their grandparents died and their mom passed away shortly thereafter.

- *Whatever you want.* It's your will. You can name whoever you want to as the beneficiary if the first person is no longer here. You could name your son-in-law, a charity, your best friend, or whatever feels right to you.

▓ **Let's Get Real**   Default contingent beneficiaries are a key example of why relying on state law may not get you where you want to go. In New Jersey, for example, the default is right of representation. I have never in over 15 years of practice had a client actually select that method. But if you made a will and didn't know any better, that would be the result in New Jersey if Person A predeceased you. Remember, the purpose of the will is to pass your assets the way that *you* want to, not how the state tells you to.

How Do Your Beneficiaries Benefit?

The next few floors of your will's structure vary based on who your beneficiaries are, how you want to leave assets to them, and whether you're engaging in any estate tax planning. Think of all these options like bedrooms that are decorated very specifically to match the needs and desires of their occupants. I discuss these options in great detail in the Resource Guides found in this Part 2 of the book.

Fiduciaries: The People in Charge

Moving right along, now that you've said who will get your estate and how they're going to get it, you progress into the part of the will that talks about who will be in charge. Selecting your fiduciaries and their successors is so important that I've dedicated an entire chapter to it (Chapter 12, "Fiduciaries"). However, to understand the blueprint of your estate plan, it's important that you have a quick overview of roles of fiduciaries:

- *Executor/Administrator/Personal Representative.* This is the one job that must be filled when you pass away. This person is in charge of gathering up all your assets, paying any liabilities or taxes, and distributing the assets to the beneficiaries.

- *Trustee.* This person has the long-term job of managing the assets for the beneficiary's benefit either during the beneficiary's lifetime or until a certain condition has occurred (such as they've reached a certain age or graduated from college).

- *Guardian.* This person is in charge of making decisions for minors until they reach age 18 or 21 (depending on state law). They work in conjunction with the trustee (who is in charge of the money) to exercise substitute parental guidance to your children until they reach adulthood.

Generally speaking, you could have one person or multiple people acting in any of the fiduciary roles. The identity of your fiduciaries is the element that is most frequently modified when reviewing an existing estate plan. Luckily, these changes can be handled very easily through a codicil to your will or amendment to a trust.

■ **Ask the Attorney** "Deirdre, help! I can't make a will because I don't know who to name as guardian." Tough. If you have minor children, naming a guardian is the single most important reason to create a will. If you don't create a will naming guardians for your minor children, the decision will be made by some judge you've never met, who quite frankly is going to be peeved that you put more thought into what to buy at the grocery store than who should raise your children. Yes, it's a difficult decision. Yes, there are no perfect answers. But you agonize over much less important decisions for your kids every single day. As their parent, you owe it to them not only to say who will be in charge if something happens to you, but to speak to that person about how you want your children raised. Can't make a decision between two people? Put into your will that if you die between January and June, Grandma M will act, and between July and December Grandma D will act; but don't let indecision be an excuse. Yeah, your mom may be angry that you named your mother-in-law as guardian, but your kids will have just lost their parents, so the adults need to step to the back of the line. (And it's not like you'll be here to hear her moan about it anyway.)

Boilerplate: This Is Important Stuff, Folks!

First, I really dislike the word *boilerplate*. It makes all these parts of the will seem unimportant and beneath your notice. "Oh, it's just boilerplate," sounds like "Oh, it's just garbage." All these boilerplate provisions are as important to your estate plan as the framework, plumbing, electrical system, ventilation, and insulation are to your home—not sexy, but absolutely necessary.

The boilerplate in an estate plan is your instructions for how the plan will work. It says how taxes are paid, what filings your executor must make, what happens if a beneficiary is under 18, how to prevent creditors from attacking your estate, and so on. Remember, you aren't here to say how your estate operates. Your will must do that for you. And if you don't leave operating instructions in your will, your state statutes provide those instructions by default. Do you really want to figure out what those statutes say? And they may not say what you want them to say.

Definitions

Your will uses a lot of legalese. That includes some shorthand for more complex terms, some that's old-fashioned by custom, and some legal terms of art. A will normally has a section of definitions for terms of art used in the will (generally found at the very front or the very back). If it doesn't, you can turn to the legalese Rosetta Stone found in Chapter 25, "Glossary," where I translate those phrases and terms into plain English. After all, what good is your estate plan if you can't understand what it says?

Alternate or Ultimate Distribution Clause

It's an icky question, but what happens to your assets if all your beneficiaries die? Although unlikely and tragic, it's not impossible. If you don't provide otherwise, your wealth will be distributed as described in your state's intestacy statutes—rules about what happens when you die without a will. And if you don't have any relatives in the right categories, the state you live in gets 100 percent of your money. Now I don't know about you, but I think the state gets plenty of my money, thank you very much. And I have never had a client, when going through their desired beneficiaries, say "Kansas" or "Kentucky" as their beneficiary. Instead, this clause directs that in the absence of named beneficiaries, your estate passes to a group of people ("my siblings and their descendants," for example) or a charity, either named or to be selected by the fiduciary.

As a practical matter, I often have clients get hung up on this particular provision. A few things can help keep it in perspective: it's highly unlikely to ever happen; you can always change your will as long as you're living; and you won't be here in the end anyway, so make a decision you can live with *today*.

Powers of the Fiduciary

This segment of your will says what your fiduciary can and can't do with your assets. Can they invest them in the stock market? Buy, sell, or operate real estate? Act without court approval? Finish a tax appeal? Keep the family business open? Take advantage of tax elections to reduce taxes? Move the jurisdiction of a trust? This section will be either the longest in your will, with paragraph upon paragraph enumerating these powers, or a short sentence that says essentially, "My fiduciary can do anything my state statutes say he can do."

I of course think it's very important that you specifically lay out what your fiduciary can do and not simply rely on state statutes. The law is very slow to change, and one of the reasons you can specify the powers of your fiduciary and not just rely on the state statutes is so you can craft a will that meets the realities of today, not those of 1994, or even 1884, which may be the last time some sections of your probate code were updated. Great example: at present, only one state, Oklahoma, has bothered to create laws that address who controls any of your social media upon your death. Only five other states are considering such laws. And how many Americans do you think use social media?

Spendthrift Clause

From an asset-protection perspective, this is the single most important piece of boilerplate. It says something along the lines of, "I direct that no beneficiary shall sell, transfer, pledge, or in any other manner anticipate or encumber his interest in my estate or any trust hereunder, and that such interest shall not be subject to attachment or other legal process of any creditor or spouse of any beneficiary." Come again? In English? Essentially, this little paragraph is the equivalent of rock-solid pest control for your house. With limited exceptions, it provides that the trustees can use whatever money is in a trust for the beneficiaries, but that as long as the money stays in trust, other people (the pests in this example) can't get their hands on the money. If your will creates any trusts, this provision must be in your will to prevent any creditors of the beneficiaries, or soon-to-be ex-spouses, from being able to reach into the trust to take out money for themselves.

Survivorship Clause

What happens if you and a beneficiary die at close to the same time? Should your will or theirs be in control? This provision creates a rule that a beneficiary must survive you by some period of time—30 to 90 days, generally—to have met the conditions of being a beneficiary under your will. Why? Let's say you love your son but only tolerate his wife, who never met a dime she didn't spend. You and your son are in the car, and a bus hits it. If there is no survivorship provision, your estate passes to your son, whose estate immediately gives your hard-earned dollars to your spend-happy daughter-in-law. If you had a survivorship provision, your will could have provided that because your son didn't survive you for the specified amount of time, any assets you left him would be held in trust for your grandchildren, thus ensuring that the money is there to pay for their college.

State Law

Common situation: you create a will when you live in North Carolina, but then you move to Ohio. Because your will was written under the laws of one state, this clause says your will should be interpreted under the laws of the state you were living in at the time you wrote it if there is any ambiguity. This helps avoid a translation situation, like when you try to read instructions to build a cabinet made in China that just don't make sense translated to English.

▧ **Ask the Attorney** "Deirdre. Do I have to change my will when I move?" The short answer is "No," but you may want to have it reviewed by an attorney in your new state. The US Constitution contains a provision called the Full Faith and Credit Clause, which basically says that whatever documents or agreements are created under the laws of one state must be respected by the other 49. Because of this, a will created when you lived in Maine is valid when you die in Illinois. However, the will created when you lived in Maine may not make sense in Illinois, because there may be different tax laws or a different probate process. That's why I always recommend that a will be reviewed by an attorney who practices in your new state of residence whenever you move.

Blue-Line Provision

This clause provides that if any one part of the will is invalid for any reason (for example, if you crossed out the section that Maine law governed the will, even though I told you not to write on the original will!), then only that provision is struck from the will. It doesn't invalidate the whole will. After all, you don't want some random change that you'll likely never thought about to invalidate your entire estate plan.

Identity of Children

I talked earlier about the importance of identifying a group of beneficiaries. When it comes to children, it's customary to name them in the will with their full legal name. If the biological possibility exists for more children, you want to specifically declare that if there is an additional child, they will share in the same manner.

██ **Let's Get Real** Your will is in many ways your last communication with your children. For children born after you made your will, how do you think they will feel if they aren't identified by name and their brother and sister are? Regardless of whether that child receives the same amount of assets, the child won't feel treated the same. Instead, in my office, if a client has another child, we add that child's name to their documents at no charge—think of it as a baby gift for your new bundle of joy!

Rule Against Perpetuities

Shiver ... this one brings back some very bad memories of my property law exam in law school. In some states, a trust can only last for a certain period of time before it must be distributed outright to the beneficiaries. This period of time could be measured by the age to which some of your beneficiaries live, 90 years, or some other set timeframe. Only a few states have gotten rid of the rule against perpetuities, so you're likely to find a provision in your will describing when a trust must vest or be distributed outright to the beneficiaries, notwithstanding the trust terms. Even if you live in a state without a rule against perpetuities, there are proposals with reference to the federal estate tax law (for example, those currently in the Obama administration's 2013 budget proposal) that will similarly limit the longevity of a trust.

Waiver of Dower, Curtsey, and Rights of Election

I mentioned earlier that nobody has a right to your estate except a spouse.[4] In many states, there must be a specific waiver of these rights in the will so the property-distribution plan that you and your spouse create for your assets is in control, not state statute. Alternatively, in the event of a second marriage, the spouses may agree to waive these rights in a prenuptial agreement, which then needs to be carried into the will.

Tax Clause

This article says who pays any taxes that are due on your estate. As with everything else in your will, if you don't say who pays the taxes, state law will control, and you and your family may be very displeased with the results. Some common options are as follows:

---

[4] Except for Louisiana, where some children have a right of inheritance.

- *All from the residuary.* Whatever taxes are due come off the top before any assets are distributed among the residuary beneficiaries. This is the most common tax clause, and it's generally used when all the beneficiaries have an equal interest in the estate.

- *Allocated among the beneficiaries.* Each beneficiary pays their proportional share of taxes. So, if you received 22.78 percent of the estate, you pay 22.78 percent of the taxes. This is generally used when different people have different interests in the estate, such as one group getting 25 percent of the estate, another group 50 percent, and two other groups 12.5 percent each.

- *Allocated among the beneficiaries of non-probate assets, and the balance from the residue.* Sometimes people leave certain non-probate assets or specific bequests to one set of people, but then the residue goes to somebody else. In this event, it would be unfair if people receiving the residue had to pay all the taxes, because some of the money is going to people who aren't sharing in the residue. This hybrid approach is fairer because one group isn't stuck paying the taxes while another group receives 100 percent of an asset.

The answer to the question "Who pays the taxes?" is central to efficient estate tax planning. Generally speaking, you don't want taxes paid out of assets passing to a surviving spouse or out of retirement plan assets. In some states, where there's an inheritance tax, assets passing to a step-grandchild might be subject to tax, but assets passing to a step-child aren't. If your goal is to have a more complicated distribution scheme (two examples that come to mind are a second marriage and a disproportionate estate plan where some assets go to some children and other assets to others), you and your attorney should spend some time making sure the tax clause matches your goals.

Waiver of Accounting

Unless you say otherwise, the default rule in many states is that your fiduciaries must provide an annual accounting to the court of what they have done with the estate or trust. The concept of an accounting is a good one, because it means the beneficiaries know what's going on with the trust. However, in today's age of electronic communications, monthly investment statements, and online banking, the beneficiaries may very easily be able to get this information without the need and expense of putting together a formal accounting and having it approved by a judge. Accordingly, it's common in your will to waive the need for an annual accounting in order to defeat any state statute that calls for one. A formal accounting is expensive and unnecessary in many estates, because the beneficiaries can simply review an informal accounting to verify that they're getting the "right" amount.

Small Trust Provision

Another unnecessary expense may be to continue to hold assets in a trust that has gotten too small to justify the annual cost of administration, or when the reasons for the trust no longer exist. For example, Grandma Martha set up her will to leave some funds in trust for the benefit of her granddaughter Emma until she turned 30. When Martha set this up, Emma was 16 and Martha thought she'd be leaving her around $100,000. However, Martha ended up spending 3 years in a nursing home, the amount going to Emma is now closer to $20,000, and Emma is 26. It doesn't make sense to create a trust for such a small amount or to maintain a trust that was larger but has now been spent down. This provision in a will allows your fiduciary either to not create the trust or to terminate the trust when it no longer makes economic sense.

■ **Let's Get Real** Your will by its nature is planning for an unknown future—you don't know right now when you're going to die, what you'll own at that point in time, or what your family will be like. The key to all the provisions in the will is a single word: flexibility. You want to create your will in such a manner that it allows your fiduciaries to look at your building plans but modify them to fit the then-current environment.

Will Execution

If you don't execute your will correctly, it will be wrong, as in invalid—as in, it doesn't matter what it says, because it won't be accepted as your final will. I'm sure you've heard stories of people leaving their will on a birthday card, on a napkin, or written on the back of a dollar bill (which is illegal, by the way). The sad-but-true and much-less published stories are when a person thought she was making out her will and had every intention in the world of it being a will, but because it wasn't executed properly, it couldn't be used as her Last Will and Testament.

Remember, you won't be here to point to your will and say, "This is my will. This is what I intend to have happen with my assets when I die." There's lots of room for fraud, and whether you have a small estate or hang out with Warren Buffett, there are always people in this world looking to cash in on your money. When you die, it's sort of easy, because you aren't here to argue. Make up a will, forge a signature, and it all goes to you. The courts have been battling this problem for centuries, and they've come up with some very specific safeguards against fraud:

- *Signature.* You need to sign your will with your actual signature (no electronic signatures allowed). In practice, most attorneys have you initial or sign each page of the will as well, so no pages are mysteriously inserted between the time you leave your lawyer's office and the time you die.

- *Witnesses.* Generally speaking, you must have two witnesses who sign their names saying that they witnessed you signing the will on a certain date and time. If there are questions about your will, these witnesses will be called to court to attest whether this is the document they witnessed. Without the witnesses, the will may not be accepted.

- *Notary public.* In addition to the witnesses, your will should also be notarized. Back in the day, when you died, the court would actually "call the witnesses" who had to come forth and say, "Yes. I saw Oliver McDermott sign his name to that specific will on November 11, 1952, and that's my signature as witness to the will." An obvious issue with the calling of the witnesses is what happens when they're dead or you can't find them. In modern times, this problem is overcome by having the will notarized at the time you and the witnesses sign it. You sign an affidavit in front of a notary indicating that you are who you are, and that this document is intended to be your will. If your will isn't notarized, I suggest you do it over now to save your beneficiaries a huge amount of hassle when you die.

- *Holographic will.* You're stuck on a sinking ship, and there's no time for lawyers or witnesses or notaries. Most courts will accept a *holographic will*, which is a will that is entirely in your own handwriting. Not partially typed or printed out and then signed by you. Not a form with the blanks filled in by you. Although holographic wills can be offered for probate, needless to say lots of questions can arise if the language you use isn't entirely clear to the people who are reading it.

■ **Ask The Attorney** "Deirdre, can I do my will online?" You absolutely can, and for many people it's the most cost efficient way of making their estate plan. However, as an attorney I often see circumstances where a do-it-yourself will is incomplete. Either the language is ambiguous (it looks like you meant one thing but said another), or the will wasn't properly executed (you had only one witness, or you signed it when it was half typed and half filled out). A court won't accept this document as a will in most states, and no state will accept it without a formal hearing. Your desire to save a few bucks can result in thousands in legal fees, all because you aren't trained in writing wills. Even for the best weekend DIYer, some jobs require a professional. A truly simple will ("all to my spouse, then my kids at 25") might be appropriate online, just like you can change out flooring by yourself. More complicated wills (any tax planning, second marriage, unequal distributions) are more like revising your electric system. You'd better bring in an expert. The online programs can only ask the programmed questions. They can't see that a certain line of questions is confusing you and you need more information or that perhaps there is something else to uncover. And you can't be sure the online program has your state law down pat.

So, you now have the blueprint of your will in front of you, and it makes sense. You can see the logic within the structure. Now what? Remember that your will only controls your probate assets. We still need to look at what to do with non-probate assets. And a will doesn't make a complete estate plan. To round it out, a power of attorney, a living will, and an advance directive are in order. Most important, this blueprint is two-dimensional. You're building your legacy—literally, what you're leaving behind when you're gone. The heart and soul of your estate plan is what you create from the blueprint.

To come up with that, I throw lots of ideas at you in the Resource Guides; some you'll love and will cause you to have that "aha" moment; others you'll reject out of hand; and still more you'll put aside in the "to be considered later" pile. My goal for you is that at the end of the Resource Guides, you'll have a picture of your estate plan in your mind. You can then look at the Action Guides to turn that picture into reality!

5

Will Alternatives and Avoiding Probate

Sometimes a Will Isn't What You Want

These days, a will isn't the end-all and be-all of estate planning. A world of will alternatives are out there: joint ownership; pay-on-death accounts; naming beneficiaries of retirement accounts and life insurance; and the granddaddy of them all, the revocable trust. First I want to educate you about how these are part of your estate plan without being part of your will. Then I'll show you some smart ways to weave these will alternatives into your estate plan to bring your assets and goals together.

I can't talk about will alternatives without talking about probate, so that's where I start in this chapter. Decades or even centuries ago, one the primary purposes of probate was to notify creditors that you had died and give them an opportunity to be repaid before the assets were transferred to the beneficiaries. In order to do this, court filings were required, notice had to be given to the public, and a delay of transfer of ownership was purposefully instituted, all to give rightful creditors an opportunity to stake their claim. Today, many people find the probate process to be antiquated, expensive, and unnecessary. Hence the goal of wanting to avoid probate and have more assets distributed at death outside of the probate process (also called *by operation of law*).

But more questions need to be answered than simply "Who gets my assets when I die?" and "Can I avoid probate?" There are questions, for example, about who *doesn't* get your assets—such as creditors and the IRS. There are other questions related to "How quickly can my beneficiaries get my assets?" Remember, you died, but your mortgage didn't, and where's that money coming from each month?

You also need to consider the expense of an estate plan. Your investment in this book may be the most money you intend to put into your estate plan. If that's the case, you need methodologies to set up your estate plan that don't involve a lawyer.

Be careful! Will alternatives cut both ways. You may have set up your estate plan to minimize taxes, reduce arguments, provide asset management, or ensure that the ultimate beneficiaries are who you want them to be. Use of will alternatives might actually defeat your goals or, in a worst-case scenario, lead to confusion and litigation.

▨ **Chapter Brief**   Probate can be expensive and time-consuming. Having property owned in a manner other than just in your own name avoids that. Some forms of joint ownership avoid probate, and others don't—the devil is in the details of title. Pay-on-death or transfer-on-death accounts are alternatives to joint ownership. A revocable trust may be the best way for you to reach your goals, but you need to understand its role and anatomy.

The Probate Process: Transferring Title from You to Them

The probate process is part of property law. The goal of probate is to transfer *clear title* (that is, property ownership where nobody else can claim to be an owner) at death from you to the person who should have the asset. Some people think of probate as a dirty word or something to be avoided at all costs—"Oh no! Not probate!" Like many things in life, probate is often misunderstood.

The purpose of probate is important. If you inherit a house from your mother, and you want to sell it to me, I'm not going to buy the house unless I know that nobody else has any claims to ownership of the house (such as your siblings, who think you took advantage of mom to get the house, and who may be right). By going through the process of probate and obtaining clear title to the assets, you let your fiduciaries and beneficiaries know that they can sell the assets and nobody's going to come after them. Remember, you're dead. You aren't there to remind your daughter that you borrowed $20,000 from the neighbor and promised to pay it back when you sold the house.

The element of formality of the probate process is actually what leads to clear title (so there is a purpose to it, after all!). Statutes in each state provide for a period of time during which creditors must make claims against the estate assets. If a creditor doesn't make a claim within that period of time, their claim is barred. You can think of it as, "Make your claim or forever hold your peace."

Probate Avoidance Isn't a Magic Pill— Taxes and Expenses Must Still Be Paid

To be clear, avoiding probate doesn't mean you don't have to pay your creditors (if only death was so easy). Each state has its own rules, but even assets that don't pass through probate are generally available to satisfy the claims of the decedent's creditors (subject to some notable exceptions I'll go over later). Some people mistakenly believe that by merely having a revocable trust instead of a will, their kids won't have to pay their debts when they die. Remember, this is the law we're talking about—if it seems too good to be true, it probably is.

▓ **Let's Get Real** The cost of probate is only one element of the total expense of administering your estate. I listen to the same talking heads on TV that you do—"Probate will steal 10 percent to 15 percent from your family!" This line might be good for ratings, but it's not necessarily accurate. The direct cost of probate might be limited to the filing fees (which tend to depend on the total size of the probate estate) and any attorney or accounting fees related to making the filings required by your state. In New Jersey, these are next to nothing. In Florida, they're in the thousands of dollars (if not tens of thousands).[1] However, there are significant additional expenses in the overall administration of your estate that have nothing to do with probate, such as executor fees, personal representative fees, trustee fees, attorney and accountant fees for preparing any tax returns, taxes, and general costs of maintaining and transferring your assets. I often find that the totality of "estate administration expenses" is incorrectly lumped under the heading of "probate expenses." Even when probate is avoided altogether, these other expenses of your estate may continue to exist. The best way to save money and reduce your estate's expenses is to have a clear vision of your assets, the people you want to benefit, and your goals, and use that vision to create a well-written and comprehensive plan that meets your objectives.

---

[1] If you're really curious about what the costs of probate could entail and how they vary between states, I present a summary comparing Florida, New York, and California in terms of attorney fees for handling a probate estate in Chapter 12, "Fiduciaries."

Joint Ownership

The only assets that are subject to probate, and also the only assets that are controlled by your will, are those that are in your own name, with no beneficiary designation, at the time of your death. Other assets, such as joint accounts, pass by operation of law. This means that no matter what your will says, the assets pass to the other owner. But (and as with all things to do with the law, there is always a "but") there are important caveats you need to be aware of in order to arrive at your intended result—not all joint ownership is the same. Hey, if this stuff was logical and straightforward, I would be writing a very short book!

Joint Tenants with Right of Survivorship (JTWROS): Or, the Survivor Gets It All

JTWROS assets represent both the best and the worst of will alternatives. On a positive note, as soon as person A dies, person B owns 100 percent of the assets. That means the money is available without any court intervention to be spent by the family as needed. It's a quick, easy, and cheap way of distributing your assets upon your death. On a negative note, people (particularly seniors) often put a joint name on an account for convenience purposes, not understanding that this means the account will pass to that person upon death. Estate litigation is an ugly business, and most estate litigations that I'm involved in share this particular issue.

Convenience Account or Specific Bequest?

How do you recognize a JTWROS asset? There'll be more than one person's name on the asset, and the connector between the names will be "or." Yes, it can come down to the lowly conjunction "or" to determine who gets the asset when you die. Now, a JTWROS asset doesn't need to be an account; it could be real estate, a bond, a car, or any other type of property.

I think an example is in order. Consider Matthew, who is 78 and has three children: Jason, Crystal, and Ryan. Crystal lives close to her dad and has been helping him out for the past couple of years as he's slowed down. One of the things Crystal does is write checks for her dad, and a couple of years ago they went to the bank to "put her name on the account." The bank manager was happy to oblige and changed the account to "Matthew or Crystal, JTWROS."

Who can withdraw money from a JTWROS account? Either owner (or any owner, if there are more than two) is treated as owning the account and can withdraw 100 percent of the assets at any time. In Matthew's example, this means there's no reason why Crystal can't write a check out to herself, with or without her dad's OK. This might not be what Matthew intended, but that is the result of a JTWROS account. Oh, and Crystal writing a check to herself from the account can be a gift for gift tax purposes, which may have other consequences.[2]

What happens when one owner of a JTWROS account dies? Whatever is in the account goes directly to the other owner. In my example, Matthew has two assets: a house worth $300,000 and the joint account with Crystal worth $200,000. Matthew's will directs everything to be divided three ways among his children. Had Mathew owned everything in his own name, each of the children would receive about $166,000. However, because the account was held with Crystal as JTWROS, she receives the account plus one third of the house, or $300,000, and Jason and Ryan each receive only $100,000.

Here is the $200,000 question. Did Matthew *intend* for Crystal to receive the same amount as her brothers upon his death? Or was Matthew totally unaware of the consequences of how the account was titled, and he still believed that each of his children would share equally in his estate? Do you know the answer? I sure don't. Situations just like this, full of uninformed actions and unintended consequences, lead to family disputes, resentment, hard feelings, and, in extreme cases, litigation.

Let's Get Real The lesson to be learned from Matthew is to be clear about your intentions and make sure your actions match those intentions. If Matthew only wanted Crystal to be able to write checks from his account, a better way would've been to identify her at the bank as a power of attorney over Matthew's account, which would give her check writing authority. Or Matthew could have provided in his will that if one child received assets as a result of his death outside of the will, then his other children would receive an equal amount from the will (as a specific bequest) before the residuary estate was divided among the children. If it was Mathew's goal for Crystal to receive the entire account, he could have underscored that intention by making a statement in his will that he wanted the joint account with Crystal to go to her at his death, with no offsetting provisions to be made to his other children. Anything is better than ambiguity.

---

[2] I go over all sorts of gifts, intended and unintended, in Chapter 9, "Gifting." Suffice it to say that when you make a gift, you potentially reduce the amount of assets that will be sheltered from estate tax upon your death. So Mathew's "gift" to Crystal could have even more far-reaching consequences to Jason and Ryan.

Married Couples—Did You Mean to Gut Your Estate Tax Planning?

Another negative point of JTWROS ownership is that for married couples this type of ownership totally undermines any tax savings that are structured in their will. I talk about this in much more detail in Chapter 14, "Planning Guide for Marrieds," but for now you should be aware that a fundamental part of estate tax savings is for each spouse to have assets in their own name that are used to fund a credit from estate taxes upon their death. If all the assets are in joint names, then it doesn't matter what the will says, because the assets pass directly to the surviving spouse and none of the tax savings are achieved. (And you wasted the money you spent on an attorney to put the estate plan in place.)

Unmarried Couples: JTWROS Could Be the Plan for You

On a positive note, JTWROS is an excellent way for couples who aren't married (dating, life partners, LGBT, ex-spouses with children), but who share common economic interests, to provide for those common interests. It's cheap and easy estate planning you can do without having anybody else involved.

To give you a sense of how this works, let's take Chris and Pat, who live in a condo together and contribute equally to all the expenses of the household. Their condo is titled in Chris's name because he had a higher-paying job at the time they bought it. Without any other planning, upon Chris's death, the condo won't pass to Pat, who lives there and contributes to it. Instead, the condo will be distributed as part of Chris's will, which might leave everything to his parents. Or, more realistically, Chris may not have a will, and state law would give the condo to his parents.

If instead the condo and the bank account that they use for living expenses are titled as JTWROS between Chris and Pat, then those specific assets, over which they have a joint economic relationship, will pass to the partner. The rest of the assets will be distributed as provided in the deceased partner's estate plan (which could go to other partner or not—it's your estate plan and up to you, after all!).[3]

---

[3] Are you an unmarried couple, or a same-sex couple, or even a former couple who still have children, pets, or assets together? Chapter 16, "Planning Guide for Unmarried and Same-Sex Couples," is full of ideas for you to think about in making an estate plan that fits your life.

Tenants by the Entireties

Tenants by the entireties (TBE) is JTWROS on steroids. This form of joint ownership is available only for married couples. It has all the same benefits and drawbacks of JTWROS, with one very important additional benefit: property held as TBE is protected from the creditors of either spouse.

There is a common misconception that anything owned jointly with a spouse is safe from one spouse's creditors. Not true. The extent to which TBE exists as a form of ownership depends on your state law. In some states, any asset jointly owned by a married couple could be owned as TBE; in others, TBE ownership is limited to real estate. Also, it isn't enough to just be married to get the TBE protection—you need to have acquired the asset jointly while you were married.

Time for another example. Andrew's business closed in 2010 because of the economy, and he has a business loan he can't repay. Generally speaking, a creditor can insist that a joint asset be liquidated and that the debtor's interest in the joint asset be used to pay his debts. The bank gets a judgment against Andrew. Andrew and his wife, Christina, have a JTWROS investment account. The bank can seek a court order to have 50 percent of the account distributed to the bank to pay down the loan.

However, if the joint asset was Andrew's primary residence that he and Christina bought after they were married and owned as TBE, and Christina was in no way responsible for the unpaid business loan, the bank couldn't force the house to be sold to collect on that judgment.

Does your house qualify for TBE protection? Look at the deed and see if it says something like "Andrew Lee and Christina Lee, husband-and-wife." If you bought the property before you got married, it won't have that protection unless you modify the deed. If you become divorced, or one spouse dies, the assets protection will fall off. Notwithstanding this, ownership of assets as TBE to the extent possible is a quick, cheap, and effective way to protect assets from creditors.

Tenants in Common: What's Mine Is Mine

Tenants in common (TiC) looks a lot like JTWROS, but it isn't the same creature at all. With TiC, each person owns a proportionate share of the asset—unless otherwise specified. Very important: each owner's own will and estate plan control their share of TiC property at death; the property does *not* pass to the co-owner by operation of law at death, and the transfer of property does *not* avoid probate.

How do you recognize a TiC asset? There'll be more than one person's name on the asset, and the connector between the names will be "and" (yup—it all comes down to a conjunction again—see how those details matter?). Unless otherwise specified, each person owns a proportionate share of the asset. So, if 4 people are named on a deed, they each own 25 percent of the property. However, with TiC you can specify different amounts of ownership, which is why this type of ownership is commonly found with investment properties. Terry puts in $50,000, and Vickie and Peter each contribute $25,000 to a property. They own the property as TiC with Terry having 50 percent, and Vickie and Peter each having 25 percent.

Who can withdraw money from a TiC account? Each owner can withdraw only up to their share (compare this to a JTWROS account, where each owner can withdraw up to 100 percent). My example of this: Jordan and Hallie Lapp are siblings who purchased a vacation home in Wyoming. The deed is titled "Jordan Lapp and Hallie Lapp." They have an "and" bank account that they use for the property expenses. They each own 50 percent of the property and account, contribute 50 percent of the costs, and would get 50 percent of the proceeds from any sale.

What happens when one owner of a TiC account dies? Unlike JTWROS, each TiC owner's interest passes to the deceased owner's estate, not the other owner. This is terrific if Hallie's intention is that her share of the property goes to her husband Dave. However, if Hallie was under the mistaken impression that because she and Jordan owned the property jointly, the property would pass to Jordan upon her death, this won't be accomplished through a TiC form of ownership. They should own the property and account as JTWROS instead.

■ **Ask the Attorney**   "So Deirdre, how should my assets be titled?" In a nutshell, if a married couple purchases real estate, it's held as TBE and passes to the surviving spouse upon death. If anybody, married or unmarried, opens a joint bank account or investment account, the default is likely JTWROS, and whatever is in that account will pass to the co-owner upon death. If an unmarried couple purchases real estate, the default is TiC. The key point? You need to check exactly how joint assets are titled and address them appropriately either by modifying the title or by making changes to your estate plan so the assets pass to whom you want them to upon your death, not as a result of some arbitrary property law rules.

Plan Your Own Estate 65

Community Property

If you're a married couple and live in one of the nine community property states—Arizona, California, Idaho, Louisiana, Nevada, New Mexico, Texas, Wisconsin, or Washington—or have lived in one of those states, then you and your spouse have *community property*. This is a type of ownership where most items acquired during the marriage are deemed to be owned 50 percent by each spouse. Community property comes from Spanish civil law (which is why it's mostly found in western states) and is based on the theory that because both spouses contribute to the joint economic unit of the marital household, everything should be joint.

Having said that, even if you live in a community property state, each spouse can have separate property. This might include property you had before the marriage, gifts, inheritances, and income earned on separate property. What is and isn't community property, and whether a creditor can get to it, varies from state to state, so you need to talk to an attorney licensed in your state.

How do you recognize community property? This can be a bit difficult because ownership isn't solely dependent on how the property is titled. A couple could purchase a home in Nevada in husband Harry's sole name, but wife Wanda owns 50 percent of it. Or the house could have been purchased with funds Harry received when his mother died and be separate property.

What happens when one spouse dies? With community property, the surviving spouse already owns half of all the community property assets, so the deceased spouse's will only controls (1) half of the community property and (2) any separate property. That separate property can be left to the spouse or others, depending on your goals and objectives.

Pay-on-Death Accounts: An Alternative to Joint Ownership

So you want to give a certain bank account to your niece when you die, but because you're still here, you don't want her to have access to it right now. The solution? A pay-on-death (POD) or transfer-on-death (TOD) account.

During your lifetime, you're the sole owner of a POD or TOD account. Nobody else has access to it, and you're 100 percent in control. Upon your death, the POD or TOD account passes to the person or persons whom you name as the beneficiary of the account.

Using POD or TOD accounts provides quick, easy, and cheap estate planning. You simply identify the account and who is to get the account when you pass away. There is a "but," of course. Significant limitations come with such a simple form of ownership. First, POD or TOD is available only for certain types of assets, such as bank accounts, brokerage accounts, stocks, and bonds. It's not available for your personal property, and it isn't commonly used in real estate ownership. The fact that an asset is "payable on death" comes from the contract you enter into with the institution that holds the asset. In a POD or TOD account, you're directing the institution to make payment of the asset to a specific person in the event of your death.

Real Stories from Around My Conference Table   A real problem with relying on POD or TOD estate planning is that it can give rise to inequities upon your death. I have a client who had six CDs, each naming a grandchild as the beneficiary. For years she meticulously maintained even amounts of money in each CD. However, when she became ill, the family started spending her assets on her care. They liquidated one CD first and then moved to another. By the time she died, two of the six CDs no longer existed, and only about half of a third CD remained. This meant that two of the six grandchildren got nothing, one grandchild got 50 percent of the original CD value, and the other three grandchildren got 100 percent. This clearly wasn't what the client intended. Fortunately, litigation was avoided when we helped the family agree to pool the money and divided it six ways. However, you can see how relying on a POD account can lead to the wrong result.

Another limitation with a POD or TOD account is that it doesn't provide for any complexity of beneficiary arrangements. What happens if the beneficiary predeceases you? What if you want more to go to one person than another?

When does a POD or TOD account do a great job? When you want to provide a specific asset outside of the balance of your estate to a specific person. From a practical standpoint, a POD or TOD account works particularly well when the person getting the TOD or POD asset has no relationship to the other beneficiaries of your estate. Examples: Your girlfriend gets a joint account, and your kids (who don't like your girlfriend) get the balance; you leave CDs to your former spouse's kids to recognize your relationship but everything else to your kids. A POD or TOD account payable to one of your beneficiaries also creates some immediately available cash to help with your estate. Your goal might be, "I want my son to get this account when I die so that I know there'll be cash immediately available, and he won't have to wait for the probate process." Looked at in this light, a POD or TOD account is an alternative to a specific bequest in a will that is carried out more quickly.

Name a Beneficiary: You Go, They Get

For some assets, such as life insurance and retirement benefits, there's not a question of "if" you should name a beneficiary but "Who should my beneficiary be?" This is because life insurance and retirement benefits are designed to have you name a beneficiary in the event of your death. Even if you don't name a beneficiary, the contract itself has a default beneficiary.

It's critically important that the beneficiary designations of your life insurance and retirement benefits be coordinated with your overall estate plan. Consider these nightmare scenarios when they're not coordinated:

- You and your spouse spend hours agonizing over exactly how to leave assets to your minor children. Fifty percent of your estate is in your retirement plans. You don't change the beneficiary on those plans to pass into the trust you so carefully crafted, so your children receive half of your estate at 18 and blow it all on cars and partying.

- You live in a state where life insurance is an asset exempt from creditors. You don't bother to fill out the beneficiary designation portion, so by default the life insurance passes to your estate. Because the death benefit goes your estate, instead of to a named beneficiary, the money goes your creditors instead of to your family.

- And the biggie—you got divorced but forgot to change the beneficiary in your 401(k) plan. You (to put it politely) loathe your ex—and the @#$&^% gets your entire 401(k) plan because federal law, which governs 401(k) plans, trumps state law, which governs your will.

Coordinating your named beneficiaries with your estate plan goes beyond merely making sure the designations match at the time you create your estate plan. You're much more likely to obtain new assets that have named beneficiaries (you change your job and get new employee benefits, you roll over your 401(k) into an IRA, you buy a new life insurance policy) than you are to update your will. It's important that whenever any of these things happen, you check back with your overall estate plan to make sure these new assets will go to people in a manner that meets your goals.

Retirement plan assets (401(k), IRA, 403(b), and so on) have very significant income tax ramifications for the beneficiary. Coordinating the distribution of retirement plan assets in your estate plan is only one element. You also need to make sure the retirement plan distributions will be made in the most tax-efficient manner, because all those assets sitting in your retirement plans are still subject to income tax, not to mention estate or inheritance tax. Isn't tax law lovely?

Revocable Trusts

I know that some of you flipped right to this chapter. You've seen commentators on TV or ads in the newspaper that scream, "You must have a revocable trust—a will is no good!" I've devoted an entire chapter to trusts (Chapter 6, "Trust in Trusts"), so you might be thinking to yourself, "Why is the discussion of revocable trusts here instead of there?" A revocable trust is a will substitute—it does all the same things that a will does in terms of distributing your estate, but it can do so in a manner that avoids probate. It may also make it easier for a person to have authority over your assets in the event you become incapacitated. It can provide a high level of privacy. For some people, a revocable trust is just the thing. The trusts I talk about in Chapter 6 are subtrusts that are created within a will or a revocable trust (or even an irrevocable trust, for that matter).

▓ **Real Stories from Around My Conference Table**   Unfortunately, a good tool in the hands of someone with bad intentions can be an instrument of destruction. There are companies known as *trust mills* that proffer the revocable trust as a magic pill to solve all the problems associated with dying. You know what they say about something that sounds too good to be true. I've seen clients come in with very impressive-looking three-ring binders of documents that are hundreds of pages long—and that don't meet the clients' basic goals. The clients believe that because they have a revocable trust, (1) they won't be subject to estate taxes—wrong, and (2) their creditors can't get to their assets—wrong. Some of the documents I've seen don't even give the assets to the person who was intended to have them. In others, the attorney who prepared the document implies that the attorney needs to be named as trustee at death, or there are instructions that their law firm has to handle the estate (wrong and wrong). All this stuff is important, folks. It determines what your family has when you aren't here to provide for them anymore. You owe it to yourself to make sure you're working with a professional who has your best interest at heart, not theirs.

Should I Have a Revocable Trust or a Will?

This question gets my favorite lawyerly answer: it depends. The primary factor is which state you live in. As I've said, some states have very high cost of probate, and you can get a lot of value out of having a revocable trust as the centerpiece of your estate plan instead of just a will. In other states, a revocable trust is the customary way of creating an estate plan—it's what the financial institutions, courts, lawyers, and families are used to seeing. With estate planning, doing what is "customarily done in your area" is of high value because the people around you will be carrying the plan out.

Two other considerations are cost and comfort level. A revocable trust as the centerpiece of your estate plan is likely to be more expensive than a will. You're creating an additional document, after all. Accordingly, you should make sure there is value to that additional document for you. Finally, if you're reading this book, you clearly want to educate yourself before creating an estate plan. Which type of plan do you believe is more closely aligned with your goals? It's your money and your family, after all.

What Can a Revocable Trust Do That a Will Can't?

Revocable trusts differ from wills in important ways. Let's look at a few.

Avoids Probate

I may have mentioned this once or twice (OK, or even a lot more), but assets passing from a revocable trust to a beneficiary at death avoid probate. In states where probate is an incredibly long and expensive process, it may be so complicated that from a practical perspective you have to involve an attorney and pay for those services. Also, it could be months of probate before your executor is able to take control of your assets. In the meantime, your mortgage and bills still need to be paid—and where is the money coming from?

Why is a revocable trust different? Although you'll die at some point, the trust won't. Because it doesn't die, the assets it owns don't go through probate. Beware! To get the benefit of probate avoidance, you must, absolutely must, *fund* the revocable trust. What does this mean? You need to retitle assets so they're not in the name of Harry Henderson but instead in the name of the Harry Henderson Revocable Trust. If you don't fund the trust, the assets will still be distributed in the way the trust says, but they'll have to go through probate before they pass to the trust, negating the benefit you were looking for in the first place.

Pourover Will

A will is always a companion document to a revocable trust. Even if you do the best job possible to fund your revocable trust, you may still end up with assets in your own name when you pass away. Example: Great-aunt Hilda died and left you an inheritance, and you passed away before you actually received the inheritance, so that is an asset in your own name. This will is known as a *pourover* will, and it generally says (1) who gets your personal property, (2) that all other assets are paid over (or "poured over") to the revocable trust, (3) who your executors are, and (4) who your guardians are. The pourover will also has some additional shortened boilerplate language regarding how to administer any of these assets.

■ **Let's Get Real**   Before you spend a lot of money trying to avoid probate, make sure probate is an expensive process in the state where you live. In New Jersey, probate is simple and inexpensive. If you live in New York, even if you have a revocable trust, it must be admitted to probate. This is why you need to speak to an attorney in your jurisdiction to see what's customary and appropriate.

Privacy

A will is a public document—if you go to Google right now, you can look up the wills of Whitney Houston and Jacqueline Onassis. But you can't find the estate plans of Steve Jobs and Michael Jackson—they had revocable trusts as the centerpiece of their estate plans. Although you may not be one of the greatest moguls or entertainers of our time, you may also firmly believe that it's nobody else's business how you distribute wealth among your family. If that's the case, you should use a revocable trust. You'll have a very bland pourover will that merely gives everything over to your revocable trust, away from the prying eyes of your mother-in-law, a nosy neighbor, or the person who wants to scam your widow.

Real Estate in Multiple Jurisdictions

If you live in Michigan and have a vacation home in Illinois, your estate will be subject to two probate proceedings when you die: one in Michigan, your state of residence; and one in Illinois, because you own real property located there. The second probate is known as an *ancillary probate*.

Two probates means two sets of expenses, and maybe even two lawyers—as if one isn't bad enough! However, if your revocable trust owns the out-of-state real estate, the property owned by the trust won't be subject to probate, because the trust doesn't die. Even in states where probate avoidance isn't a driving concern, it may make sense to create a revocable trust to own your out-of-state property.

Oh, and avoiding probate does *not* mean you avoid taxes. If you own real estate in a jurisdiction has its own estate tax, your real estate may be subject to tax when you die, even though your own state doesn't have a state-level estate tax. (For example, Michigan doesn't have a state estate tax, but Illinois does.)

Where Might You Live Next?

An estate plan is an investment. If you know that you're planning to relocate from Connecticut to California in the next two years, it would be wise to find out what's customary in California before doing your estate planning in Connecticut, so that you can incorporate standard practices of both states into the investment you're making in your estate plan today. A revocable trust might be a more flexible document in the event that a will doesn't make sense in California, but there's no downside to having a revocable trust in Connecticut.

Disability

Just as a revocable trust doesn't die, it doesn't become disabled. As such, it can be an alternative to a general durable power of attorney. The concept is that a trustee is a defined role—when one individual steps out, another individual merely steps in. Because the trust remains the owner of the property, only the mouthpiece of the trust is changed. This is no different than when Bill Gates stepped down as CEO of Microsoft and Steve Ballmer stepped in—the change in leadership didn't affect the validity of the corporation.

▓ **Let's Get Real**   Like probate avoidance, the use of a revocable trust in the event of disability can be more theoretical than practical. If you're in a jurisdiction where it's customary to use a power of attorney in the event of disability, there may be more paperwork involved in having institutions consent to the change of trustee than to use a power of attorney in the first place. (The converse is true in a jurisdiction where revocable trusts are the custom.) Although theoretically there's no reason a third party needs to consent to a change of trustee, that is irrelevant if the bank manager "isn't sure" about whether you can act as successor trustee. From a practical perspective, it's the person at the bank whom you need to satisfy, whether they're right or not. This is why the customs of your area of the country have a direct impact on the effectiveness of your estate planning. In New York, financial institutions are used to seeing a statutory form of power of attorney. They're reasonably (if not correctly) reluctant to accept a trustee change without additional documentation that the new trustee is indeed the authorized person to act. Remember, they're sued if they're wrong.

Anatomy of a Revocable Trust

Because the revocable trust is a will substitute, it's structured much the same as a will. There's a logical progression from one floor to the next as you create the revocable trust. I went through a lot of this in detail in Chapter 4, "What Goes into a Will?" so here I focus on what makes a revocable trust different from a will and give you an abbreviated description of the building blocks.

Will Substitute

When you die with a revocable trust, it says who your ultimate beneficiaries are, instead of your will. This type of trust is a creature of many names. It could be referred to as a revocable trust, a living trust, or even a loving trust. Get ready—I'm going to pull out the legal guns. Attorneys refer to it as an *inter vivos trust* (meaning a trust that was created during your lifetime), as opposed to a *testamentary trust* (which comes into being upon your death). Its key feature is that it's revocable because the person who created the trust (you) can change the trust or take money out of the trust any time you want to. This is distinguished from an irrevocable trust, which is a totally different animal.[4]

Terminology

Because a trust isn't a will, the terminology is different. The person who creates a trust is known as the *grantor*, *trustor*, or *settlor*, depending on what's common in your jurisdiction. Instead of an executor, you have a trustee who is in charge of the trust.

▓ **Ask the Attorney** "Deirdre, can I name guardians for my children in my revocable trust?" No! In some states, guardians can only be named in your will. This is one of the reasons a revocable trust is always accompanied by a pourover will (flip back a few pages if you need to). Because you don't know what state you'll live in when you die, you must create a will that names guardians if you have minor children.

Blueprint of a Revocable Trust

What's different when you're constructing a trust instead of a will?

---

[4] Irrevocable trusts are the beasts that can beat back Uncle Sam. If your goal is to save taxes, spend some time in Chapter 6, "Trust in Trusts"; Chapter 10, "Insurance Trusts"; and Chapter 11, "Advanced Tax Strategies."

Lifetime Trust: What Happens While the Grantor Is Alive?

By its nature, a will only takes effect upon your death—therefore, there's no need to talk about what happens to your property while you're still alive. In comparison, your revocable trust comes to life when you create it. It may own assets during your lifetime (and must own assets during your lifetime if your goal is to avoid probate upon your death). So, the first part of your revocable trust always talks about whom the assets can be distributed to during your lifetime. Your trustee (normally you, while you're still alive and competent) has the power to distribute the assets of the trust to you, and to your spouse if you're married, for any reason. Normally there are no other beneficiaries of the trust during your lifetime, because any amount you give to anyone other than yourself or your spouse is potentially subject to gift tax.[5] You can amend and change the terms of the trust at any time. Because the trust is revocable, you as the grantor can add assets to and remove assets from the trust at any time for any reason.

Be aware of three key things that result from you having this power to add and remove assets, and change or amend the trust:

- Assets in a revocable trust aren't protected from creditors. If you can get your hands on your assets, your creditors can get their hands on your assets.

- Assets in a revocable trust are yours for estate tax purposes. The value of property owned by the trust will be added to everything else you own to see if you owe any tax and how much.

- You're the income tax payer for any money earned by property in the revocable trust. Some people have "read" that if money is in a trust, nobody has to pay income taxes on it. That kind of thinking will land you in jail. Your revocable trust uses your Social Security number while you're alive.

Administrative Fund: Distribution Provisions

Moving on to the next section of your revocable trust, you find instructions to your trustee about what to do with the assets in the trust upon your death. The first part of the instructions talk about your trustee "gathering" all the assets. This means changing title of any probate assets to the trust so the trustee has authority over the assets. Next, the trustee will pay debts, taxes,

---

[5] They tax me if I keep it; they tax me if I give it away. Sad but true. Look at Chapter 9 for strategies to reduce the tax man's share.

and liabilities (if this sounds familiar, these are the same steps that your executor is directed to take under your will). After everyone else has been paid, the revocable trust gives the trustee instructions about who are the beneficiaries of the remaining assets. There could be specific bequests, as in a will, or just a residuary bequest. There are also instructions about tax elections so your trustee can work with your executor (who may be the same person) to minimize the tax impact of the distribution of your wealth on your family.

Subtrusts: Further Trusts to Accomplish the Grantor's Objective

After the assets are gathered, the debts and expenses are paid, and the trustee identifies who gets what, the trust outlines the criteria you designed for the long-term management of the assets in any subtrust that was created. A subtrust is merely a specific trust created within the overall structure of the revocable trust. The subtrusts don't come into effect until you've passed away, so they're very similar in purpose and description to the testamentary trusts that might be created under your will. I describe all different types of subtrusts in Chapter 6.

Who's in Charge? Trustees and Successors

The trustee is the person in charge of the property owned by the trust. The individual (or individuals) who fill this role change over time.

While you're alive, you'll likely want to be the trustee of your revocable trust. In some rare exceptions where the person who's creating the trust doesn't want to manage their own money, they can name another person to act as trustee (I usually see this only with the very young or very old).

Upon your death, the person who's in charge of carrying out your immediate instructions needs to meet the short-term goals of figuring out what you have and what you owe, and getting it to the right people. This job description is very similar to the executor in your will, and you may have somebody in mind to do this who has certain financial skills.

Any subtrusts that are created are for the long-term benefit of your family. It may be appropriate to have different trustees for these subtrusts—perhaps the beneficiary should be acting as a trustee or co-trustee of any trust created for their benefit.[6]

---

[6] Naming the trustee is arguably the most important decision you'll make about your estate plan. After all, what does it matter what you say if the person carrying out your wishes doesn't do a good job? You don't need to decide now. I've dedicated Chapter 12 to

The Rest of the Trust—Beautiful Boilerplate

Just like a will, the trust is a creature of your own design, and you have to give it powers to act in the manner that you want it (think Wall-E, not Frankenstein). Accordingly, the bulk of the trust consists of lovely boilerplate provisions, just like a will.

What Tools to Use

At the end of the day, the answer to "which type of document?" (a revocable trust or just a will) and "how to title assets?" (individual, joint, community, pay on death, and beneficiary designation) that's best for you is unique to your situation. Part of the consideration is the knowledge level of the professional you're speaking to, which is one of the reasons I strongly suggest working with an attorney who focuses in estate planning to put your estate plan together. All I ask is that you please don't choose one form of asset transfer over another based on what your neighbor, hairdresser, father-in-law, seminar speaker, or television personality said—they don't have the knowledge or experience to evaluate your unique situation and guide you to the right answers (and yes, I've had clients come into my office and tell me that they "needed a trust" because that's what their hairdresser said).

---

everything you need to think about in naming a trustee. They key in naming a trustee is to actually name one. Don't let fear of decision about this issue defeat the goal of putting your estate plan in place.

6

Trust in Trusts

The Secret to a Great Estate Plan

You don't just want a good estate plan—or an adequate or OK estate plan—you want a *great* estate plan. You want an estate plan that takes your wealth, filters it through your goals, and produces a final package that provides security and peace of mind. The secret ingredient that will bring your estate plan to life is effective use of trusts.

▦ **Chapter Brief** Trusts have extreme value for your family regardless of the amount of your wealth. Whatever you have, trusts can be used to protect those assets so your goals are met and the assets aren't lost due to waste, creditors, or influences outside your family. It's incredibly hard to earn wealth, and you can use trusts to make sure the wealth stays in place as security for your family and under their control.

What Is a Trust?

You can view a trust as if it were a mini family business whose goals and purposes are aligned with your own. Just like a business, a trust can own any type of asset that you can, such as bank accounts, real estate, investment accounts, stocks, bonds, limited liability company interests, and so on. A trust is responsible for paying income taxes, just like any business, and has a tax rate different from individuals, like businesses do. Even though the assets in a trust are used to reach the family's goals and objectives, they're separate and distinct from the beneficiaries' individual assets, which protects those assets from any creditors. Trusts are the vehicle that will allow you to reach your tax savings goals.

Trust Triangle

There are three parties to every trust:

- *Grantor, trustor, settlor.* Regardless of the name, this is the person creating the trust and transferring their money to it. This role is like the founder of the family company. The name varies by custom depending on what state you live in. There is usually a single grantor, but a married couple may both be grantor of the same trust.

- *Trustee.* This person is in charge of making all the decisions about the trust. This is like the president of the family company. There must be one trustee, but there can be multiple co-trustees.

- *Beneficiary.* These are the people who are like the shareholders of the family business. All the profits and assets flow to them. Who the beneficiaries are and how the assets flow to them varies depending on (1) the grantor's goals and objectives and the values they they're trying to pass along and (2) whether the trust is designed to meet any specific tax-savings goals.

One person can have multiple roles in the trust triangle, but having more than one role may change the tax treatment of the trust. If one person is both grantor and trustee, it's generally a revocable trust. In some states, a person can be a trustee and a beneficiary. But in order to maintain tax savings and asset protection, there are certain restrictions on a beneficiary/trustee's ability to make distributions to themselves. The extent to which you can maintain control of the trust and not have the trust assets either subject to estate tax or available to your creditors comes down to the old adage "You can't have your cake and eat it too." However, with some informed estate planning, you can nibble on the cake and enjoy the frosting!

Asset Protection and the Spendthrift

Trusts are near and dear to an estate planning attorney's heart for one fundamental reason: money in a trust that someone else created for your benefit can't (absent very special, specific circumstances) be used or taken by a third party who isn't a beneficiary of the trust. What does this mean in English? Trusts provide protection from what I call *creditors* and *predators*. So, if your parents leave your inheritance to you in a trust, and you later can't pay back a loan, the lender can't make you go into the trust to get money to pay the loan.

Why is this? A well-drafted trust contains a *spendthrift provision* that essentially says, "No interest in any trust hereunder shall be subject to a beneficiary's liabilities or creditor claims, assignment, or anticipation." This means even if the beneficiary wants to, the trustee doesn't have the power to use the money in the trust to pay the beneficiary's debts. The beneficiary also can't give the trust to a soon-to-be ex-spouse or creditor because they don't have the power to "assign" their interest in the trust.

Who Could Be Creditors?

The creditor situation that most people fear is the future divorce of one of the beneficiaries. Let's say you leave your daughter, Mary, one third of your estate. A very reasonable concern is, "If Mary gets divorced in the future, could my soon-to-be ex-son-in-law Steve share the inheritance? I don't want that to happen." This isn't to say that you don't adore Steve now. The point is that Steve only gets to share in the benefit of your wealth as long as he is married to Mary; if that relationship ends, so should his access to any money you've left to Mary and her children.[1]

Assets that are left in trust to children are generally exempt from being distributed as part of the marital estate in a divorce. This is true in both common law and community property states. In a practical sense, this means if you leave the inheritance in trust for Mary, Steve has no claims to it if the marriage ends.

■ **Ask the Attorney** "Deirdre, do I have to leave assets to my kids' spouses?" No. Ninety-five percent or more of my clients exclude sons-in-law and daughters-in-law from their estate plans. When we get to the point in our conversations about "Whom do you want to leave your assets to?" some families are straightforward that they want the spouses excluded, whereas others feel it might somehow be "wrong" to do so. Remember, you worked a lifetime for your wealth, and you can leave assets to whomever you want. Excluding your children's spouses is most definitely the norm.

Other creditors could show up in the event of a downturn in the family finances. The sad reality is that your family members might mismanage money, overextend themselves with "wants" and not "needs," lose their jobs, get

---

[1] Even if Steve isn't a direct beneficiary of your estate, the reality is that he will likely be an indirect beneficiary as long as he is married to Mary. If Mary decides to hold her inheritance for the kids' college, then Steve benefits because instead of saving for education, he can save for retirement.

sick, or otherwise be unable to keep up with their obligations.[2] But if an inheritance is left to them in trust, then the assets (as long as they stay in the trust) are exempt from the claims of credit card companies, banks, tax liens, or any other liability in which the beneficiary might find themselves.

Creditors also often crop up when the beneficiary isn't financially mature. Turning 18, 21, 25, or 30 doesn't automatically mean a person has the skills to manage the large sum of money they suddenly have control over. Remember, everything you have is cash to them. And it's much more fun to throw a party than it is to consider the effect of rates of return on cash flow over 20 years. A trust can give the beneficiary time to learn how to manage money by having another person as trustee for a period of time. After all, your wealth grew over decades. You probably made mistakes along the way and learned from them. Your beneficiaries are receiving a very large amount of money at once. Ever see what happens to lottery winners? You can protect your heirs from the temptation of burning through a lot of money all at once by leaving it to them in a trust that provides distribution controls.

Who Could Be Predators?

Creditors seek to enforce legal obligations against assets that you've left to your beneficiary. Predators, on the other hand, have no real claims on the money. They simply want what's yours. These predators are often disguised as friends or even family members, but at the end of the day they're more interested in using your beneficiary's money for their benefit than in making sure the beneficiary is secure and protected. In our office, we often see this with younger beneficiaries who haven't attained financial maturity and are swayed to invest in a business or buy a fancy house or car that's well beyond their means. The predator might even be one of those deadly sins, like greed or sloth. The beneficiary might use the inheritance as an excuse to not work and become a productive adult. Even when people are older and married, there can be pressure from the spouse to get a vacation home, or upgrade the kitchen, or go on one more vacation, instead of setting aside the money for college education or retirement.

---

[2] An *Atlantic* article found, "[T]otal household debt currently stands at $11.44 trillion [...] the average American owes $47,500." Jordan Weissmann, "Americans Are Still Swimming in Debt They Can't Repay," *The Atlantic*, June 1, 2012, www.theatlantic.com/business/archive/2012/06/americans-are-still-swimming-in-debt-they-cant-pay/257996./

▓ **Real Stories from Around My Conference Table**   You may be thinking to yourself right now, "This asset protection stuff doesn't apply to me; this only happens to the Britney Spears of the world." You need to keep in mind that your family will only have this money as a result of your death. They will be going through a period of emotional devastation and may have just lost one of the anchors in their lives. The fact that they're hurting and submerged in stormy waters will attract sharks. A number of real-life examples quickly come to mind: a gypsy came to a widow's door because he was "in the neighborhood" sealing driveways, and charged her $4,000 to do a $500 job; an elderly widower was targeted by an unscrupulous financial planner to purchase annuities in his IRA because they would give him "tax protection," even though IRAs are already tax deferred (but annuities give huge commissions to the salesman); a 22-year-old bought an expensive car and then couldn't buy a house because he didn't have the down payment; a 42-year-old son-in-law ran the family's finances, convinced the daughter to put the entire inheritance in joint names, and walked away with half of it to spend on his next wife; and a 27-year-old's "friends" convinced him to take his entire inheritance from his mother and invest in their paintball company, but they never gave him ownership and he ended up with nothing.

You can't protect your loved ones from the jerks they come across in life (or marry). What a trust can do is prevent those people from destroying the security you've worked so hard to create for your family.

Asset Protection for Successful People

Asset protection isn't needed solely because a person is facing financial pitfalls or may be influenced by bad people; some of the people in your life who need asset protection the most are the ones who are the most successful! There are risks inherent with success. If you're an accomplished business person, you may need to borrow from a bank on a regular basis. If you're a professional (doctor, lawyer, accountant, chiropractor, architect, and so on), your professional liability creates a greater risk profile than that of the average person. Sometimes claims are made against people who have achieved great things merely because they have done so. We live in a litigious society, and you can't control who might sue you for anything. One thing you can control is whether any inheritance you're leaving to your family is available to satisfy that lawsuit. Put the inheritance in a trust so all your hard work isn't victim to somebody else's greed.

The Limits of Asset Protection

Except for in certain states and foreign jurisdictions, you generally can't set up a trust for your own benefit that is also protected from your own creditors.[3] The asset protection I'm talking about is for the benefit of your beneficiaries, not you. Think about it. The assets are protected from creditors and predators either because (1) you've died and created a trust, or (2) you've given away assets to a trust that you don't control. Your beneficiaries enjoy the gift of asset protection due to the high bar crossed to set it up.

Asset protection is available only as long as the assets stay in the trust. As soon as the assets come out of the trust, they're fair game to creditors. Example: Your son Kevin loses his job and finds himself in the midst of a bankruptcy proceeding. His grandmother left an inheritance to him in trust. The assets in the trust are generally exempt from the bankruptcy proceeding. But if Kevin starts taking money out of the trust to fund his lifestyle, that money might be available to satisfy the creditors. This is one reason I recommend that a trust potentially have multiple beneficiaries. If Kevin's children are also beneficiaries of the trust, the trustee could use the trust assets for their benefit without involving Kevin. Or the trust could buy things for Kevin instead of distributing money to him.

Asset protection can be lost based on the actual use of the trust. For example, suppose the trust regularly distributes $1,000 per month to you, and you file for divorce and tell the trustee, "Don't give me the $1,000 per month anymore." The court might find that the longstanding nature of the $1,000 each month is a mandatory distribution to you and direct that it needs to continue to be paid, thus affecting support and alimony. Additionally, if you're the trustee of a trust for your own benefit, and you don't respect the parameters the trust and instead treat it as your personal checking account, a creditor won't have to respect the parameters either.

Trusts and Money

I'm super excited to tell you about all the different types of trusts there are in the world. (I'm serious! People tell you to do what you're passionate about, and for me, that's helping you understand how to protect your money for your family.)

---

[3] Alaska, Delaware, Nevada, and South Dakota allow you to create a trust in which you're a beneficiary but the assets are beyond the reach of your creditors. This is the real "having your cake and eating it too" scenario. If protecting your assets from your own creditors is a concern for you, you need to make an appointment with an attorney who specializes in asset protection.

Do You Need One to Have the Other?

You may be thinking to yourself that trusts are for people who are fabulously wealthy, and that's not you. Not true. If you've ever been concerned about what your beneficiaries will do with the money you leave them, then you can design a trust to target those specific concerns. I'm pretty confident that I've already outlined lots of other reasons to use trusts that have nothing to do with the amount of wealth you have, but have everything to do with maximizing that hard-earned wealth for your beneficiaries. All I'm asking you to do is keep reading to see whether a trust might be a better way for you to meet your goals for your family instead of an outright "whatever happens, happens" inheritance.

It could be that after reading this chapter you decide that for your family an outright inheritance is the best thing. After all, it's simple, straightforward, and easy to implement. That's terrific! It means you've educated yourself about the options and decided on an estate plan that works for you (now, call your attorney or hit legalzoom.com to get it done). But it could also be that your situation doesn't lend itself to this type of simplicity, and a trust can be used as a tool to address your "what if ...."

Two Trust Types: At Death, During Life

To start with, the world of trusts is broken into two distinct territories: is the trust created as a result of your death, or did it come into being during your lifetime?

- *Testamentary trust.* This is a trust that's created as a result of a person's death. A testamentary trust can be created either in a will or in a revocable trust. This trust isn't funded (doesn't contain assets) until items are distributed to it as a result of a person's death.

- *Inter-vivos trust.* In comparison, this trust is not only created but also funded and fully operational during your lifetime. The territory that an inter-vivos trust covers encompasses two areas:

  - *Revocable trust.* This type of inter-vivos trust is likely to be used as the centerpiece of an estate plan. It has no asset protection or estate tax advantages while you're alive, but it can be a super-efficient way to transfer assets at death, as I describe in Chapter 5, "Will Alternatives and Avoiding Probate."

- *Irrevocable trust.* If you're creating a trust during your lifetime and putting money into it that you can't get back, you have a specific reason to do so. You're also likely to have some excess wealth. Irrevocable trusts are usually used to achieve advanced estate and gift tax minimization strategies, or to satisfy a specific asset protection purpose (such as for a child with special needs).

Each trust I introduce you to can be created either upon your death (testamentary) or during your life (inter-vivos). My intention here is to give you an overview of the different structures you might use to connect your money to your goals.

Two Trust Parts: Income and Principal

The assets in any type of trust are divided into two categories:

- *Income.* This is what the trust earns in interest, dividends, lease payments, or royalties. It doesn't include any capital gains from selling an asset. Income is taxed to the trust at trust income tax rates, which are higher than individual income tax rates. If the trust income is distributed to a beneficiary during the year, the beneficiary then pays the income taxes on the income distributed to them. This makes sense, because if the beneficiary ends up with the money, they have the dollars to pay the tax.

- *Principal.* This is what the grantor originally contributed to the trust. Added to principal are (1) any income that the trust earned during the year that wasn't distributed to the beneficiaries and (2) any appreciation on the assets during the year. Trusts pay the same capital gains tax rates that individuals do.

Let's Get Real When a trust earns income, it pays taxes on it at the highest income tax rate (35 percent right now) starting at $11,650 of earnings. Compare this to a single individual tax payer who doesn't hit the 35 percent tax rate until $388,350 of earnings. All things being equal, it may make sense to have the trust income distributed to a beneficiary each year so that less income tax is paid. However, things aren't always equal. If the beneficiary is a minor, or going through a divorce, or the trust is related to special needs, it may defeat the goal of the trust to distribute all the income to the beneficiary. In this case, the cost of asset protection is higher income tax. Bear in mind that the tax rate differential only applies to income and not to capital gains, so a trust in that situation could pursue an investment strategy to minimize growth through income and maximize capital gains.

What Kind of Trust Is Best for You?

Trusts are structured depending on your needs and goals. Some are put into place for tax savings, and others with more of an asset protection objective. Some are for groups of people and others for only one. Here I want to give you a flavor of different types of trusts so you can start thinking about which might appeal to you.

Family Trust

A family trust might also be called a *credit shelter trust,* or *trust B* in an A/B trust plan[4], or a *sprinkle trust.* Whatever the name, the family trust is just what it says: a trust for the benefit of a group of family members. A family trust is commonly used when a married person passes away in order to capture their exemption from estate taxes (be they federal or state taxes). The concept of how to plan to minimize taxes is discussed more fully in Chapter 8, "Taxes." In that case, the family trust would be for the benefit of the surviving spouse and children.

Whom Does It Benefit?

When you went through the exercise of who you want to have your money and what values you want to share, did you have a group of people in mind? For married couples, the answer is generally "my spouse and children." Often you want to leave it up to your spouse to use the money to support your values with your children. In other words, you want to create a family business where your spouse is in charge and your spouse and children receive the benefit of the assets, but the assets are secure and are being used to satisfy your long-term goals and vision. That family business is the family trust.

Although a family trust is always used to minimize estate taxes, you should consider it part of your estate plan even if estate taxes aren't your concern. Do you have misgivings about your spouse managing money? You could name

---

[4] Some attorneys refer to an estate plan designed to minimize estate taxes as an "A/B" plan, where a marital trust (described below) is Trust A and the family trust is Trust B. I personally don't like this nomenclature because it isn't descriptive of what the trusts do, so I don't use these terms in my conversations with clients or with you.

a child or third party as the trustee or co-trustee. Does the idea of your spouse remarrying and giving your wealth to a new spouse and their children keep you up at night? You can limit the beneficiaries to only your spouse and biological children in any distribution. Do your beneficiaries consist of your sister and her kids? The family trust isn't limited to benefiting a spouse and children but could be used for other multigenerational family groups.

A Sprinkle Here, a Sprinkle There

A common design element of a family trust is that it's a *sprinkle* trust, meaning the trustee has the discretion to give more or less to any one or more of the beneficiaries as their needs dictate. Imagine if all the beneficiaries were plants in a garden. The trustee could sprinkle a little water on plant A one day, a lot of water on plant B the next day, and no water on any plant the third day. Here, the water being sprinkled is money. So, if your spouse and children are all beneficiaries of the family trust, the trustee can use the money for the spouse, or for one of the children, or for all of the children, in the trustee's discretion based on what the family's needs are.[5]

Income and Principal

The family trust can be designed so the distribution of income or principal is made in the same manner or differently. Some people want to make sure all the income goes to their spouse. In this case, this family trust would mandate that all income is paid to the spouse (quarterly is most common). I refer to this as a *mandatory income distribution*. Other people want to leave it up to the trustee to distribute income or principal. After all, the trustee will actually be there in the future to evaluate the needs of the beneficiaries and the tax laws in place at that time. I call this a *discretionary distribution*.

Marital Trust

A marital trust is a trust created solely for the benefit of the surviving spouse. I'll talk about this more in Chapter 8, but for now know that any assets passing to a surviving spouse aren't subject to estate tax due to an unlimited marital deduction from estate taxes. However, assets passing in a trust are by definition not passing directly to the surviving spouse. How do you reconcile the two? You create a very specific type of trust known as a *qualified terminable interest property (QTIP)* trust. I use the more descriptive vernacular—marital

---

[5] Don't forget that if your goal is to maintain control in the family, your spouse can act as trustee or co-trustee. For more ideas on how to create an estate plan using a family trust, or any trust I'm describing here, you should look at the Planning Guides later in the book.

trust. (Tax attorneys love acronyms to describe tax-savings vehicles. I dedicate all of Chapter 25, "Glossary," to the alphabet soup of tax planning.) With a marital trust, assets can pass to a trust for the benefit of the surviving spouse *and* receive the marital deduction from estate taxes. One upside is that the person creating the marital trust can direct how the assets of the trust are used, subject to certain restrictions.

Because this is a "have your cake and eat it too" situation, a marital trust must follows some very specific rules:[6]

- The surviving spouse must be the only beneficiary of a marital trust during their lifetime.

- The surviving spouse must receive all the income of the trust each year (a mandatory income distribution). The surviving spouse also has the right to demand that the trust invest in income-producing property.

- Whatever assets are in the trust when the surviving spouse dies must be included in the surviving spouse's taxable estate. The marital trust provides for estate tax deferral, not estate tax reduction. (Compare this to a family trust, which can minimize estate taxes.)

Single-Beneficiary Trust

A beneficiary trust is a testamentary or inter-vivos trust for the benefit of a single person. A beneficiary trust can be used to achieve a host of goals: financial management, asset protection, funding an education, building retirement security, creating an income stream, encouraging certain behavior to support your values, and basically anything else you want to achieve via the way you leave money to a beneficiary.

Depending on what your goals are, you can structure a beneficiary trust either to have a certain end date or to continue for the beneficiary's lifetime.

Age-Restrictions Trust

This type of beneficiary trust has an end date. The age-restrictions trust directs that the assets in the trust must be distributed outright to the beneficiary at a certain age or ages, or when a fixed period of time has elapsed.

---

[6] A special note for anyone who is in a civil union or same-sex marriage: estate tax rules are federal in nature, and the estate tax deferral of a marital trust doesn't apply to you. Look to Chapter 16, "Planning Guide for Unmarried and Same-Sex Couples," for alternative estate tax savings ideas.

For example, you might direct that the beneficiary receives everything outright at age 21, or half of the assets at 25 and the remaining half at 30. Other ideas are for the assets to be held in trust for five years from when the second parent passes away, or ten years after the first grandchild is born. The general theory is that you want the assets held in trust until a certain amount of life experience has been achieved, which you're marking by the passage of time. The trust will then dissolve, and you leave it up to the beneficiaries to do what they will with the money.

Another way of structuring an age-restrictions trust is to say that the person will have a right of withdrawal over, let's say, 50 percent of the trust at age 30, and the remaining trust at age 35. The right of withdrawal achieves the same result as an outright distribution in that the money is theirs when a beneficiary reaches the milestone, but the beneficiary can elect to continue the trust for management purposes. *Caution:* Once the milestone is reached, there will no longer be any asset protection over the trust. If the beneficiary can withdraw the money, so can their creditors.

Bear in mind that in an age-restrictions trust, the milestones represent when the beneficiary *must* get the money. You can give the trustee the ability to distribute the trust income and principal to or for the beneficiary at any time before the milestone in the trustee's discretion, or as you otherwise direct.

Income and Principal

In an age-restrictions trust, income and principal can be treated separately. For example, the trust might provide for "income starting at age 22, with mandatory distributions of one half of the principal at 30 and the remaining balance at 35." By setting up the age-restrictions trust in this manner, the beneficiary will receive some money without the trustee's control or interference (depending on your perspective). This provides the beneficiary with an excellent opportunity to make good or bad decisions with a small part of their inheritance before they receive the bulk of it. Sometimes the most valuable lessons we learn are from bad decisions. Of course, it's helpful if the impact of the bad decisions is limited by the amount of money involved.

Pros and Cons

The age-restrictions trust provides the simplicity of having a time certain as to when the trust ends: X happens, and the money is distributed. It also supports the belief that at some point, the beneficiary should have control over their own inheritance. (This can also be achieved with a lifetime trust where the beneficiary is the trustee, which I talk about later.) The age-restrictions trust also satisfies the sense of "I can only do so much, and at some point it's their responsibility," in that when the milestones are reached, the torch is completely passed to the next generation. Another benefit is that the trust can be designed to terminate after it accomplishes its goal, such as "By age 25, Pamela should have completed her education."

The key downside of mandating a time to make a distribution is that you don't know today what situation a beneficiary will be in at some future point in time. What if you set a distribution age of 25, and Pamela decides to go on to graduate school, has never had a real job, and has no idea how to manage an inheritance? What if at the time of the distribution Pamela is in the middle of a divorce or bankruptcy? What if Pamela is a successful professional or business owner, and she has an increased liability profile? Distributing assets at a time certain in the future could actually be harmful instead of helpful.

Lifetime Trust

As its name suggests, this type of beneficiary trust lasts for the beneficiary's lifetime. It's an age-restrictions trust that doesn't end. The lifetime trust can be set up in most any manner you like: all of the distributions of income and principal are within the control of the trustee; distributing income is mandatory, distributing the principal is discretionary; or even that a fixed percentage of the trust principal must be distributed on an annual basis (a *unitrust*).

Pros and Cons

The key benefit of a lifetime trust is that third parties never have access to the trust assets unless and until the assets are distributed from the trust. This negates all the worry about "What position will the beneficiary be in at the time a distribution is called for?" because there are no mandatory distributions. Instead, all distributions are in the power of the trustee.

The downsides of the lifetime trust are primarily (1) the ongoing expenses of maintaining the trust, which will need to file its own separate tax returns and potentially pay the trustee, and (2) the fundamental issue to the beneficiary of having somebody else control their money.

Who Controls the Trust Over a Lifetime?

The question of who controls the trust is a very real roadblock as to whether setting up a lifetime trust makes sense. Luckily, there is a very elegant solution to this problem: you can name the beneficiary as the trustee of their own trust. Think about it. Instead of mandating a distribution at a certain age, just name the beneficiary as trustee (or co-trustee) at that age instead. If you were considering two distribution ages, name the beneficiary as co-trustee at the younger age and sole trustee at the older. A caveat: In certain states, you can be the sole trustee of your trust; in others, if you're a beneficiary, you need to have a co-trustee.

This solution creates a situation where your son Adam can act in the role of beneficiary and trustee. Adam can have the income of the trust distributed to himself quarterly and have the principal of the trust available to satisfy his needs for health, education, and maintenance and support of his lifestyle. Adam can also enjoy a super-benefit: the lifetime trust will be (1) excluded from his taxable estate and (2) unavailable to his creditors. We call this a home run!

■ **Ask the Attorney**   "Deirdre, how do you most often recommend leaving assets to children?" In my office, the default planning technique is to leave assets in trust for a child's lifetime and name the child as a trustee of their own trust at a certain age (normally 25 or 30). It's the best of all worlds. As long as the assets remain in the trust, they're beyond the reach of creditors and predators, thus creating a level of security over the assets that the child couldn't create themselves. By naming the child as the trustee or co-trustee at a certain age, the child is in control of their inheritance and will participate in investment decisions, distribution decisions, and how to utilize the gift to best support the child's family's needs and values.

Special-Needs Trust

I have found that special-needs trusts (SNTs) are becoming more and more common as families have beneficiaries with physical or mental disabilities.

Types of Beneficiaries

When considering a SNT, you need to think about two distinct classes of beneficiaries. The first are family members who may be either mentally or physically disabled and who, because of their disability, may require ongoing financial assistance. This group could include people of any age. This is the situation that most people think about in conjunction with a SNT.

There are two issues with the first group of special-needs beneficiaries: first, you might fear that the family member will never be able to manage an inheritance independently. But you also might be concerned that your loved one may need public benefits at some point in the future (for medical care, housing benefits, or food and transportation, for instance). Most public benefit programs are asset-based. To the extent that a person has what is deemed to be "too much" in assets, they don't qualify for the public benefit program. You also need to stir uncertainty into the mix. You may not know now whether a grandchild who has been diagnosed with Asperger's will be independent in the future.

The second group of beneficiaries is often overlooked: your parents. Sad to say, but the Greatest Generation is facing a scary reality where the cost of long-term healthcare may outstrip their resources. The baby boomers are right behind them. Nursing-home costs can range from $8,000 to $12,000 per month. People are living longer but not necessarily healthier, and the need for long-term care is growing. This need could put your parents (or other older relatives) in a position where they have to consider some sort of governmental assistance program to either provide for their needs or supplement their own resources in paying for a nursing home, assisted-living facility, or in-home care.

The thing these two groups of beneficiaries have in common is that in order to get the benefits they may need, they must financially qualify. The threshold to qualify can be as low as $2,000. Any of the special-needs beneficiary's assets over the qualification threshold must be spent down to the threshold to obtain or maintain qualification for benefits. If an inheritance is made outright, it will be deemed to be an asset of the special-needs beneficiary and must be spent down. This mandatory spend-down leaves the beneficiary in the position of having no security and being entirely dependent on the state for their needs. A better solution is to direct the inheritance to a SNT that can be used to supplement the special-needs beneficiary's lifestyle but can't be forced to be spent down in order to qualify for necessary assistance.[7]

Types of Special-Needs Trusts

One type of SNT is a *statutory special-needs trust*. This trust is created with the beneficiary's own money. This is typically the situation where a disabled beneficiary receives an inheritance, and no SNT provisions were created in the estate plan. In order for a statutory SNT to not be an available asset that must be spent down in order to qualify for care, the statutory SNT must be used only to supplement the disabled beneficiary's needs, and it must contain a payback provision. The payback provision directs that the state in which the special-needs beneficiary resides must be the primary beneficiary of the statutory SNT upon the special-needs beneficiary's death, to the extent of any money the state has spent on their care. Remember when you considered who you wanted to be your beneficiaries? Did you name Indiana or any other

---

[7] If these concerns resonate with you, examine Chapter 21, "Planning Guide for Special-Needs Children" and Chapter 20, "Planning Guide for Your Parents." I give you concrete ideas of how to incorporate these beneficiaries' needs into your plan.

state? Didn't think so. The good news? A statutory SNT is totally avoidable with an informed estate plan.

The other SNT is a *discretionary special-needs trust*. Unlike the statutory SNT, the discretionary SNT is set up by Dad with Dad's money for the benefit of the disabled child, Kristin. The discretionary SNT needs to be very specifically crafted so the trust won't interfere with Kristin's qualifications for public benefits. Is this type of trust needed in your family? If it is, you need to see an experienced attorney in your state. A discretionary SNT must follow very specific language that varies by state. A properly drafted discretionary SNT structures the inheritance for the disabled beneficiary as a supplemental security blanket to provide for those things that the state doesn't.

Multiple Beneficiaries: Common-Pot Trust

A common-pot trust is like a family trust, but for a group of the same generation. Consider Wade and Cheryl, who have two daughters ages 18 and 12. They feel that their older daughter Jessica is more "set" than her sibling. Jessica is a freshman in college and has a well-funded 529 plan. Wade and Cheryl want anything they leave to their children to get them both to the same place: graduated from college. They recognize that each daughter will have different expenses to reach that place. Instead of dividing the inheritance into two shares now and putting their younger daughter Ashley at a disadvantage because she has more expenses to reach the goal of being a college graduate, they want both girls to share in the inheritance until Ashley graduates from college.

The solution? All of their assets are left in a common-pot trust until Ashley turns 22. The trustee is directed to sprinkle the income and principal among the girls as the trustee sees fit, bearing in mind that to the extent possible Wade and Cheryl want the trust to pay for college. When Ashley turns 22, whatever balance exists at that point is divided into two equal shares and distributed into a lifetime trust for each child (where the child is co-trustee at 25).

Generation-Skipping Trust

This is a taste of a tax-savings technique that I'm saving (yup, pun intended) for the Chapter 11 "Advanced Tax Strategies". Remember that each person has an exemption from estate taxes, and married couples can take advantage of it by creating a family trust. Well, each person can also set aside an amount in a trust for their children, have their children as beneficiaries during their lifetime, but pass that amount tax free to the grandchildren on the child's death. That's right, I said tax free! This is known as a *generation-skipping trust,* but I think it's better described as a *generation-sharing trust.*[8]

Charitable Trust

Although charitable trusts satisfy the desire to give to others, I find that the driving force behind them is generally tax motivated. With a charitable trust, both charitable and individual beneficiaries share in the income and principal of the trust over time. However, because the goals are so often tax motivated, I have put the detailed discussion of these types of trusts in Chapter 11.

Powers of Appointment: Changing the Trust

Any trust—a family trust, marital trust, or beneficiary trust—suffers from the same basic issue of "what if?" "What if" there is an unexpected illness, divorce, incompetency, addiction, death, and so on, and the terms of the trust no longer make sense? Do you not create a trust for fear of an unknown future? No. You use the magic clause that makes everything all right: the power of appointment.

At its heart, a power of appointment gives someone other than you the right to (1) change the trust after you're dead, (2) make distributions to designated beneficiaries outside of the trustee's authority, and (3) terminate the trust and distribute everything to the beneficiaries (so an irrevocable trust isn't so irrevocable after all). You can name a beneficiary of the trust (typical) or a third party as the power holder.

The power of appointment comes in four mix-and-match varieties:

- *Limited.* The holder of this power can direct the assets to a class of individuals, but the holder's use of the power doesn't make the asset theirs for estate tax purposes. This class could be defined narrowly, such as the beneficiary's descendants, your descendants, or your parent's descendants. Or it could be defined as broadly as anyone other than (1) the person holding the power, (2) the estate of the person holding the power, (3) the creditors of the person holding the power, or (4) the creditors of the estate of the person holding the power. This power should be in almost every trust.

---

[8] If this paragraph has you thinking "I want to know more about generation-sharing trusts!" then you should immerse yourself in Chapter 8. There I go over how the GST tax works and how you can take advantage of it.

- *General.* Holders of this power can direct the assets to anyone, including themselves. A general power of appointment makes the asset theirs for estate tax purposes. You'll usually find this in limited situations, such as a generation-sharing trust.

- *Inter-vivos.* This power of appointment, whether general or limited, can be exercised by power holders during their lifetime. I use an inter-vivos power of appointment when the family wants to give as much control and flexibility to the beneficiary as possible while still enjoying the benefits that a trust provides.[9]

- *Testamentary.* This power of appointment, whether general or limited, can be exercised by the power holder upon their death in their will. I put a testamentary power of appointment in almost every trust I draft, unless there is a very specific situation when it doesn't make sense. You can provide for both a lifetime and a testamentary power of appointment.

Ask the Attorney "Deirdre, other than the fact that you see them as competition, what's the real reason you don't like online wills?" To be honest, I have no more issue with online wills than I do with attorneys who don't focus in estate planning preparing estate planning documents. Both instances tend to miss the nuances. The power of appointment is a case in point. I never, ever, ever prepare a trust without a power of appointment unless the client, after lots of discussion, indicates that they don't want the trust to be changed, no matter what. (In real life, this usually only occurs in a marital trust left to a second spouse where the client wants to be absolutely sure the balance will go to the client's kids when the spouse dies.) Powers of appointment are invaluable. But they're a nuance, not part of the standard plan. I see online and attorney-prepared estate plans alike that have all sorts of problems that could be easily solved without court intervention by the lowly power of appointment. But because those plans are made to a standard, and not necessarily customized to your situation, this small but important detail is missed. This is why I'm writing this book. I want to empower you to take charge of your estate plan, no matter how you get it prepared, and make sure it includes all the features you need to best pass your wealth and values to your family.

---

[9] A marital trust can't have an inter-vivos power of appointment, only a testamentary one. In a marriage with common children, you should have a testamentary power of appointment in the marital trust so the surviving spouse has the flexibility to change how the children inherit assets over time as the spouse's and children's experiences and circumstances change.

7

Rounding Out the Plan

Documents for When You're Not Dead Yet

A complete estate plan doesn't stop at the question, "What happens if I die?" It also provides for "What happens if I get sick or can no longer make decisions for myself?" To answer that question, you'll need a few other documents to round out your estate plan.

■ **Chapter Brief**   A *power of attorney* says who controls your money when you can't. A *living will* or *advance directive* outlines the medical care you want in a terminal situation. A *health care proxy* or *medical power of attorney* names someone to make medical decisions for you when you can't. Organ donation is a laudable goal, but like your funeral, it needs to be discussed in advance.

Power of Attorney

No estate plan is complete without a power of attorney. It's great to do all this planning for your loved ones, but you can't forget to take care of yourself or, in this case, your money.

What Does It Do?

A power of attorney gives another person, your *attorney-in-fact* or *agent*, the ability to make financial decisions for you in the event you can't make them for yourself. In my opinion, this is in many ways even more important than a will, because a power of attorney is about who makes decisions while you're still alive. Let's face it, when you're dead, what happens to your assets doesn't really matter to you anymore.

A power of attorney is an incredibly powerful document. It allows somebody to withdraw your entire bank account. It's also an incredibly necessary document. Just because you get sick doesn't mean your bills and obligations stop: somebody needs to have the authority to make financial decisions for you. It's almost easier when you die, because at least then a process is in place (probate) for someone to control your assets.

What Does It Look Like?

Your power of attorney identifies you and your attorney-in-fact or agent. The name used varies depending on where you live in the country. It should list the person's relationship to you and their full name and address so they can be identified as the correct "John Smith." It includes a list of actions that the attorney-in-fact can take on your behalf. *Caution!* Make sure this list is tailored to your state. Although your document might say "My attorney-in-fact can do all the things I can do," for us lawyers, "all" doesn't necessarily mean "all." For example, your power of attorney might not authorize the ability to make gifts unless you specifically say so, regardless of "all."[1]

The power of attorney should be witnessed (by two people) and notarized. This isn't called for in all states, but you don't know what state your power of attorney might be needed in, so it's best to be as expansive as possible. After all, you want your power of attorney to be accepted when needed.

■ **Let's Get Real** In some states, the actual form of a power of attorney (that is, word-for-word what a power of attorney document looks like) is set by statute. (New York has a specific form for power of attorney that everyone in the state is supposed to use). As a practical matter, banks, financial institutions, and other people who are in a position to accept a power of attorney are used to seeing that specific format. If your form of document is noncompliant, it may be a *valid* power of attorney, but you may not be able to use it in an immediate, practical manner. It's important to check with legal representatives in your state to determine what form of power of attorney is commonly used. I have some clients who recently moved to New York, where their will is perfectly acceptable; but I had them change their power of attorney, not because it was bad, but because it was in a form that I knew wouldn't be immediately accepted should the document need to be used.

---

[1] Question: "If a power of attorney is such a powerful document, should I be concerned about the person I name taking my money?" Well, this depends on your relationship with the attorney-in-fact. If you have any doubts about whether the person will put your needs first, a quick solution is to name co-power holders who have to act together. I discuss other points to consider when naming your attorney-in-fact in Chapter 12, "Fiduciaries."

What Happens If You Don't Have a Power of Attorney and Become Incapacitated?

Scenario: You're hit by a texting teen and suffer a traumatic brain injury. Or you have a stroke or Alzheimer's or Parkinson's. You aren't dead, but you're looking at a long life without all your faculties to help you through it. You need your money to work for you now. If you didn't take the time to create a power of attorney, the only other option is a guardianship proceeding. A *guardianship* is a formal judicial proceeding in which a judge you've never met decides whether you're competent. Sounds fun, right? If you're found to be incompetent, the judge nominates somebody to manage your money for you. You may or may not have any relationship with this person who is now in charge of everything that has to do with you and your money.

A guardianship proceeding comes under the heading of "things to be avoided in life." It's expensive (involving at least two doctors testifying to your incompetency, as well as two lawyers: the one bringing the action and one appointed to represent your interests). It's embarrassing (you and your lack of competency are public record, and sometimes the judge insists that you be brought to court). And it's time consuming (it can take months to see a judge). The most critical point? A guardianship is totally avoidable. If you make out a power of attorney (running you a couple hundred dollars if an attorney customizes it for you and your state, or less if you download the form), a guardianship is unnecessary. Most important, you get to say who is in charge of your money, not some judge.

Reminder: A revocable trust may achieve the same objective, but the assets must be owned by the revocable trust in order for the successor trustee to take title to them.[2]

Types of Powers of Attorney

Not all powers of attorney are the same. You need to make sure you're using the right one for your situation:

- *General.* A general power of attorney is just that; your attorney-in-fact has the ability to make any type of financial decision for you that you could otherwise make for yourself. A general durable power of attorney is what is most commonly used as part of an estate plan.

---

[2] Look back at Chapter 5, "Will Alternatives and Avoiding Probate," for my discussion of how you can use a revocable trust in the event of your disability.

- *Limited.* A limited or *special* power of attorney governs a specific asset or transaction. You might use one to facilitate a single transaction such as purchasing a house or closing a business deal where you, the person granting the power, aren't otherwise available to act on your own behalf. It's of limited use (pun intended) in an estate planning situation.

- *Durable.* A power of attorney is *durable* if it includes specific language stating that the power of attorney continues to be effective in the event of your disability. In one of the strange ironies of property law, if your power of attorney isn't durable, then the law's default position is that the power of attorney becomes ineffective as soon as you become incapacitated. Of course, it's only when you become incapacitated that you really need the power of attorney. (Yeah, I have no idea how that bit of logic got through.) So, a properly drafted general durable power of attorney says that it continues to be effective even if the person making it becomes incapacitated.

- *Immediate.* An immediate power of attorney empowers your agent to act for you now. There are no other requirements or conditions to acting as your power of attorney. I almost always prepare an immediate general durable power of attorney for my clients.

■ **Let's Get Real** Given that this is such a powerful document, you don't want to leave the original power of attorney around for anyone to find and use. There isn't a requirement that a person being given the power of attorney verify that you're in fact incapacitated or need to have the power of attorney used when it's presented to them. The whole purpose of the power of attorney is to sidestep any need for independent verification so your attorney-in-fact can act for you *now*. My practice is to maintain client originals in our vault to safeguard them.

- *Springing.* The authority of the attorney-in-fact only springs into power when certain criteria have been met. This normally involves one or two physicians certifying that you're incompetent.

■ **Let's Get Real** There are several practical issues with springing powers. First, a power of attorney tends to be used in an emergency situation. In real life, it's time consuming to make an appointment with a doctor, have a consultation, and get the report—more so if you need to see two doctors. Second, once you have the doctors' certifications, the issue of staleness arises. How does the bank manager know you're still incapacitated if the doctor's letter is three months old? The bank may reasonably require a fresh letter, causing you to have to go through the earlier hassle again. Instead of using a springing power, consider how you choose your fiduciaries and maybe name more than one person if you're concerned with the power being misused.

Revoking a Power of Attorney

There are three ways to revoke a power of attorney. The first is to directly revoke it (write on the face "revoked," and sign and date) or indirectly revoke it by signing a new power of attorney that revokes the old one. *Caution:* States differ on whether you need to let your prior attorney-in-fact know that you've revoked the old power of attorney. It's best practice to advise them in writing, to avoid a situation in which the prior attorney-in-fact acts on your behalf (after all, if you're naming someone else, it's likely because you don't trust the old person as much as the new person, so you really don't want them to have the power to mislead the bank). This also underscores why you (or your attorney) should always keep the original power of attorney document. It will be pretty hard to revoke if the attorney-in-fact has the original.

I talked earlier about the second way to revoke a power of attorney. If you create one that isn't durable, and then you become disabled, the power of attorney is revoked.

The third way to revoke a power of attorney is to die. Your power of attorney dies with you. Once you go, your agent no longer has authority to act. The authority to control your assets now belongs to your executor. And no, using a power of attorney after death isn't a good way to avoid probate or "correct" a person's will.

Living Will or Advance Directive

This is a statement of the type of medical care you want in a terminal medical situation, crassly known as a *pull the plug* authorization. In some states, the term *living will* is used; in others, it's called an *advance directive*. The statement of your wishes about end-of-life medical care might even be part of a health care proxy or medical directive, which I talk about next.

Whatever the document is called, the point is that without a clear statement of your final wishes, your family may find themselves in a long moral or legal battle about your intentions one way or the other. Some famous cases are Karen Ann Quinlan and Terry Schiavo, who were in vegetative states for 10 and 15 years, respectively. The important thing here is, what are your wishes and beliefs? If you were Karen Ann Quinlan or Terry Schiavo, what would you want to happen? Do you want all medical measures taken at that point if you have a terminal disease? Do you want pain relief even if it hastens your death? Only you can answer these questions and tell your family what you want. A living will or advance directive prevents your family from agonizing and sometimes fighting over "what mom would have wanted." Don't leave it to a doctor you never met, or to your kids, to guess what you want—write it down.

■ **Let's Get Real**   I'm hoping that one reason you're reading this book is that you want to educate yourself about the best way to plan to leave your assets to your loved ones. That process takes time. The question of who to name to make financial or medical decisions for you, or what end-of-life care you want, may be straightforward for you. If that's the case, there's no reason you can't go online now and read and prepare your power of attorney, living will, and health care proxy. Some state bar associations have even created forms for you to use: that makes preparing them free and easy! Google "living will" and your state as a starting point.

Health Care Proxy or Medical Power of Attorney

The health care proxy or medical power of attorney is the companion document to the living will or advance directive. Again, what the document is called varies by state, and sometimes the living will/advance directive statement is combined into the health care proxy/medical power of attorney document. Whereas the living will/advance directive specifies what medical care you want, the health care proxy or medical power of attorney names a person (the *health care representative*) to make medical decisions for you when you can't.

You don't have to be terminally ill for your health care representative to act, just incapable of making decisions. Some real-life examples: You're in the emergency room in no condition to make decisions, and there are two treatment options. Or you just came out of anesthesia, and your home care needs to be reviewed. Or you just had a baby and the doctors want to give you treatment, but they don't know whether you're breast feeding. Nothing life-threatening is happening, but due to the temporary circumstances you're in, you aren't the best person to critically evaluate a medical decision. This is where the health care representative comes in.

In more serious situations, the health care representative is also the person making end-of-life decisions. It's a heavy burden, but better a person you choose than a stranger (or a committee of strangers, if the hospital is involved). Look at the positives of creating a health care proxy document. You're empowered to make the medical decisions that are right for you, and you can talk to your surrogate decision-maker in advance about your values and wishes.

■ **Ask the Attorney.** "Deirdre, how often do I need to update my health care documents?" You need to make sure they're fresh. Under the federal Health Insurance Portability and Accountability Act of 1996 (HIPAA) you have something called PHI (no, it's not a disease—it stands for Protected Health Information). HIPAA is the law that mandated the volume of privacy forms you now need to fill out at the doctor's office and hospital. In short, you need to give written authorization for any other person to view your PHI. A health care proxy older than 2003 won't include a statement about PHI, and many newer ones use old forms that don't reference HIPAA either.

From a practical perspective, you want to name a single person, not a group of people, as your health care representative. Health care decisions are often time sensitive, and the medical staff needs to know who the single person is whom they should be talking to. End-of-life care by committee doesn't work.

■ **Ask the Attorney** "Deirdre, I filled out a health care proxy at the hospital and checked some boxes about the care I wanted. Isn't that enough?" Here is my problem with the "check the box" approach. You can't tell me right now what illness you'll experience in the future and what the treatment options will be. Absent a crystal ball, I recommend that you have a heath care proxy that gives your health care representative the broadest possible powers, because that person will be in possession of all the facts when you become ill in the future and won't be guessing like you are right now.

Organ Donation

Organ donation literally saves lives.[3] If you're reading this book and considering what will happen to your money and family, you should also think about what will happen to you. If your beliefs and values permit it, and you want to be an organ donor, you need to put your plans in place in advance. In some states, you select to be an organ donor on your driver's license or carry an organ-

---

[3] I have personally benefited from organ donation. Each of you who might consider organ, tissue, or eye donation after reading this book is helping me thank the unknown family who made the decision that their loss could be another's gain. So, thank you.

donor card. The best place to go is organdonor.gov and select Becoming a Donor. This will take you to a registry and rules for your specific state.

It's Your Funeral

And the fun never ends. From organ donation to funeral arrangements—I appreciate your sticking with me! Let's talk facts. Dying sucks, but it's unavoidable. When you're gone, you're gone. But your family is still here to deal with the aftermath. Wouldn't it be a gift to them if you had thought about what your funeral should be like and communicated your wishes to them? What if your parents are very religious, but you aren't? Should your spouse feel pressure to have a ceremony for them and not you? What about burial versus cremation? Or who should have your ashes? Don't leave it to your kids to agonize over, or fight over, what you would have wanted. Whether you want a somber memorial or a big party, communicate it, and set aside the funds (this is where a pay-on-death or joint account may be perfect).

Your will isn't the best place for your funeral wishes. Most times, the will isn't looked at until well after the deed is done. Better to have your funeral wishes as part of your living will or as separate instructions that you keep with your estate-planning documents. Some people even take matters into their own hands and plan the event down to the music and décor. Although it might sound morbid, for those who are ill it can be empowering to design their own send-off and use the event as a source of celebration of life for the family, instead of mourning a loss.

8

Taxes

The Government as Your Beneficiary

When I asked you who your estate plan will benefit, I'm pretty sure you didn't mention the government. The good news? Although you might not be able to disinherit Uncle Sam entirely, there are lots of ways to reduce the government's stake as a beneficiary of your estate. Before we go there, let's take a stroll through the tax code.

> **Chapter Brief**   Taxes affect every estate, no matter how modest or massive. Any death has income tax and capital gains tax consequences. The federal government and many states have an estate tax. There are also inheritance taxes and generation-skipping taxes to contend with, so arm yourself with knowledge.

Taxes Aren't Emotional ... They Just Are

Look, there are lots of reasons to get riled up about taxes. Taxes are too high; the government does a bad job of spending your money; estate taxes are taxing your money twice. It's unfair. It's too much.

But the fact is ... taxes just are. If you want roads, an army, a currency system, and all that stuff, taxes are what is used to pay for them.

Complaining about taxes won't make them go away. Neither will ignoring them. The US tax code provides all sorts of opportunities to reduce taxes at death. Some taxes are even eliminated entirely! I'm devoting this chapter to educating you about how to maximize what your beneficiaries receive. An informed taxpayer is a happy taxpayer when it comes to estate taxes, because you can end up paying less.

Why Care About Taxes at Death?

There is a great misunderstanding about death and taxes. Taxes affect *each and every* estate. I shake my head at the campaign to reduce or eliminate the estate tax, or what some call the "death tax." Federal estate taxes only affect about 2 percent of the US population, so 98 percent of us could care less! In comparison, income taxes and capital gains taxes impact 100 percent of deaths, and they get no press. Death is what we tax attorneys call a *tax realization event.*

Although estate taxes can be expensive for those who have wealth (the top estate tax rate is set to be 55 percent for deaths in 2013 and forward, although that may change), for the vast majority of US families federal estate taxes are avoidable. But don't stop reading here. If you don't have a taxable estate right now, you may have one in the future. At least spend time understanding how the "other taxes" work in the context of your estate.

As of the publication of this book, 23 states and the District of Columbia have their own estate or inheritance tax.[1] To add to the confusion, state estate taxes change all the time. Look to my website, www.deirdrewheatleyliss.com, for the most up-to-date information. If you live or have property in one of these states, you need to see a local attorney so your estate plan will contain strategies to minimize state and federal estate taxes.

Estate and Inheritance Taxes

An estate tax is a tax on your ability to pass wealth to another person upon your death. It only applies once you have certain level of wealth. The estate tax is separate from income tax, capital gain tax, property tax, or any other type of taxes. It works hand in hand with gift taxes.

Let's start with a super-quick example to paint the picture. Robert dies August 3, 2012, as a resident of Georgia (which has no state estate tax). His assets total $6 million. As is common with his generation, he has no debt. Robert's will leaves everything to his two children, William and Barbara. For people who die in 2012, the first $5,120,000 of wealth escapes federal estate tax due to the estate tax exemption amount. The federal estate tax due is about

---

[1] Those of you living in one of these states are in the joyful position of needing to worry about two estate or inheritance tax scenarios when you die: federal and state. Are you reading this in Connecticut, Delaware, District of Columbia, Hawaii, Illinois, Indiana, Iowa, Kansas, Kentucky, Maine, Maryland, Massachusetts, Minnesota, Nebraska, New Jersey, New York, North Carolina, Ohio, Oregon, Pennsylvania, Rhode Island, Tennessee, Vermont, or Washington? Sorry! (See the "State Estate or Inheritance Tax" section of this chapter.)

$306,000 (I'm ignoring any deductions). Robert's after-tax estate is $5,694,000, and William and Barbara each receive $2,847,000.

As of this writing, the federal estate tax is up in the air. Will Congress repeal it, or won't they? What will the exemption be? The current exemption amount of $5,120,000 is scheduled to be reduced to $1 million for deaths starting in 2013. So, what would happen under the current law if Robert died March 3, 2013? He would have the same taxable $6,000,000 estate, but his estate tax would now be $2,580,000 (by the way, that's an increase of over 800 percent just for living another year). Robert's after-tax estate is reduced to $3,420,000, and William and Barbara each receive $1,710,000.

■ **Let's Get Real**   I've tried not to rant, but I can't take it anymore! Congress has abandoned its responsibility to provide citizens with a reliable tax code. We've gone from an exemption of $3.5 million in 2009, to no estate tax in 2010, to a $5 million exemption in 2011–12, and back to $1 million in 2013. It's impossible to plan in this environment. It's even more impossible to write a book trying to educate *you*! Estate taxes result in real checks (with big numbers) that need to be written and real families who are affected. Oh, and don't forget that this all comes about because somebody *died*, which is a tragedy in the first place! I'm writing this book about the situation today. My publisher knows that this chapter could be out of date as soon as it's published, because who knows what Congress will and won't do? As a solution, I've agreed to update this chapter as soon as new federal estate tax laws are issued, which will bring e-books and future publications up to date. I'll also post to my website at www.deirdrewheatleyliss.com, so please look there as well to make sure you're getting as much information as you can. OK—I feel better now. Rant over.

There are two big exceptions to the estate tax. The tax doesn't apply to assets passing to a US citizen spouse or to charity. But don't stop reading! To minimize taxes on the assets passing to your children, a tax-savings structure must be created in the estate plan of the *first* spouse to die. If you leave all your assets to your spouse, you *defer* estate taxes until your spouse dies. However, your family will likely end up paying *more taxes* overall on the second spouse's death because you didn't put a plan in place to minimize them.[2] So read on.

---

[2] I'll give you specific estate plan blueprints to minimize taxes in Chapter 14, "Planning Guide for Marrieds," but you need to understand the structure of the estate tax to evaluate which options work best for you. That's what this chapter is about.

Federal Estate Tax

The federal estate tax applies to all US citizens and residents.[3] Even if you aren't a citizen or resident, if you own real estate in the US, the federal estate tax applies to that property as well.

Just because you're subject to the federal estate tax doesn't mean you need to worry about it. If your taxable estate is less than the exemption amount of the federal estate tax at the time you die, then there is no need to file a federal estate tax return (Form 706) or pay the tax.

Of course, the trick question is, "What will the exemption amount be when I die?" For deaths in 2012, the exemption amount is $5,120,000. If Congress does nothing (which they excel at doing), then starting January 1, 2013, the exemption amount will be $1 million. President Obama has proposed a permanent exemption amount of $3.5 million, but that is going nowhere right now. And who knows what changes future presidents and Congresses will bring?

What Assets Are Counted for Estate Tax?

For estate tax purposes, the United States government taxes anything you own, anywhere on Earth, or even off Earth if it comes down to it. I've spent a lot of time talking about different forms of ownership. Anything you directly own or are deemed to have control over and benefit from is "yours" for estate tax purposes.

Here are some general rules for what's included in your taxable estate:

If you own it in your own name, then 100 percent of it is yours.

If you own it with your spouse, then 50 percent of it is yours. Note that there won't be any tax on the other 50 percent, because it passes to your spouse by operation of law, and I already told you that there's no estate tax on assets passing to your spouse.

If you own it with somebody other than your spouse, then 100 percent of it is yours unless you can prove that you didn't contribute 100 percent of the value of the joint property. As an example, Linda owns a piece of property in North Carolina with her daughter, Jennifer. Linda contributed 75 percent of the purchase price and Jennifer contributed 25 percent of the purchase price, and they have documents to substantiate this. On Linda's death, 75 percent of

---

[3] Special estate tax laws govern noncitizens. If this applies to you, you should look at Chapter 19, "Planning Guide for Noncitizens," for the rules you need to be aware of as well as the ways to structure an estate plan to comply with them.

the value of the North Carolina property is included in her taxable estate. The other 25 percent of the value is Jennifer's.

How do you figure out what is part of your estate for estate tax purposes? First, go back to the list of assets you created at the beginning of this journey. Then, categorize them by value, ownership, and estate inclusion. For a married couple, that might look something like Table 8-1.

Table 8-1. Example of a Rough List of Assets for Estate Tax Planning Purposes (James and Karen)

James and Karen - December, 2012

Asset	Value	James	Karen	Both	Included in Estate
Home	$550,000.00			$550,000.00	$550,000.00
Vacation Home	$325,000.00			$325,000.00	$325,000.00
James 401(k)	$365,000.00	$365,000.00			$365,000.00
Karen IRA	$110,000.00		$110,000.00		$110,000.00
Joint checking	$15,000.00			$15,000.00	$15,000.00
Investments	$280,000.00			$280,000.00	$280,000.00
Vehicles	$25,000.00	$10,000.00	$15,000.00		$25,000.00
Personal Property	$15,000.00			$15,000.00	$15,000.00
James Life Insurance	$500,000.00	$500,000.00			$500,000.00
Totals	$2,185,000.00	$875,000.00	$125,000.00	$1,185,000.00	$2,185,000.00

Notice a couple of things. First, I didn't use exact figures. This is just a snapshot to see where you are, so exact figures aren't necessary (and it takes a lot less work). After all, you aren't going to add up the numbers until the first person dies, and everything will be different then. Second, this example doesn't include every detail about the accounts. Again, the goal is to get a picture, so you don't need to go crazy figuring it all out. Third, the key number is what is included in the taxable estate. If this amount exceeds the exemption for a single person under your state or federal law, then you need to have a plan to reduce estate taxes in your estate plan. Here, the total assets in James's and Karen's estate exceeds the 2013 scheduled federal exemption of $1,000,000, so I would recommend that they do estate tax minimization planning in their wills.

How Do You Value Assets for Estate Tax Purposes?

When I talked about what your assets are, I mentioned that value is a grey area. The legal standard is the *fair market value* (FMV). Strap yourself in for some legalese (and get a sense of what I wade through all day). The IRS says:

> *The fair market value is the price at which the property would change hands between a willing buyer and a willing seller, neither being under any compulsion*

to buy or to sell and both having reasonable knowledge of relevant facts. The fair market value of a particular item of property includible in the decedent's gross estate is not to be determined by a forced sale price. Nor is the fair market value of an item of property to be determined by the sale price of the item in a market other than that in which such item is most commonly sold to the public, taking into account the location of the item wherever appropriate.

—Regulation §20.2031-1

Huh? This means you can't use the lowest value you can find for your asset for estate tax purposes. Telling the realtor to lowball your house's value won't save you taxes. The IRS may be slow, but it isn't dumb. This type of move invites an underpayment notice, together with interest and penalties.

The FMVs of some assets are easy. For bank accounts, investment accounts, retirement accounts, and life insurance, the FMV is essentially the value of the account on the date of death, which you can get from the institution holding the asset. For real estate and closely held businesses, you need an appraisal of what a third party would pay for the assets (which may be a far different number than what you think the property is "worth").

What Can You Deduct?

You don't pay estate taxes on the value of all your assets when you die (your *gross estate*). Instead, you pay estate tax on your *net estate*:

Net Estate = Gross Estate − Deductions

One of the best ways to reduce your estate tax is to maximize deductions to reduce your net estate.

Marital Deduction

Anything passing to a US citizen spouse is a deduction from the estate tax. This is why there is effectively no tax on assets that go to a spouse. This includes amounts passing to the surviving spouse either outright or in trust.[4]

---

[4] Look back at Chapter 6, "Trust in Trusts," for my description of a QTIP trust, which is a trust for the surviving spouse who qualifies for the marital deduction. Same-sex couples and unmarried couples need to remember that this doesn't apply in your situation. You need to be more creative to minimize estate tax. See Chapter 16, "Planning Guide for Unmarried and Same-Sex Couples."

Ask the Attorney "Deirdre, if there is no estate tax when assets go to the spouse, why do married couples need to do estate tax planning?" In short, because you need to use the estate tax exemption amount of the *first* spouse to die in order to shelter assets from estate tax when the second spouse dies. Let's look at James and Karen again (Table 8-1), whose combined gross estate is $2,185,000. If James dies in 2013 without an estate plan, everything passes to Karen with no estate tax. So far, so good. However, if Karen dies later in 2013, her estate includes 100 percent of their assets and generates a tax of $525,650. Not so good. Instead, if James and Karen had invested in an estate plan, they could have directed $1 million of assets (the assumed 2013 exemption amount) to a family trust when James died. That family trust would *not* be included in Karen's taxable estate, so her gross estate would be reduced to $1,185,000, and the taxes would be reduced to $75,850. Scenario A, no estate plan, kids get $1,659,350. Scenario B, with tax-minimization estate plan, kids get $2,109,150. That's a difference of $449,800—just for doing your will right. See? Attorneys are good people after all!

Charitable Deduction

Anything passing to a qualified charity (such as any public 501(c)(3) charity, school, or charitable foundation) isn't subject to estate tax. Another way to consider it is that you can either pay taxes or give money to charity. For wealthy families, maximizing the estate tax exemption amount only gets you so far. At the end of the day, estate tax may still be due. However, because any amount given to charity is a deduction from the estate tax, some people make charitable bequests to direct the funds to charity instead of to the government in the form of taxes.

Let's Get Real Retirement plans (401(k), 403(b), IRAs, and so on) are great assets to distribute to charity upon your death. I've said it before, and I'll say it again: when you inherit a retirement plan, you also inherit the unpaid income tax obligations. This means there could be an estate tax on the overall retirement plan *and* an income tax to be paid whenever distributions are made. The net result could be that less than 50 percent of the retirement plan goes to your beneficiary. Consider instead leaving the retirement plan to charity. Charities don't pay income tax, so they get 100 percent of the dollars and don't have to share with Uncle Sam. Also, the bequest to the charity is a deduction from the estate tax.[5]

---

[5] Two points of clarification. First, if you pay estate tax on your retirement plan, then your beneficiary can credit a portion of the estate tax paid against their income taxes when a distribution from the retirement plan is made. Also, charitable planning for a retirement account makes the best sense in a single individual's estate plan, because there would be no estate tax on the retirement plan if it passed to a spouse.

Debts

You don't pay estate tax on money you owe. The estate tax is a tax on the total amount of wealth passing to your family. If some of that wealth is going to your creditors, that amount isn't subject to estate taxes. The big deduction here tends to come from a mortgage. Other deductions include car loans, credit card bills, and anything else you owe.

I talked about how to calculate the total amount of your debt early in the book when I went over your assets. You can subtract that debt from your total assets right now to get a more realistic picture of what the estate tax might be if you died today.

You may have noticed that I ignored James's and Karen's debts when coming up with an estimate of their taxable estate (Table 8-1). I did this on purpose, because you're unlikely to die the day after you calculate your taxable estate. As time goes on, I find that people tend to pay down their debt, so it becomes a smaller and smaller number. At the same time, their assets increase. Because this is just a snapshot, I estimate only the assets to very roughly account for the growth of the assets over time.

Expenses

Dealing with somebody's estate is similar to running a mini-business. As with all businesses, running an estate involves expenses. These come in the form of funeral expenses, probate fees, valuations, expenses to maintain the property, and attorney and accountant fees, among others. Certain expenses are deductible against the estate tax; others aren't. Remember that the mantra of the estate tax is that it's a tax on wealth you're passing to your family. If the IRS finds that an expense is for the benefit of the beneficiaries, not to administer the estate, it won't be allowed (for example, fixing up the house for sale or maintaining the property before it's deeded to the beneficiary). However, to the extent that expenses are deemed to be purely related to your death and the things that must be done to transfer your property from you to your beneficiaries, they're deducted from the gross estate and thereby reduce the estate tax.

State Death Taxes Paid

If you're lucky enough to live in one of the 23 states or District of Columbia that have their own estate or inheritance tax, you may find yourself paying taxes to two government authorities (for example, the IRS and the state of New York). If this is the case, any tax payment to New York will be a deduction against the federal estate taxes. This is similar to how you can deduct your state income taxes and property taxes on your federal income tax return each year.

Exemption Amount

A federal estate tax exemption amount, set by law, is applied to your net estate (the value of your estate after payment of debts and expenses) to determine the amount of estate taxes you need to pay. In 2012, that exemption amount is $5,120,000. It's scheduled to be $1 million for deaths in 2013 going forward. There are proposals to institute a permanent exemption amount of $3.5 million for deaths starting in 2013, but those don't have any traction so far.

I want to walk you through exactly how the federal estate tax is calculated, to demonstrate the roles of asset values, debts, expenses, and the federal estate tax exemption amount. I'll use Carol's estate as an example. Carol dies in 2013 when the federal estate tax exemption amount is $1,000,000:

1	Gross Estate	$ 3,200,000.00
2	Less Debts and Expenses	$ (375,000.00)
3	Net Estate	$ 2,825,000.00
4	Tentative Tax on Net Estate	$ 1,187,500.00
5	Less Federal Applicable Credit	$ (345,000.00)
6	Net Federal Estate Tax Due	$ 842,500.00

Figure 8-1. Example of federal estate tax calculation (Carol's estate)

Some points of clarification. The first thing I did was determine Carol's net estate by subtracting any debts and expenses from her assets (Line 3 = Line 1 – Line 2). The next step was to figure out the tentative taxable estate tax, which is the estate tax calculated on the net estate before applying any exemption amount (Line 4). I arrived at this amount by applying the estate tax rates in effect to the net estate on Line 3 (this is where the estate tax rate comes into play). So far, so good. But where is that $1 million exemption amount I've been talking about all through the chapter?

For purposes of calculating the estate tax, the $1 million estate tax exemption amount is converted into its worth in actual taxes and called the *federal applicable credit*, which you see on line 5 of Figure 8-1. The $345,000 represents the tax that would be paid on $1 million of assets. I credited that tax amount against the tentative estate tax to arrive at the federal estate tax due (Line 6.)

Why do I talk about the federal estate tax exemption amount if it isn't even part of the calculation? Because I'm applying the before-tax amount of the credit to the before-tax assets. It gets us to the same place, but it's far easier to think about the amount of money that goes tax-free to your heirs than to think of a credit against taxes paid by your estate.

In addition, if you made prior taxable gifts (a large gift for which you filed a gift tax return), those amounts are added back to the gross estate for the purposes of calculating the tax.[6]

■ **A Bit of History** If you'd like to know why the estate tax exemption amount has been ping-ponging about, I'd like to share some recent history with you. It's important because it shows how the political process directly affects your estate plan.

When George W. Bush became president in 2000, he ran on a platform of massive tax-cuts. The 2001 Tax Act significantly changed estate taxes by gradually increasing the federal estate tax exemption amount from $675,000 in 2001 to $3.5 million in 2009, followed by a year (2010) with no estate tax (before you get excited, other taxes were levied on beneficiaries of those who died in 2010). However, the 2001 Tax Act wasn't a permanent tax law; it was scheduled to sunset or expire on 12/31/10, bringing the estate tax exemption back down to $1 million. "Oh no! This can't happen!" cried Congress in December 2010 (note that they had 10 years to address the issue but waited until the last month). "We know the answer!" exclaimed the wise voices in Washington. "We'll create another temporary tax law—and this time we'll increase the exemption to $5 million. But the law will only be in effect for the next two years, effectively making it another Congress's headache to find a permanent estate tax solution."

It's that two-year extension that will expire on December 31, 2012, bringing us back by default to a $1 million exemption amount.

Portability

The 2010 Tax Act, set to expire December 31, 2012, introduced the concept of *portability* of the exemption amount between spouses. Essentially, when the first spouse dies (before December 31, 2012), that spouse's estate can file an estate tax return providing that when the second spouse dies, the second spouse's estate can use any unused federal estate tax exemption amount from the first spouse. The kicker? The second spouse also has to die before December 31, 2012. Although it's a great concept, both spouses must die

---

[6] If you've made large gifts in the past or are considering making such a gift in the future, you should study Chapter 9, "Gifting."

before December 31, 2012, so I hope this isn't relevant to those of you reading this book.

Estate Tax Rates

Congress has had great fun with estate tax rates along with the federal estate tax exemption amount. The 2001 Tax Act gradually lowered the estate tax rate from a maximum of 55 percent to a maximum of 45 percent.[7] The two-year temporary tax law that is in place right now taxes estates at the maximum of 35 percent. The scheduled new tax law with a mere $1 million exemption amount for deaths in 2013 and forward is coupled with an increase in the estate tax rate back to 55 percent. The proposed $3.5 million permanent estate tax exemption is coupled with a maximum 45 percent estate tax rate.

Estate Tax Return: The Final Step

What happens when a person dies and has a taxable estate? The executor needs to prepare and file an estate tax return (Form 706). The estate tax return and any tax payment are due within nine months of the date of death. Although preparing and filing a Form 706 is well beyond the scope of this book, I'll give you some free advice: get professional assistance from an attorney or accountant.

State Estate or Inheritance Tax

If you live in or own real estate in a state with its own estate tax, your estate plan just got more complicated. Depending on the type and amount of tax, you may need to do state estate tax planning, separate from federal estate tax planning. This is where seeing a local attorney will be of value.

In 2012, 19 jurisdictions have their own estate tax: Connecticut, Delaware, District of Columbia, Hawaii, Illinois, Kansas, Maine, Maryland, Massachusetts, Minnesota, New Jersey, New York, North Carolina, Ohio, Oregon, Rhode Island, Tennessee, Vermont, and Washington.

Many more states could have an estate tax in 2013. This is because, before the 2001 Tax Act, you only paid estate taxes the federal government. A credit for part of the estate tax was owed to the state you lived in. So, you paid the feds, and the feds paid your state. Most states had a law on their books saying their estate tax was equal to the federal "state death tax credit" amount.

---

[7] In case you think these tax rates are ridiculously high, they're actually at a historic low. From 1942 to 1976, the top estate tax rate was 77 percent, with a mere $60,000 estate tax exemption amount.

Fast-forward to the 2001 Tax Act, which eliminated the credit to the states. Some states responded by instituting their own estate tax. Others did nothing but still have the law on their books that the estate tax is equal to the federal state death tax credit amount.

Fast-forward again to 2013, when the credit will be reintroduced unless Congress acts (not holding my breath). That means more states will collect an estate tax. However, you won't pay more tax, because your state will collect part of the federal tax.

States with Inheritance Tax

An inheritance tax is a tax based on who receives your money and how they're related to you. Generally speaking, people who are more closely related to you pay a lower tax rate or no inheritance tax at all.

Seven states collect inheritance tax: Indiana, Iowa, Kentucky, Maryland, Nebraska, New Jersey, and Pennsylvania. The rates and due dates vary by state. Notice how New Jersey and Maryland have both an estate tax and an inheritance tax? Gotta love being a Jersey girl!

Income Tax

What? After all that talk about estate and inheritance taxes, you thought I was finished with taxes? Not so fast. I'll show you how capital gains taxes are eliminated at death, but some income taxes are here to stay.

Inheritances and Income Tax

Good news first. The general rule is that your beneficiaries don't pay income tax on an inheritance. That's right—an inheritance is (usually) income tax free. Why is this? Well, your estate is responsible for estate taxes, so your beneficiaries receive after-tax dollars. This is the case whether your estate had to pay an estate tax or not.

Remember how I keep saying retirement assets are "special"? The special part is the surprise that you still need to pay income taxes on them when they're inherited. Unless your retirement account is a Roth account, you never paid income taxes on those dollars when they went into the account. Retirement accounts are tax-*deferred*, not tax-free. The income taxes on distributions from the retirement account must be paid by the beneficiaries who inherit the account. This is true for any other asset for which income taxes haven't yet been paid, such as a tax-deferred annuity or fixed pension payments.

Your estate itself must pay income taxes on the income it earns. If your estate has $100,000 in a bank account and earns $5,000 in interest (don't laugh, banks actually used to pay you money to keep your money with them), then your estate will have to pay income tax on the income earned.

Capital Gains Tax: Magical Step-Up in Basis

I'll let you in on the true magic of the estate tax. The existence of the estate tax makes capital gains taxes disappear at death.

Normally, you have to pay taxes on any appreciation in an asset from the time you got it to the time you sell it. But death changes everything.

Let's say Larry bought a share of Apple for $10 (what a lucky duck). It's now trading at $510. If he sells that share of stock, he earns $500. He has to pay federal capital gains taxes (currently 15 percent) on his earnings plus any state income taxes based on where he lives. Larry's *basis* in this example is $10 (what he paid for the share), the FMV is $510 (what someone else will buy it for), and Larry's *gain* (or *amount realized* in tax parlance) is $500. Larry will pay $75 in federal capital gains taxes plus some additional state tax. Start adding zeros to my example to see how those taxes add up!

When you die, all that appreciation or gain disappears because your beneficiaries' tax basis is stepped-up to the FMV at the day you died. This step-up in basis means that when Larry's daughter Julie inherits his share of Apple, her basis is $510 (the FMV when Larry passed away). If Julie now sells the share for $510, she owes no capital gains tax (the $75 that Larry would have paid had he sold the share when he was alive is eliminated).

If Julie sells the Apple stock for $600, she owes capital gains tax on the $90 of gains earned after Larry's death. Conversely, if the stock sells for $400, Julie has a capital loss of $110 that she can incorporate into her own income tax calculations.

"Wow, this is great!" you must be saying to yourself. "All those taxes just disappear." This is true, but let's look at the details.

First, you need to die to get this step-up in basis. That's a big primary hurdle.

Second, an estate tax must be in effect. You may recall that 2010 was billed as "a great year to die" (I won't even get into the mixed-up priorities that led to those headlines). The step-up in basis is predicated on the fact that an estate tax is in place. No estate tax, no step-up in basis.

Stay with me for one second. Without delving deeply into tax policy theory, the IRS considers death a *realization event*—a time to square up on taxes.

Instead of making your executor try to count up the basis *and* FMV of everything you own, an estate tax is applied. It's a lot easier to figure out the FMV of what exists when you die than what you paid for the asset way back when. You may or may not have an estate large enough to generate a tax, but the existence of an estate tax is what allows your assets to pass capital gains tax free to your family.

Generation-Skipping Taxes

The *generation-skipping transfer* tax (GST tax) is the government's way to keep you from giving all your money away and cheating it out of its share. In the normal course, Uncle Sam gets a bite of your family's pie of wealth at every generation. When the second parent dies, an estate tax may possibly be assessed on the assets passing to the children.

Let's say Helen is 90 years old, her kids are retired and set, she really likes her grandkids, and she understands how estate taxes work. Helen might say to herself, "If I leave all my assets to my grandchildren, although they will be taxed in my estate, they won't be taxed again when my kids die." Great idea, right? Well, the government isn't dumb. The tax code says, "Not so fast there. We'll let you 'skip' over your kids to your grandkids, but only for *some* of your assets. If you give away too much to your grandkids, then we'll assess a flat 55 percent tax." Ouch! Although the government gives you a chance to some generation planning, there are real teeth if you try to do too much.

How Does the GST Exemption Work?

Each person has a certain exemption amount from GST taxes ("exemption amount" sound familiar?). You can designate assets up to that amount to pass either directly or eventually to grandchildren without being subject to the GST tax. The GST exemption amount is usually captured by a trust for the benefit of the child and their children (sounding even more familiar?). In the same way that the estate tax exemption amount is put in a family trust to reduce taxes when the second spouse dies, the GST exemption amount is put in a generation-skipping trust to reduce taxes when a child dies.

The GST exemption amount is fixed by law and is traditionally the same as the estate tax exemption amount (currently $5.120 million and scheduled to return to $1 million adjusted for inflation in 2013). You can use the exemption either during your life or at your death. If you use $1 million of the GST exemption amount when you're alive by making a gift to your grandchildren, and a $3.5 million GST exemption amount remains upon your death, then you can use only $2.5 million to fund a GST trust at your death because you already used part of your GST exemption during your lifetime.

Ask the Attorney   "I'm not a Rockefeller or Gates. How does all this GST stuff apply to me?" Well, remember that I strongly recommend that you consider leaving assets in trust for a person's lifetime and name that person as trustee to get asset protection. Who knows what the tax laws will be in the future? I can't even tell you what they will be next year. Why not set up the inheritance so that if your beneficiaries don't use it, it can go tax-free to their kids?

9

Gifting
Give It Away Now

After I go through the whole discussion of what estate taxes a family might be facing, I often get this question: "What happens if I give my stuff away now instead of waiting until I die?" The answer isn't as simple as you may think. My initial reply is, "Does making a gift move you toward your goals?" After all, once you give away dollars, they're gone; you can't take them back. If that isn't a roadblock, what about the fact that gifting could create taxes instead of saving them? Read on.

■ **Chapter Brief**   Don't let the tax tail wag the dog. The primary questions are whether you can afford the gift and whether it forwards your goals. If yes, will making the gift create taxes instead of saving them? You have both an annual exclusion and a lifetime exclusion from gift taxes. Some gifts are totally exempt from tax. If you're making a gift, what is the best way to do it? That's what this chapter is about.

You Give, It's Gone

The first question about gifting, before we get to all the neat tax stuff, is, "Can you afford it?" If the stock market goes down 40 percent, can you still afford it? What if you get sick? Your answer might be, "Well, my kids will take care of me." Really? And what is your Plan B if they don't? I don't mean to be harsh, but I have clients in their 70s who are supporting their kids in their 40s and 50s. This isn't the place for social commentary, but you worked hard for your wealth. You have dreams and bucket lists to fulfill. It's OK to use your money for yourself. So, before you start thinking about giving away your assets, make sure doing so makes sense for you.

A second point, when you give away an asset, is that you can't attach a string to get any part of the asset back. If you do, that string will pull the asset back into your taxable estate, thus defeating the tax purpose of making the gift in the first place.

What might this string look like? You give the family vacation home to your children, but you continue to use it rent-free every summer. You retain the benefits of the vacation home, and that string pulls it back into your taxable estate. Or suppose you give stock to your children but tell them they have to direct all the dividends to you. Because you keep the income, this pulls the value of all the stock back into your taxable estate. Or perhaps you create a trust and name yourself as one of the beneficiaries "just in case." You retain the possibility of continuing benefit from the assets, so the entire asset is pulled back into your taxable estate.[1]

Third, the income goes with the gift. If you own a commercial property that generates $30,000 a year in rent, and you give the property to your children, they now get the $30,000 instead of you. It's not just a question of whether you can live without the commercial property, but whether you can live without the rental income that the commercial property generates.

■ **Let's Get Real**   You can't rely on your kids to give back your money in case you need it. It's harsh but true. Bear in mind that people call their attorney when they have problems, so I've seen some of the worst that families can do to each other. Not to be rude, but have you looked at the financial tendencies of your children's generation? There is clearly more of a sense of "finance it" than the "deferred gratification" that marks older generations. If your kids take what you give them and spend it, it's gone; there is nothing for you to get back. What if the issue isn't your kids, but their spouses? What if a spouse pressures them to spend the money they're supposed to be saving for you? What if your child dies unexpectedly and the spouse now has your money because it passes through your child's estate plan? What if you and your child have a falling out? You know these are real possibilities, because you've seen friends and neighbors go through them. I'm not telling you to not consider gifting. I'm suggesting that you need to be smart about it.

Income Tax and the Carryover Basis

If you've reached this point, I assume I haven't totally scared you away from the idea of gifting. Gifting is a terrific tool in an overall estate plan, but you need to understand some of the nasty little tricks of the tax code.

Let's start with the good stuff. Gifts aren't income to the recipient. You paid income taxes on the money you're giving away when you earned it. Because

---

[1] Fear not. There are exceptions to all these examples and ways to have your cake and eat it too. I'll go over some of them in Chapter 11, "Advanced Tax Strategies."

you already paid income taxes on it, your beneficiaries don't have to. If you give somebody $10,000, they receive $10,000 of value.

Let's revisit the magic trick of the estate tax: when you die, capital gains taxes disappear. Have you ever said to yourself, "I don't want to sell *xyz* because I would have to pay taxes?" The taxes you're avoiding are capital gains on the asset's appreciation since you bought it. The good thing about dying? The slate is wiped clean. The cost basis of the asset steps-up to the fair market value (FMV) at the date of death.[2]

The first nasty little tax code secret? When you give away an asset during your life, you haven't yet paid that ultimate price of dying. Because your beneficiaries still have you, they don't get a step-up in basis in the assets gifted. Instead, there is a *carryover basis*, which means the recipient of the gift takes your basis in the asset.

Remember my discussion in Chapter 8, "Taxes," about the step-up in basis of a share of Apple stock on Larry's death when he left his stock to his daughter Julie? Let's see what happens when Larry gifts that same share of stock instead.

Larry still bought a share of Apple for $10. It's now trading at $510. If he sells that share of stock, he has earned $500. He has to pay federal capital gains taxes (currently 15 percent) and any state income taxes based on where he lives. Larry's basis in this example is $10, the FMV is $510, and Larry's gain or amount realized is $500. Larry pays $75 in federal capital gains taxes and some additional state tax.

In the example in Chapter 8, Larry died and left the Apple stock to Julie, and her basis became $510. If she had sold it for that amount, there would've been no capital gains.

Here, however, Larry is gifting the stock to Julie. Julie takes Larry's basis of $10. When Julie sells the stock for $510, she has a $500 capital gain, and she pays $75 of taxes on it. To take this further, what if Larry doesn't have just 1 share of Apple, but instead has 100 shares of Apple? By making a gift of the stock to Julie, Larry locks in that Julie must pay tax of $7,500 on a $50,000 capital gain. And what if the capital gains tax rates go up? Julie will have to pay even more in taxes.

Here is the zinger question: what if Larry doesn't have a taxable estate because the total value of his assets is below the federal estate tax exemption amount? In that case, had Larry done no gifting, Julie would've inherited the Apple

---

[2] If you want a refresher on how the step-up in basis works, flip back to Chapter 8, "Taxes." I presented an example about Apple stock that I repeat here, but with totally different capital gains tax consequences.

shares with the stepped-up basis and owed zero capital gains tax. By gifting the Apple shares instead of leaving them to Julie at death, Larry actually *creates* a $7,500 tax that would be totally avoided if he didn't make the gift. See what I mean about nasty little tricks of the tax code?

▓ **Real Stories from Around My Conference Table**   Here's a situation of misguided good intentions that I see time and again. Mom and dad are elderly and have had a health scare. They're close to their kids and concerned that the government will "take their money" if they need to go into a nursing home. Out of fear (and without guidance), they transfer their home to their kids. They bought their house in 1949 for $23,000. It's worth $400,000 today. They don't have a lot of assets outside of the house, so estate taxes aren't a worry for them. By making a gift, which is done with the best of intentions, they lock in a tax for their children of at least $56,550. "But wait," you say. "There is an exclusion on capital gains taxes for the sale of the house." No. There is exclusion on capital gains taxes for the sale of your *primary residence*. Because the kids don't live in the house, they don't get the benefit of the exclusion. See why it's important to get good advice?

Annual Exclusion Amount

OK, I'm pretty much done with all the bad stuff about gifting. Let's get to the good stuff, starting with the renewable tax-free gift. Not much in life is tax-free, but one thing is: the *annual exclusion* from gift taxes. On January 1 each year, Uncle Sam gives you the right to give up to $13,000 per person to anyone in the world with no gift tax consequences whatsoever. If you're married, you can give away up to $26,000 per person, even if the source of the gift comes from the assets of only one spouse. On January 1 of the next year, the annual exclusion from gift taxes replenishes itself, and you can give away a new $13,000 or $26,000 per person per year, as the case may be. The annual exclusion is even indexed for inflation, so over time it will grow to $14,000 per person, $15,000 for person, and so on.[3]

Making annual exclusion gifts is an easy way to reduce the value of your estate. Because the gift is tax-free, no gift tax returns need to be filed. It's calculated per recipient, so it's easy to treat every family member equally. However, you may want to consider making the annual exclusion gift in a trust versus writing a check every year, because the total amount gifted can become very substantial over time.

---

[3] In fact, the annual exclusion amount in scheduled to go up to $14,000 per person in 2013. Sometimes inflation can be a good thing!

Lifetime Exemption Amount

What if you want to give someone more than $13,000 per year? What if you would like to give them $100,000 or more? You can certainly do that, but these larger gifts will affect your *lifetime exemption amount*. Hmmm ... *exemption amount*. Didn't she talk about that when she was discussing estate taxes? Why, yes, I did. That's a very astute question, because the estate tax exemption amount and the gift tax exemption amount are actually one and the same. They're *unified*, which means that if you use your lifetime exemption amount today, you'll effectively have less exemption amount available to shelter your estate from estate taxes upon your death. I know this sounds tricky, but let's break it down.

One quick aside, to be clear: Any use of the lifetime exemption amount is in addition to the annual exclusion amount. Annual exclusion = tax free.

What Is the Gift Tax Exemption Amount?

In 2012, the gift tax exemption amount is $5,120,000. It's scheduled to return to $1 million in 2013.

You need to understand that the gift tax is the backstop to the estate tax. Without a gift tax, everybody could give away all their assets right before they died, and the government would never collect any estate tax revenue. It bears repeating: the IRS may be slow, but it's not stupid. Also, the incredibly high exemption in 2012 is an anomaly. Even during the period from 2001 through 2010 when the estate tax exemption amount was increasing or disappearing as the result of the 2001 Tax Act, the gift tax exemption amount remained fixed at $1 million.

What Are the Estate Tax Consequences?

There are estate tax consequences to making a gift above the exclusion amount of $13,000 per person? You betcha. And you thought the whole purpose of gifting was to remove the assets from your estate. The gift tax and the estate tax are integrated or linked. That is to say, whatever gift tax exemption you use during your life reduces the estate tax exemption amount available at your death.

An example is definitely in order. Sandra gives her son Jason $113,000. She uses her annual exclusion for $13,000 and her lifetime exclusion for $100,000. Let's assume that the estate tax exemption amount is $1 million when Sandra dies. Because Sandra used $100,000 of her lifetime exemption amount in the gift to Jason, her actual estate tax exemption amount will be considered to be only $900,000. When you use any of your lifetime exemption amount, it reduces, dollar for dollar, the estate tax exemption amount available upon your death.

I hope that example make sense, because it's a bit of an oversimplification. The last nasty little nuance about gift taxes is that, when you make a gift, it's included in your estate tax calculation. I've gone through how you add up all your assets to figure the gross estate, subtract from that any debts or expenses to find the net estate, and calculate the estate tax after applying the estate tax exemption amount. What I didn't mention earlier is that any *prior taxable gifts* are added back into the estate tax calculation.

Bear with me. When you make a gift during your life using your lifetime exemption amount, you're effectively using part of your estate tax exemption amount. In reality, though, you add the amount of the gift you made to your gross estate, and then apply the full amount of the estate tax exemption amount to the estate. In Sandra's estate, this calculation looks something like Figure 9-1.

1	Gross Estate	$	3,400,000.00
2	Less Debts and Expenses	$	(200,000.00)
3	Plus Prior Taxable Gifts	$	100,000.00
4	Net Estate	$	3,300,000.00
5	Tentative Tax on Net Estate	$	1,495,000.00
6	Less Federal Applicable Credit	$	(345,000.00)
7	Net Federal Estate Tax Due	$	1,150,000.00

Figure 9-1. Example of the estate tax consequences of making a gift above the annual exclusion amount (Sandra's estate)

The prior taxable gifts (gifts to which you applied your lifetime exemption amount) are added back in Line 3 of Figure 9-1 as part of the calculation of the estate tax. Why this level of complexity? To make sure you didn't put yourself in a lower estate tax bracket by virtue of making the gifts. The tentative tax on Line 5 is calculated on the net estate on Line 4, which includes the prior use of the lifetime exemption amount (reflected on Line 3). You then subtract from the tentative tax the tax value of the full estate exemption amount (the applicable credit on Line 6) to arrive at the estate tax due. Sandra's estate tax on a $3.4 million gross estate with $200,000 in expenses and a $100,000 prior gifts ends of being *exactly the same* as the estate tax calculated on a $3.5 million gross estate with $200,000 of expense.

So why bother making gifts? The point is that when you make a gift using your lifetime exemption amount, it's *not* the gift that achieves the tax savings. The tax savings are generated by the fact that any *growth or earnings* on the gift after it's made aren't included in your taxable estate. Remember, gifts made using the annual exclusion aren't added back into the estate tax calculation, so they truly are tax free.

What Are the Generation-Skipping Tax Consequences?

The gift tax and the generation-skipping tax (GST) are also unified. This means if Donald makes a gift of $100,000 to his granddaughter Nicole during his lifetime, then upon Donald's death, he has already used $100,000 of his GST exemption amount. He has only $900,000 available to put into a generation-sharing trust (assuming a $1 million GST exemption amount).

What Assets to Gift?

Let's recap the nasty nuances of the gift tax. First, the recipient takes your cost basis. Second, the true power of gifting comes from the growth of an asset after you give it away, because the amount of the gift is included in your estate tax calculation. What conclusions can you draw? When making a gift, it's best to select assets that have one or more of the characteristics of (1) high cost basis in comparison to value and (2) high growth potential.

The highest cost basis asset is cash. Sometimes a good time to make a gift is right after you've liquidated something (a piece of real estate, a business interest, and so on). Also bear in mind that basis is irrelevant if there are no plans to sell the asset. So, another ideal asset to gift may be one where there is no intention of the asset leaving the family (real estate and business interests again come to mind).

The gift for which you'll get the most bang for your gift tax buck is one where you expect significant growth over time. The best example that comes to mind is something you transfer before it becomes valuable. For instance, if you give a plot of land to a trust for your children, and then you develop the land, you're leveraging your gift. Or you transfer an interest in a startup business to a trust for your grandchildren, and then you work hard to make the business successful. Now, when the trust sells the asset, there will be capital gains taxes on all the appreciation. However, the 2013 scheduled top federal capital gains tax rate of 20 percent is way less than the top gift and estate tax rate of 55 percent.

But what happens if the asset goes down in value? Too bad. When you use your lifetime exemption amount, you're taking a snapshot of the value of the asset at the time you make the gift. You're banking on the assets going up in value and thereby on being able to pass assets to your family members at a low tax cost insofar as the growth will occur on their balance sheet and not yours. If you make a bad bet, the consequence is that you wasted some of your lifetime exemption amount, because the asset your beneficiaries now have is less valuable than the amount of lifetime gift tax exemption you used.

Gifts Exempt from Gift Tax

Certain categories of gifts are exempt from both the annual exclusion and the lifetime exemption amount. You can make as many of these gifts as you want, with no limitations or gift tax consequences:

- *Spouse.* As long as your spouse is a US citizen, you can give them as much money you want to with no tax consequences. These gifts can either be made directly or in a qualified terminable interest property (QTIP) marital trust.

- *Charity.* Transfers to charities aren't taxable gifts. However, there are limitations on the amount of charitable gifts you can deduct from your income taxes each year.

- *Political organizations.* Whether you support elephants or donkeys, or something in between, transfers to political organizations aren't subject to gift tax.

- *Education.* Tuition expenses that are paid directly to the educational institution aren't subject to gift tax. The check must be written for tuition (not room and board) and must be paid to the institution. If the check is made out to the beneficiary, even if it's for educational purposes, it doesn't qualify for this exemption.

- *Health care.* Medical expenses that are paid directly to the medical provider aren't subject to gift tax. If the check is made out to the beneficiary, even if it's for health care purposes, it doesn't qualify for this exemption.

How to Make Gifts

The government doesn't want you to give away all your money. The more money you have when you die, the more tax revenue Uncle Sam gets. Remember my example about how the marital deduction on jointly owned assets can actually result in more money going to pay estate taxes when the second spouse dies, because the federal estate tax exemption amount of the first spouse to die wasn't utilized? The trick with the gift tax exemption amount is to use it very wisely.

One of the beautiful things about making a gift is that you get to see the beneficiary enjoy your generosity while you're still here. Because it's your money, feel free to direct your generosity in a way that support your values and makes you feel good.

There is no single "best way" to make a gift, so you should consider the pros and cons of various options:

- *Outright.* The benefit of making an outright gift is its simplicity. You write a check, and the money is theirs. The downside is that there is no asset protection, and you have no control over the money. This is best for gifts of smaller amounts of money (potentially utilizing the annual exclusion) or gifts of dollars that you know will be spent right away and not invested.

- *Custodial account.* Minors under the age of 18 or 21 (depending on the state) can't legally hold title to money. Each state authorizes either a Uniform Gift to Minors Account (UGMA) or Uniform Transfers to Minors Account (UTMA), in which a custodian (the parent or some other responsible party) manages the account for the minor's behalf. Whatever is in the account is turned over to the minor when he or she reaches the age of majority (18 or 21). The benefit of these accounts is they're easy to set up. The downside is that 18 or 21 isn't generally the best age to be turning large sums of money over to a kid. So, if you're going to use these types of accounts, the intention is generally that they be spent (usually for education) prior to the time the funds are turned over.

- *529 account.* These are special accounts that grow tax-deferred as long as the funds are used for education. They're very popular with both parents and grandparents as a way of funding a child's education. 529 accounts have a neat feature that when making a transfer to the account, you can contribute five years' worth of annual exclusion gifts at one time. This means you can fund the account with up to $65,000 ($13,000 x 5) in year one and apply the $65,000 to your annual exclusions over the next five years. Even though you're making a gift in excess of $13,000 in year one, you don't need to use your lifetime exemption amount.

- *Single-purpose trust.* These are trusts that are funded and designed to meet a specific goal, such as education, language studies, or a special-needs trust. The trust terms are structured to have the trustee not use the money for items other than your goal, and the trust is funded to a level appropriate to meet your goal. The trust can be funded on an ongoing basis using annual exclusion gifts or through one-time use of the lifetime exemption amount.

- *Discretionary trust.* A trust implemented primarily for estate tax reduction purposes is typically created as a discretionary trust where the trustee is charged with using the assets for the beneficiaries' needs over time as those needs may change. The trust can be funded on an ongoing basis using annual exclusion gifts or through one-time use of the lifetime exemption amount.

- *Insurance trust.* This is a trust specifically designed to remove the death benefit of insurance policies from your taxable estate for pure estate tax minimization purposes. This is such a powerful tool as part of an estate plan that I've dedicated Chapter 10, "Insurance Trust," entirely to its design and purpose.

Gift Tax Return

Whenever you're doing gifting, you need to bear in mind that you may need to file a gift tax return (Form 709). The gift tax return is due April 15 of the year following the year in which the gift was made. Many people overlook the requirement to file a gift tax return because, for the most part, when you make a gift you aren't paying taxes. The only time you pay gift taxes is when you make a gift in excess of your lifetime exemption amount. Years of experience has demonstrated that most people are loath to pay taxes when they don't have to, so they limit their gifting to whatever they can do on a tax payment-free basis.

Situations where you need to file a gift tax return include:

- Any use of the lifetime exemption amount.

- Use of the annual exclusion of both spouses when the assets being gifted only come from the assets of one of the spouses.

- Any time you transfer something where its FMV could be in question, such as a business interest, real estate, or artwork.

By filing a gift tax return that discloses what you believe to be the FMV of the asset and how you arrived at the FMV, you start a three-year statute of limitations period. If the IRS doesn't challenge the value within that three-year period, then the amount of the gift is fixed and complete. If you don't file a gift tax return, then the IRS can always go back and challenge the valuation you used when you file an estate tax return in the future in which you disclose these prior gifts. This applies to annual exclusion gifts when the thing being gifted has a value in question.

- An indirect gift. Any transfer of value from one person to another without compensation is potentially a taxable gift. The gift doesn't need to be intentional; it arises from any transfer of value. Situations that I've seen included parents transferring real estate to an LLC and then including the child as a member of the LLC without the child making any contribution of capital; or a parent voiding their stock certificates in the company, which resulted in the children's stock certificates being worth more.

Ask the Attorney "Deirdre, my parents transferred stuff into my name over the years, like real estate. They never filed a gift tax return. This isn't really a gift, is it?" Of course it's a gift. A failure to file a gift tax return doesn't mean something isn't a gift. The estate tax return specifically asks if the decedent made any "prior taxable gifts." It doesn't ask if the decedent "filed any gift tax returns." Lying on a tax return is punishable by penalties, interest, and even criminal actions in extreme cases. Furthermore, if an executor knowingly files an incorrect estate tax return, they're personally liable for all those penalties, interest, and criminal actions. More self-reporting is involved with the gift tax return and the estate tax return than with income tax returns, where you know the IRS receives duplicate copies of your income information. The best course of action is to be truthful, disclose whatever issues exist, and deal with them, so the family isn't subject to lingering problems.

10

Insurance Trusts

Magic Tax-Reduction Trick

For those of you who have (1) a taxable estate (or an estate potentially subject to estate tax) and (2) life insurance, this chapter is a must read. A life insurance trust can literally make hundreds of thousands of dollars of taxes disappear. For you, a life insurance trust is a "have to have" document, as much as a will, a power of attorney, a living will, and a health care proxy.

■ **Chapter Brief**   Life insurance gives your family choices at death through cold cash. Term versus permanent insurance—which might be right for you? An insurance trust directs all that cash to your beneficiaries and none to the government. An insurance trust needs to be properly structured for the death benefit to be out of your taxable estate. Annual documentation is required to keep it out of your taxable estate. Flexibility is the hallmark of a trust that will fit you today and in the future.

Integrating Insurance into Your Estate Plan

Why is life insurance so important in estate planning? First, cash is king in estate administration. From a practical perspective, death both ends an income stream and creates a lot of new expenses on top of needing to maintain normal household expenses. Life insurance creates dollars at death to take care of immediate expenses as well as provide a source for future ones.

Second, life insurance is unique as an asset because it doesn't have real value until you die. Sure, your policy might have a cash surrender value that you could tap into if you needed it. Or you might be investing in a policy as a way to save for retirement. But the big bang for your buck with life insurance is the death benefit. To get that, you need to be dead.

What are the implications of my observations? Well, because life insurance isn't an asset you're likely to want to spend during your lifetime, it's a pretty painless asset to give away. Also, remember that 100 percent of the death benefit is included in your taxable estate. So, the life insurance policy that had zero value to you right before you died could add $1 million to your estate, with Uncle Sam waiting for his share.[1] An insurance trust leaves Uncle Sam disappointed and out in the cold.[2]

Life insurance also acts as a backstop to your other, less liquid assets. Your net worth might look great on paper, but if it consists mostly of your house and your retirement plans, it's not attractive to spend it to support your beneficiaries. If you'll essentially create new assets at death by having life insurance in the first place, why not create tax-free assets through a life insurance trust that owns the policy? If you agree, why not go a step further and make sure the death benefit stays in trust until needed by the beneficiaries, so as to avoid creditors and predators?

Must You Have Life Insurance?

No, of course you don't need to have life insurance. However, many people do have it to provide cash to their families at death. They could be motivated to cover the mortgage, to provide for college, to replace one spouse's income, to generate liquidity in their business, to create new dollars on death for a second spouse or special-needs trust, or for myriad other reasons. It could even be as simple as your employer providing a policy with a large death benefit. The point is that if you have life insurance or are considering purchasing

---

[1] If you live in a jurisdiction with a low estate tax threshold, the mere existence of life insurance can create a taxable estate. Think about it. If you have $750,000 of assets and a $500,000 life insurance policy, you may be thinking to yourself that you don't have a taxable estate if the federal estate tax exemption is $1 million. However, you're forgetting to add the death benefit of the life insurance, which will put you over the top for estate tax purposes. The life insurance trust takes the death benefit out of the equation.

[2] There's always a caveat. One very important consideration with life insurance is that if you have an existing life insurance policy and you transfer it to a life insurance trust, it doesn't leave your taxable estate until three years have elapsed. So, if you transfer the policy to a trust, and you die two years later, you get zero estate tax savings. However, if you die three years and one day later, the entire death benefit is excluded from your taxable estate.

it, you can make sure it goes estate tax free to your family (and protect that death benefit from creditors and predators).

Ask the Attorney "Deirdre, do you sell life insurance to your clients?" No, absolutely not. The only thing I sell to my clients is legal services. In my state, attorneys are barred from being compensated for services other than legal services. The reason is that, as your attorney, I'm supposed to have your best interest in mind. If I recommend an insurance policy to you, and I get a commission if you buy it, don't you think I might be inclined, if only subconsciously, to suggest that you do what is in my best interest, even if it's not in yours? This is what is called a conflict of interest. Your attorney should disclose to you if they get paid for anything you buy based on their advice. If you're unsure, ask.

Making Life Insurance Part of Your Estate Plan

Why are you creating an estate plan? You have people you want to protect, values you want to pass on, and goals you want your family to reach. Would having more money help you accomplish that end? If so, you should consider life insurance as part of your estate plan. The death benefit from a life insurance policy is generally available three to five weeks after your death, and it avoids probate. Regardless of the amount of your wealth, your family will be reeling from your death, feeling incredibly insecure, and fearful of making the wrong move. Even if they can liquidate assets (which, due to probate proceedings, they might not be able to do), your family won't be in good shape. Having new cash available goes a long way to give your family the confidence to go on.

Types of Insurance

The world of life insurance is divided into two spheres: term and permanent. The insurance companies are always coming out with different products that you invest in the stock market, or that are guaranteed, or that have great names, but these are your basic options.

Term Insurance

Term insurance is pure death benefit. Every day that you don't die, you lose 1/365 of the premium you paid for the year. This isn't the worst thing in the world, though, because you're still alive to enjoy another day. Think of it like your homeowner's insurance. It's not as if every day when you drive home, you say, "Darn, my house didn't burn down today, so I didn't make anything off my homeowners insurance."

The cost of pure term insurance goes up each year, because each year you live you're one year closer to your statistical death (cheery thought, huh?). So, if the premium is $100 at age 30, it might be $110 at 31, $122 at 32, and so on. Term insurance is usually packaged for a period of years (10, 15, or 20 years); you pay a flat premium each year, which blends the lower costs in the younger years with higher costs of the later years. What if you stop paying the premium? The policy ends, because you aren't building any equity over time.[3]

Term insurance is relatively cheap. In a quick search on the Internet I found a $1 million death-benefit 20-year term policy for a 42-year-old man for around $1,000 a year from an A++ rated company (that is, a company with a stronger financial rating than the United States). The flip side is that if you wanted to continue the coverage at age 62, you might then be paying $7,200 a year. (I leave it to the investment experts whether paying less for longer and investing the difference is a better bet.) And if you got sick between 42 and 62, you might be paying more, or you might not qualify for continued insurance at age 62 at all.

Permanent Insurance

Permanent insurance (sometimes called *whole life, variable,* or *guaranteed*) is an investment. You're paying for something more than just the pure death benefit. You may have a whole life or variable policy that accumulates cash value so that after a while, the policy can use its own earnings to pay the premium. You may have a guaranteed policy and pay to have coverage for life. With a permanent insurance policy you need to consider the additional premium costs over any about the cost of pure term insurance as part of your overall investment plan.

A permanent policy is generally designed so you pay more premiums up front, and after a period of time the premium is scheduled to *vanish*. The premium doesn't actually disappear; instead, the idea is that in the first years you overpay so much above the pure term insurance cost that the excess investment, plus the earnings on that, eventually generates enough dollars to pay the premium without you contributing more.

---

[3] Some term insurance policies are *convertible*, which means you can exchange your policy for a permanent policy during the conversion period (at a much higher premium, of course). You pay for the privilege—every bell and whistle added to an insurance policy (even the "luxury" of paying monthly instead of annually) adds to the cost.

■ **Real Stories from Around My Conference Table**   Do you have permanent life insurance? Yes? Then stop right now and make a note to contact your insurance company to get an *inforce illustration*. I'm serious—stop now and make a note. When you bought your life insurance policy, there was an *illustration* of how it would perform in the future based on certain assumptions. Among those assumptions were pure guesses about interest rates and stock market return. The illustration showed you what your life insurance policy would do assuming those assumptions came true. Well, guess what? The insurance companies have no more crystal balls than you do. We've been experiencing unprecedented low interest rates. The real result? I have had clients who haven't had to pay insurance premiums in years coming to me with notices that they now need to pony up $16,000, $24,000, or, in one case, $54,000 more dollars each year to keep the policy in force. What to do? Don't pay and lose the policy? Pay—but where to get the money? Don't be surprised. An inforce illustration uses a new set of assumptions based on where we are today so you can see whether your policy is healthy or likely to blow up in the future.

Reasons for Insurance

Here's the thing. You may want your estate plan to accomplish certain goals, but you don't have enough money at present to get there. Because your estate plan comes into effect at death, insurance is a natural investment to consider, because it also comes to fruition at death. I've listed next some of the reasons I most frequently see people incorporating life insurance into their estate plan. If any of these speak to you, consider holding the insurance in a trust, where 100 percent of the dollars will go to meeting those goals of yours:

- *Replace income.* If you're the breadwinner for your family and you die, there's no more bread. Life insurance can replace the dollars you might've earned over a period of years.

- *Replace taxes.* If you have a taxable estate, and you know that $500,000 is likely to go to estate taxes, or you want to replace the income taxes on your IRA, you could purchase $500,000 of life insurance so the tax man gets paid *and* your family receives your total net worth. This can be especially important for unmarried couples who don't get the benefit of the "no tax on assets to the spouse" rule.

- *Cover a large expense.* You want your kids to go to college, or you don't want your spouse to worry about the mortgage. You can estimate what that expense would be and get an insurance policy with a death benefit to cover the cost. Term insurance fits nicely here because these types of expenses will potentially be taken care of over a period of time if you're still here.

- *Create a bigger pool of dollars at death.* Let's say you have children from your first marriage and a spouse from your second marriage, and there's not enough money for everybody. You can leave life insurance to your kids and everything else to your spouse. Or, what if you have a special-needs child, and you want to be able to provide for her but not take away from your other children? Insurance creates new dollars for that child at death.

- *Create liquidity at death.* Perhaps your assets consist mostly of a business or real estate. Although they provide a nice income while you're managing them, no other family member may have the skill to get money out of those assets. Or they may not want to be partners with your partners. Life insurance can provide a means whereby you sell the nonliquid asset in return for liquid dollars, and those dollars come into being when you pass away.

Anatomy of an Irrevocable Life Insurance Trust

An *irrevocable life insurance trust* (ILIT, pronounced "eye-let") is a trust that you create during your lifetime. An ILIT is specifically designed to own life insurance, keep it out of your taxable estate, and pass the death benefit to your beneficiaries in a manner that's coordinated with the rest of your estate plan. What are its key characteristics?

- *Irrevocable.* Once the ILIT is created, it can't be terminated or changed by you.[4] The trust must be irrevocable for the assets to be excluded from your taxable estate.

- *Inter-vivos.* The ILIT is created by you during your lifetime. This is different from other trusts for your family members,

---

[4] Just because you can't change the trust, that doesn't mean the trust can't be changed. A well-drafted trust can give your trustee or, in some cases, your beneficiary lots of powers to modify the trust. These include changing who the beneficiaries are, changing when and how the beneficiaries receive assets, changing the trustee, and even rolling the trust assets into a new trust in the event the ILIT isn't working at some point in the future.

which might be created within your estate plan but don't come into effect until you've passed away.

- *Policy owner and beneficiary.* The ILIT owns the life insurance policy on your life and is the beneficiary of that policy. Upon your death, the death benefit passes into the ILIT for the benefit of your intended beneficiaries. Because you don't own the policy when you die, it isn't included as part of your taxable estate. Your beneficiaries receive 100 percent of the death benefits tax-free.

- *Grantor/Insured.* The person creating the ILIT is normally the person whose life is insured under the insurance policy owned by the ILIT.

- *Trustee.* The trustee is somebody other than the grantor/insured. I commonly suggest naming the spouse and/or an adult child as a trustee or co-trustee.

- *Beneficiaries.* These can be either the same beneficiaries as in the rest of your estate plan, with the exact same distribution terms, or other beneficiaries of your choosing.

- *Boilerplate.* Just like any other trust, you need to create the rules by which the ILIT operates. The bulk of the trust agreement addresses these rules.[5]

Crummey Notices

To set the stage, everything I've been talking about so far relates to the death benefit being estate-tax-free when paid to the ILIT. However, before you die, money must be contributed to the trust periodically so the trust, which owns the life insurance policy, can in turn pay the premiums. When you transfer money to an irrevocable trust, that is a *gift*. Does this gift eat away at your lifetime gift tax exemption amount?

Let me answer that question with a question: Would you trade a little bit of paperwork to avoid using your lifetime gift tax exemption amount and save it for when you die? It's not too painful, I promise.

---

[5] Need a refresher in the blueprint of building a trust? Look back at Chapter 8, "Trust in Trusts," for the building blocks.

What Is a Crummey Notice?

We tax attorneys call this paperwork *Crummey notices*. No, I'm not making up that name, nor am I referring to the fact that nobody likes to do paperwork. Instead, I refer to the great case of Mr. Crummey, who took the IRS to court and won.

What was Mr. Crummey's issue? Well, a gift has to be a "present interest" to qualify for the annual gift tax exclusion. (See how all the pieces of what I've been talking about start to come together?) In order for a gift to be a present interest, a person must have a right to take money now. The problem is that when you're making a gift to a trust, generally speaking the whole point is that the beneficiary needs to wait until a later point to get the money—and thus there's no present interest. Mr. Crummey (or more likely his very creative tax attorney) found an entirely legitimate way to have his cake and eat it, too.

What was Mr. Crummey's workaround? He suggested that if he transferred $10,000 to a trust with two beneficiaries, he would give notice to each beneficiary that they had a period of time (let's say 30 days) to withdraw $5,000 each (their share of the contribution Mr. Crummey had made to the trust). If the beneficiaries didn't withdraw the money within the 30-day period, the money would stay in the trust and be governed by all the trust distribution instructions (and be available to pay the life insurance premium). If the beneficiaries did withdraw the money, then they could spend it.

Because the beneficiaries have a right to withdraw the money for a period of time, the court agreed that the beneficiaries had a present interest in the gift, and thus that Mr. Crummey could utilize his annual exclusion from gift taxes when making gifts to the trust in this manner.

The Crummey notice is the documentation that lets the beneficiaries know about a right of withdrawal, which allows the gift to the trust to qualify for the annual exclusion from gift taxes.

How to Do Crummey Notices

I often handle the Crummey notices for my clients. This isn't because they can't do them, but because they want to make sure the Crummey notices are done each year. If you do want to it yourself, here are the basic steps that you need to follow:

1. Open a bank account in the name of the ILIT. Transfer to that account an amount of money that's at least equal to the insurance premium payment.[6]

2. Divide the total amount of the premium payment by the number of trust beneficiaries to whom you'll give the right to withdraw part of the contribution. This may not be all the trust beneficiaries, because there may be some whom you don't want to give a right of withdrawal (maybe a kid has substance-abuse issues). However, as long as each beneficiary to whom you've given a right of withdrawal can withdraw less than the annual gift tax exclusion amount ($13,000 per person currently, or $26,000 for married couple), the entire premium contribution can be sheltered by your annual gift tax exemption amount.

3. The trustee gives each beneficiary written notice that they can withdraw their share of the contribution from the trust. (If the premium payment was $10,000, and you had two beneficiaries, the trustee could advise them that they could each withdraw $5,000.) In the notice, the trustee tells the beneficiaries how long they have to withdraw the money (let's say 30 days) and that they need to advise you whether they want withdraw the money or not.

4. Each beneficiary elects to (1) withdraw the money, (2) sign a waiver indicating that they're not going to withdraw the money, or (3) do nothing.

5. If the beneficiary elects to withdraw the money, then the trustee distributes the dollars to them. If the beneficiary waives the right to withdraw the money or does nothing, then the trustee uses the dollars to pay the insurance premium.

What If I Don't Have Crummey Notices?

Well, if you don't have Crummey notices, then when you make a contribution to an ILIT (or any other irrevocable inter-vivos trust), the contributions count against your lifetime exemption from gift taxes, and not your annual exclusion amount. "Oh, what's the big deal?" you might be saying to yourself. "After all, the premiums are only $5,000 per year." OK. So after you pay the premium for 10 years, you've used $50,000 of your lifetime exemption amount. After

---

[6] Crummey notices work with any irrevocable inter-vivos trust; it doesn't need to be an ILIT. The mechanics are the same in order to have a contribution to a trust qualify for the annual exclusion from gift taxes.

20 years, you've used $100,000 of your lifetime exemption amount (which is 10 percent of the lifetime exemption amount given to you). That will increase the taxes your family pays upon your death. Instead, just by doing a little paperwork each year, you could make totally tax-free gifts to your beneficiaries. It seems to me that it's worth a couple of hours each year to save the money.

Changing Title

The single most important aspect of creating a successful ILIT (or a successful gift of any kind, for that matter) is to change the ownership and beneficiary of the life insurance policy to the trust. If the ILIT doesn't own the insurance policy, then all the paperwork you have, and all the money you spent for the attorney to prepare it, is worthless.

For a privately owned (not employer-provided) policy, in order to move it into the ILIT, you must complete (1) a Change of Owner form naming the ILIT as the new owner the policy and (2) a Change of Beneficiary form naming the ILIT as the sole beneficiary of the policy.

For employer-provided or group term insurance, in order to move it into the ILIT, you must complete (1) an Absolute Assignment Form, in which you give up all rights over the policy and instead name the ILIT as the entity that can exercise those rights; and (2) a Change of Beneficiary form naming the ILIT as the sole beneficiary of the policy.

When you sit down to change the owner and beneficiary of the policy to the ILIT, you need to have the following information on hand:

- *Full name of the trust and date of execution.* For example, "The Liss Family Trust dated October 1, 2001."

- *Name and address of the trustee.*

- *Tax identification number of the trust.* Because the trust is a separate taxpayer from you, it must have its own identification number. These numbers are issued by the IRS (Google "IRS apply for employer identification number" online). While you're alive, there shouldn't be any tax filings. The threshold to file a trust income tax return is $600 of income each year, and any earnings within the insurance policy itself aren't subject to income tax. After your death, the trust may be required to file a tax return each year, depending on the amount of income generated.

- *Copy of the trust.* Some companies want to see the cover page and the signature page; others the cover page, first page, and signature page; still others the entire trust; and some, nothing at all. See why it's frustrating? Whom you're leaving your estate to and how is nobody's business. If the insurance company asks for a full copy of the trust, speak to your attorney about whether you could merely send the first page and the execution pages, or potentially the trustee sections, or whatever else the insurance company needs to document its file.

Ask the Attorney "Deirdre, is it difficult to move insurance into an ILIT?" No. It's not difficult, but it's one of the most frustrating things about my practice. First, each insurance company has its own forms, and they don't all ask for the same things. Second, unless the form can be downloaded, our office can't obtain the forms on our client's behalf, so the client has to contact the insurance company. Human nature being what it is, this isn't always a priority on a client's plate. Third, some group policies don't permit any paperwork; you need to make election through your employer's human resources system. Finally, if the insurance forms aren't filled out exactly properly (and I've had them returned because someone couldn't make out a comma on the form), they'll be kicked back and you'll have to start all over. I give you this warning now. Once you create the ILIT, the work isn't finished. You need to push through and complete your planning. Of course, you can avoid all this paperwork if you set up the ILIT when you buy a new policy and name the ILIT as the initial owner and beneficiary of the policy.

ILIT at the End of the Day

So, you set up the ILIT, properly change the owners and beneficiary of your insurance policies to the trust, and then manage to get hit by a bus. What next? Your trustee will file a claim with the insurance company by sending the company a copy of your death certificate. Within three to five weeks, either (1) a check will be sent to the trustee or (2) an account will be opened in the name of the trust and a checkbook sent to the trustee. No income taxes, no estate taxes—just cash. Depending on the trust terms, the trustee can distribute money to the beneficiaries, pay expenses directly, or even lend money to your estate or beneficiaries to give them cash flow before the estate is settled. Whatever isn't spent stays in trust until it's time for it to be distributed based on the instructions you left your trustee. And who is never getting any money? Poor old Uncle Sam.

11

Advanced Tax Strategies
Your Family Gets More ... the IRS Gets Less

Your will, power of attorney, living will, and health care proxy are in place. You've even looked at an insurance trust or at giving away your assets now. But you still have the government as one of your beneficiaries. What else is a person to do? The tricks don't stop now. There's a whole "alphabet soup" of advanced tax planning strategies for you to explore. Think of this as an appetizer, because if any of these appeal to you, you'll need to see an attorney to find out if the techniques will enhance your plan.

▨ **Chapter Brief**   GRATs, QPRTs, and charitable trusts are split-interest trusts that allow you to give away your assets and still retain a benefit from them. IDGTs supersize a regular trust by allowing additional tax-free contributions each year. FLPs and FLLCs create a family business and leverage the concept of valuation discounts to maximize gifting. Loans and installment sales freeze value in the parents' estate and grow the children's assets.

I need to mention a couple of caveats before I get down to it. First, although the planning techniques in this chapter may seem sexy and fun, they're add-ons to the foundation of your estate plan. Sometimes I meet people who are so excited about tax savings that they don't focus on the basic questions of who gets their assets, how the beneficiaries get those assets, and what values they want to pass along. Next, I'll just be sharing an overview of each technique, not getting into the nuances. If I tried to do that, I'd need a second book! Finally, this isn't DIY planning. You need to speak to an attorney in your state who specializes in estate planning to see if any of these are actually right for you.

QPRT: Qualified Personal Residence Trust

Scenario: You transfer your home to a trust and give yourself the right to live in the home for a fixed term of years (let's say 10). Following the 10-year period, the house is distributed to your children.

Why would you do this? A *qualified personal residence trust* (QPRT) allows you to make a completed gift today of the house at a fraction of its value. Because you're giving the house to an irrevocable trust but retaining the right to live in it for a period of time, your kids aren't getting 100 percent of the value of the gift today—they have to wait 10 years to be able to use the house. If your kids aren't getting 100 percent now, then the cost of the gift in terms of how much of your lifetime exemption you're using is less than the fair market value (FMV) of the house.

An example is definitely in order. Shirley lives in Ohio and has a vacation home on Lake Erie that her kids enjoyed every summer growing up, and now her grandkids do. She is considering gifting and wants the vacation home to stay in the family. The house is valued at $550,000, and Shirley is 70 years old. The IRS says that Shirley's retained interest[1] in the house is worth $218,323, so the gift is $331,677. Ten years later, the QPRT distributes the house outright to the children. If the value of the house increases a mere 2 percent per year, Shirley will have gifted an asset that would have been worth $670,450 10 years later, for a gift tax cost of only $331,677.

The benefit of a QPRT is that it's straightforward and statutory (what we lawyers call *black-letter law*). This isn't a planning technique made up by attorneys to try to turn the tax code to their client's advantage and which may or may not work in the long run. All you need to know about a QPRT is set out in black and white in the US tax code: section 2702 to be exact. The IRS has even published a form of QPRT that you can look at.[2]

Section 2702 says that, for gift tax purposes, a *retained interest* (Shirley's right to use the vacation home for 10 years) normally has no value: the gift tax cost is 100 percent of the value, regardless of the fact that the children have to wait 10 years to enjoy the house. However, for a *qualified interest*, which includes a retained interest for a fixed period of time (10 years in Shirley's case), you can deduct the value of the retained interest from the gift. This is

---

[1] The amount of the *retained interest* in a QPRT is calculated as function of (1) the length of the QPRT and (2) the 7520 rate (named after the tax code section that references it), which is an interest rate set by the IRS based on market interest rates and used in retained interest calculations.

[2] You can find it at Rev. Proc. 2003-42, 2003-1 CB 993. Just type it in Google.

how Shirley is able to give away $550,000 and use only $331,677 of her lifetime exemption amount.

One final benefit: It's easier to give away a house than to give away money, especially if you can still live in the house for a while. It's harder to give away liquid assets that you might need in the future.

So, what are the downsides? Of course there are downsides—you didn't think it would be this easy, did you? Catch number 1: If you die before the QPRT term ends, it's as if you did nothing. The entire property, at its then-current value, is included in your taxable estate. You rolled the dice and lost. Catch number 2: You have to pay rent to the QPRT beneficiaries to use the property after the trust term ends. (In the example, Shirley would need to pay FMV rent to keep using the vacation house starting in year 11). To be honest, this is the biggest stumbling block I run across, because people who've just given a valuable property to their children aren't necessarily happy to then pay the kids rent to use it.

GRAT: Grantor Retained Annuity Trust

A *grantor retained annuity trust* (GRAT) is like a QPRT but with investments or a business interest instead of a house. Example time again!

Brian is 47, has been fortunate enough to do well for himself, and has amassed quite a bit of wealth. He invests actively in the stock market. He wants to engage in gifting, but he isn't financially secure enough to give away substantial assets now. He would, however, be happy to give away the *growth* on his assets.

Brian sits down with me to discuss a GRAT. I explain to him that he starts a GRAT by contributing money to an irrevocable trust for the benefit of his family. Brian will be repaid his initial contribution to the trust in equal installments over a term of years (let's say seven) plus the 7520 rate at the time the GRAT is created. Know for now that the *7520 rate* (named after the tax code section that references it) is an interest rate set by the IRS based on market interest rates and used in valuations of life estates, remainder interests, and annuities. I explain to Brian that in recent years, because of the low interest-rate environment, the 7520 rate has been very low. For October 2012, it's a mere 1.2 percent. In the event that the investments of the GRAT have a rate of return greater than 1.2 percent (the 7520 rate), that "excess growth" is transferred to the beneficiaries of the trust gift-tax-free.

"What?" Brian says, as his eyes light up. "All I have to do is find an investment with a rate of return of greater than 1.2 percent, and I'll get back all the money that I contributed to the trust plus 1.2 percent, and any excess earnings will pass to my kids tax-free?" Yup. That's pretty much it in a nutshell.

To show you the power of a GRAT in numbers, assume Brian is super-excited and contributes $1 million to a GRAT. Each year for the next seven years, he'll receive an annuity payment of $149,797. At the end of seven years, Brian will have gotten back a total of $1,048,579. However, if the GRAT's investing creates an actual rate of return of 10 percent per year, then at the end of the seven years there will be excess growth (growth over and above the annuity amount that must be returned to Brain) of $527,567. Where does this excess growth go? The $527,567 passes into a trust for the benefit of Brian's children. And how much gift tax will Brian pay? That would be none, nada, zero, zilch.

But wait! The savings don't stop here. Brian could create a series of GRATs. Each year as he receives his annuity payment back from the first GRAT, he could consider whether to contribute that annuity payment, plus potentially other money, to another GRAT. This GRAT could have the same term of years or a different term of years.

What's the downside to a GRAT? First, although it works well with investment assets, it doesn't always work so well with business or real estate assets. This is because in order to figure out how much of the GRAT needs to be returned as an annuity payment, you have to do a valuation of the business or real estate each year. This can quickly become very expensive. Second, as with the QPRT, if you die before the trust term ends, you lose. Whatever is in the GRAT is part of your taxable estate. Third, if your investment loses value, then although you'll receive back whatever is left of your initial contribution to the GRAT, nothing will pass to your beneficiaries because you haven't met the threshold of a rate of return in excess of the 7520 rate. I saw a lot of this in 2008/2009.

■ **Let's Get Real**   GRATs and QPRTs work best in a low-interest-rate environment. The lower the interest rate, the lower the threshold the GRAT needs to beat on its investments to transfer tax-free dollars. The lower the interest rate, the lower the gift-tax cost of a QPRT.

IDGT: Intentionally Defective Grantor Trust

Being an *intentionally defective grantor trust* (IDGT) or *grantor trust* can supercharge any trust, but is particularly effective when you sell assets to a trust. Normally, if something is "intentionally defective," that is a bad thing.

Not so with trusts. An IDGT is merely a technical name for a trust whose grantor remains the income taxpayer on the trust, even though the grantor gave away the money.

Paying Income Taxes Is a Tax-Free Gift

Why would you want to do this? It's bad enough to pay taxes on money you get—why would you want to pay taxes on income you don't receive? Well, as a super-simplified example, if a trust earns $1,000 per year and is in the 35 percent tax bracket, the trust has to pay $350 in taxes. This means the beneficiaries receive only $650 of growth that year (remember, appreciation on a gift is the true value of gifting). Instead, if the grantor remains the taxpayer of the trust, then the grantor pays the $350 in taxes out of the grantor's other assets. This achieves two very significant results: (1) all the earnings in the trust grow for the benefit of the beneficiaries, income-tax-free; and (2) the grantor pays the income tax with dollars that might otherwise be subject to estate tax in their estate, thus reducing their taxable estate. In short: more money to the family … less money to the IRS.

Estate Freeze via Sale to IDGT

If that isn't enough, the real leverage in an IDGT occurs when you sell an appreciated asset to the IDGT and achieve an *estate freeze* for a small gift tax cost. Here I'll talk about Lisa, who started a very successful textile company. She imports fabric and sells to retailers throughout the Southeast. Her business has exploded in the past five years, thanks to a savvy Internet presence. Lisa has constantly reinvested in her business, so although it's quite valuable, she doesn't have a huge amount of liquid assets outside of the business. Lisa wants to do some gifting to her kids, but she doesn't want to gift large amounts of cash and liquid investments.

Lisa and I sit down and discuss a scenario in which she sells some of her business (let's say, $1 million worth) to an IDGT. "I can't do that," Lisa says, "I'll get killed with capital gains taxes!" Not so fast. Because Lisa owns the business interest being sold to the trust, and the trust is an IDGT where Lisa is the taxpayer, there are *no capital gains* on the sale. For tax purposes, the sale is between the same taxpayer (Lisa is selling to Lisa), which isn't a tax realization event.

Mollified, Lisa asks me to tell her more. I suggest she contribute $100,000 as a gift to an IDGT. She wants this structured as a common-pot trust for her children, who are still very young. Lisa then sells $1 million worth of her business to the IDGT in return for a note payable over five years, with interest of at least the *applicable federal rate* (a minimum interest rate set by the government for transactions between family members). The September 2012 rate for a five-year loan was 0.84 percent.[3]

The result? Lisa contributed $100,000 to the IDGT as gift. She sold an asset worth $1 million to the trust. She received back $1 million in the form of a $100,000 down payment and a five-year note. The note will be paid off by distributions from the company to shareholders, which includes the IDGT. Going forward, any growth in the business or future distributions on the portion of the business that was gifted belongs to the children via the trust. This effectively freezes the value of the interest sold at $1 million, because all the growth following the sale takes place on the IDGT's ledger and outside of Lisa's taxable estate. Lisa's gift tax cost is the use of $100,000 of her lifetime estate tax exemption amount (or less if she can apply her annual gift tax exclusion amount to the gift), and her only out-of-pocket cost is the cost of doing the transaction.

What is the downside? (You knew this question was coming.) Well, if you die while the note is still outstanding, the remaining balance of the note is an asset of your estate and subject to estate tax. Second, this sale technique relies on having an absolutely solid valuation to support the price of the asset being sold. If you have a weak valuation, the IRS can contend that you made an additional gift by virtue of the value reported being less than the actual value transferred. Because of this, a gift tax return must always be filed.

Generation-Skipping Tax Trusts

I've mentioned this a time or two before, but using your generation-skipping tax (GST) exemption amount is a home run. Recall that that GST exemption amount is the most you can leave to a person in a generation more than one below yours (a grandchild or a relative 37.5 years younger). By skipping over a generation for estate tax purposes, you deny the government a bite at the apple that is your assets.

Generation-Sharing Trust

Just because it's called a generation-*skipping* tax doesn't mean that you need to exclude your children to take advantage of the GST exemption amount. A better way to describe how to leverage the power of the GST tax exemption amount is to think about the recipient of the gift or bequest as a *generation-*

---

[3] You might have noticed that our current historically low interest rates make QPRTs, GRATs, and IDGTs very attractive. As interest rates go up, so do the costs of these planning techniques—and the tax savings go down.

sharing trust. This is basically a family trust for the benefit of a person and their descendants. You create a trust for the benefit of your child and their children, or your sister and her children, or whatever multiple generations you want to benefit. The generation-sharing trust can be either inter-vivos (created during your life) or testamentary (created at your death). Your child (or sister, or partner, as the case may be) can even be the trustee or co-trustee, so they can direct how the money is used in their family. You provide that if the primary beneficiary doesn't use all the money during their lifetime, then the money will pass to their children *estate-tax-free.* Moreover, you give the primary beneficiary a limited power of appointment, so they can direct how this estate-tax-free money will pass to their children (or to whomever the person designates with the power of appointment). The grandchildren or other younger generation members now have the money, and the government is left out in the cold.

▓ **Ask the Attorney** "Deirdre, I'm not a Rockefeller or a Gates. How does all this GST stuff apply to me?" Well, remember that I strongly recommend to all my clients that they leave assets in trust for a person's lifetime and name the person as trustee to achieve asset protection. Who knows what the tax laws will be in the future? I can't even tell you what they will be next year. Why not set up the inheritance so that if your kids don't use it, it can go tax-free to their kids?

Dynasty Trust

I've mentioned this a time or two before, but powering up a GST trust into a dynasty trust is a home run. The dynasty trust is a GST trust on steroids. It's designed to last literally generations without being subject to estate tax when each successive generation passes away. This is what people like the Rockefellers and Gates would have.

Let's look at some conservative numbers. You fund a dynasty trust with $1 million. You direct that all income passes to the child (so income isn't being added to the trust principal). The principal grows at a mere 2 percent. Your child passes away 25 years after you do. At that time, the trust principal is $1,640,600 (and your kids have been receiving 4 percent income of $40,000 or more each year). If the trust was included in your child's estate, $820,300 of taxes might be due.[4] Because it isn't, the trust passes tax free to the child's children, and continues to grow. Twenty-five years later, the grandchildren have received the income (now at least $65,625 per year at 4 percent), and

---

[4] I'm illustrating this at a 50 percent estate tax rate, not taking into account any exemptions or changes in rates. I can't tell you what Congress is likely to do in 2013—much less 2038!

the principal continues to grow at 2 percent. Now the trust principal is $2,691,600. Imagine what would happen if you had a rate of return greater than 2 percent—or if the trust kept some of its income! See the power?

Forever is a very long time, though. In most states, a trust must end at some point. There is something called the *rule against perpetuities* (RAP). (I'm literally getting flashbacks to my first year in law school class thinking about RAP— and not in a good way.) In shorthand, under the common law (unless there is a statute saying otherwise), a trust can't last longer than the lifetime of all the beneficiaries who are alive when the trust is set up plus 21 years. Some states have modified RAP to make it easier to figure out the end date. A few states have even eliminated RAP in an effort to attract dynasty trusts to be located in, and thus be taxpayers in, their jurisdiction.

In considering a dynasty trust, be aware that there have been tax proposals to limit the term of a GST trust so it must end after 90 years and be distributed or taxed. And see an attorney! This isn't DIY planning.

CRT/CLT: Charitable Trusts

It's OK to be charitable but not *that* charitable. It's OK to give it away and want a little something in return. Luckily, the tax code has a special plan for you. With a *charitable lead trust* (CLT), you can give assets to a trust, provide the charity with an income for a term of years, and then give your kids whatever is left over at the end of the term. Or, with a *charitable remainder trust* (CRT), you can give assets to a charity and you or your beneficiaries receive an income from the amount gifted for a term of years.

What's the benefit? You (if you set up an inter-vivos charitable trust) or your estate (if you set up a testamentary charitable trust) get a charitable deduction for the contribution to the CLT or CRT. Of course, it isn't a deduction for 100 percent of the amount contributed, because the charity doesn't receive 100 percent of the money. The amount of the deduction is calculated based on the term of years the income stream exists.

For example, Gary and Judy have always generously supported their church. They have a lot of commercial real estate with tenants and want to provide for the church in their estate plan, but they also want to see the property stay in the family. I propose that they pick a property (Lot C) and contribute it to a CLT on their death. The CLT document provides that for 20 years, the church will receive the income generated by Lot C. At the end of the 20 year term, the property will pass back to the family, thus allowing Gary and Judy to satisfy both of their goals. Pretty neat, huh?

■ Ask the Attorney "Deirdre, is there a way for me to have my cake, nibble away at it, and enjoy the icing?" Yes! Combine the CRT or CLT with an irrevocable life insurance trust (ILIT). For example, if you create a CRT in your will, take some dollars that you might otherwise give to a charity now and use them to purchase a life insurance policy in an ILIT. When you die, the life insurance is paid to the ILIT, effectively replacing the dollars you gave to the charity on an estate tax free basis.

FLP/FLLC: Family Limited Partnership/ Family Limited Liability Company

This technique relies on the concept of *valuation discounts*. What does this mean? Let's say I have share of stock in Facebook that I want to sell and you want to buy (bless you). The stock is trading at $17.73. How much are you likely to pay for it? Well, $17.73, because if you didn't pay me that, I'd sell the share to someone who would.

Now, suppose I'm willing to sell the share of Facebook to you, but I have some conditions: you can't ever sell the stock to anyone else, I control when you receive any dividends, and you can't use the stock as security for a loan. Would you still pay me $17.73 for that stock share? Probably not. You might be willing to pay me $11 or $12, though. That is the essence of a valuation discount: when you're looking at the FMV, you need to consider what a willing seller would accept and a willing buyer would pay. This includes restrictions on the item that make it unpalatable, such as a lack of control or a lack of marketability.

How does this work in the estate planning context? Mark and Debra own a ranch that they want to begin transferring to their kids (in a GST trust, of course), and they're looking for a way to get the most bang for their buck in making the transfer. The ranch is worth $3 million, and they each want to use their full lifetime gift tax exclusion of $1 million each. If they make a plain old gift, they can give away $2 million (or 66 percent of the ranch), leaving $1 million in their taxable estate.

What if, instead, I sit down with Mark and Debra and suggest that they contribute the ranch to a *family limited liability company* (FLLC)? The FLLC has two types of ownership interest: *managing member*, representing 10 percent of the FLLC; and *non-managing member*, representing 90 percent. The non-managing member ownership interests have no control over the management of the ranch or the distribution of its profits (a *"lack of control"*). The non-managing members also can't sell their ownership interest to anyone else (a *"lack of marketability"*).

Mark and Debra will still give away $1 million each. Now, however, they're giving away $1 million of non-managing member interest in the FLLC instead of just part of the ranch. The non-managing member interest is less attractive to a buyer, just like in my Facebook example above. If a buyer discounts their offer by 25 percent to reflect the lack of control and the lack of marketability, then Mark and Debra can apply that same 25 percent discount to the value of the gift. Remember, FMV is what a willing seller and willing buyer in possession of all the facts would arrive at as the value of an item. If a 25 percent discount is applied to the non-managing member interest, then it's worth less. This means that $1 million of gift tax exemption could "buy" more of the non-managing member interest. In fact, after applying a 25 percent discount, the $1 million gift tax exemption amount represents a 44.44 percent interest in the FLLC instead of a 33 percent interest. This means that for the same use of a combined $2 million lifetime gift tax exemption, Mark and Debra are allowed to give away 88.88 percent of the FLLC instead of only 66 percent. Is that bang for your buck, or what?[5]

The downside is that you must have a real business in the FLLC with a real business purpose. It must operate like a real business. And no, saving taxes isn't a business purpose. Also, the concept of valuation discounts has been under constant attack by the IRS, with mixed results, so the effectiveness of the FLLC varies on a state-to-state basis.

■ **Ask the Attorney** "Deirdre, I love the idea of valuation discounts, but I don't want to do any gifting. Am I out of luck?" Absolutely not. If you have some kind of business, consider changing its structure so that some of your equity has all the control and most of the equity has no control. When you die, the same type of valuation discounts will be available to your estate.

---

[5] How does the math work? Mark and Debra contribute the ranch to the FLLC, so the FLLC has a total value of $3 million. This means each 1 percent of the FLLC has an undiscounted value of $30,000. If a 25 percent discount is applied, then each 1 percent of non-managing member interest has a value of $22,500 ($30,000 x 25 percent = $7,500; $30,000 – $7,500 = $22,500). With me so far? Mark and Debra want to give away $1 million each. If $22,500 is equal to 1 percent, then the question is how many times $22,500 goes into $1 million. The answer is 44.44 times. Before the discount, the value of each 1 percent was $30,000, which goes into $1 million 33.33 times. So, thanks to the discount, the same gift of $1 million now represents 44.44 percent if the FLLC instead of 33.33 percent.

Loans and Installment Sales: Estate Freeze

What happens if you make a loan or sell the asset instead of making a gift? If you didn't make a gift, you don't pay gift taxes. These techniques are an *estate freeze*. You're transferring money or an asset with the expectation of receiving back the principal sum transferred (plus market-rate interest). However, any growth following the date of transfer accumulates on your beneficiaries' balance sheet, not yours.

Loans

Consider Jeffrey and Michelle, a couple in their 40s with two children. Jeffrey is a serial entrepreneur and is good at his calling. He has a track record of investing in businesses that provide a high income stream. He has just set up an inter-vivos GST trust for his children, and he wants that trust to invest in his next project, where he anticipates a 12 percent annual rate of return.[6] However, Jeffrey doesn't want to make a large gift and use up his entire gift tax exemption amount (after all, there may be something even better to use it on later). Instead, he lends $500,000 to the GST trust. The loan note calls for 20 annual payments at an interest rate of 4 percent, secured by the assets of the trust. The GST trust uses the loaned money to invest in the new venture.

Jeffrey is right, as usual, and the investment starts kicking out 15 percent. Each payment that Jeffrey and Michelle receive back is mostly return of principal (getting back the loan amount) and 4 percent interest, which they include in their income taxes. The trust has the money to repay the loan through the money it's receiving from the investment. At the end of the day, Jeffery and Michelle get back their $500,000 loan (plus 4 percent), but everything else flows to the trust for their kids.

If Jeffrey and Michelle die, all that is included in their estate is the unpaid balance of the loan. This would have been included in their estate anyway if they had done nothing, because they had already accumulated the $500,000. Because this is a loan and not a gift, Jeffrey and Michelle are able to shift some of their accumulated assets to their kids at no gift tax cost. This gives them

---

[6] Setting up the trust to make the loan isn't necessary. Jeffery and Michelle could have made the loan directly to their kids (assuming they were of age). Because Jeffery and Michelle spoke to me, however, I shared with them all the asset-protection benefits of a trust, and they will never again consider any outright gifts or inheritances!

the flexibility to look at other planning techniques in the future that might make better use of their gift, estate, and GST tax exemption amounts.

Installment Sales

Ron and Joyce are in their 70s and own a company that engineers and produces medical instruments. Ron is very well known and holds several patents. Their son Daniel has followed in his father's engineering footsteps, and they want him to have the business, but they haven't gotten where they are in life without keeping the tax man out of their pockets.

Daniel comes to see me for help getting a bank loan to buy out his parents. The problem with a bank loan is that Ron and Joyce will be slammed with capital gains taxes on the sale. The alternative? Ron and Joyce can be the bank. They sell the business to Daniel and take back a note (with interest and security, of course). They set the sale price based on an independent valuation.

Each month, Ron and Joyce receive a payment from Daniel. Each payment has three parts for income tax purposes: return of principal investment, capital gain, and interest income. The ratios of the three parts depend on how much appreciation occurred in the business when Ron and Joyce owned it. They pay capital gains tax on the appreciated portion and income tax on the interest. This works well for them because the income stream helps fund their retirement, and deferring taxes is a good thing (after all, why pay taxes on money that they aren't going to spend yet?).

Daniel now owns his parents' business. He uses the income from the business to pay off the installment sale note. Any other profits or growth belong to Daniel and reflect his contribution to the business. When Ron and Joyce die, the business won't be included in their taxable estate. There is no worry that the business might need to be sold to pay taxes. If any balance remains on the note, it will be included in Ron's and Joyce's taxable estates.

■ **Ask the Attorney** "Deirdre, this sounds great! But I have an even better idea. Forget the valuation. Daniel and his parents should just come up with what they think is a fair price." Remember, IRS slow, not stupid. Of course there is incentive to give your kids a deal when selling something to them. We call this "deal" a gift. The gift amount is the difference between the FMV of the asset and what you sold it for. This transaction is part sale, part gift. When you die, your estate has to file an estate tax return. It will be reviewed. The IRS has copies of all your income tax returns. If the IRS sees that for 45 years Ron and Joyce received income from RJ Craft, Inc., but all of a sudden they receive none and all of RJ Craft, Inc.'s income now goes to Daniel, the IRS will reasonably wonder whether a gift was made. You need to be able to substantiate the transaction.

"We pulled the number out of the air" won't work. Because this can be hard to do 10–15 years later, I have even filed gift tax returns disclosing an installment sale and claiming there was no gift, just to put the IRS on notice and start the three-year statute of limitations running to review the transaction.

Mix and Match

This is by no means an exhaustive list of ways to save estate tax. Remember, the idea is to give you a flavor of the variety of techniques that might be used to reduce your tax bill and disinherit Uncle Sam. Each has its pros and cons. Some work better with investment assets, others with a business or real estate. Each has different estate, gift, and income tax consequences.

The beauty of tax planning is that once you understand the ingredients, you can mix and match them to make something that reflects your needs. Make a loan to a trust to purchase an investment, and use the income to pay insurance premiums on a policy in an ILIT to replace any dollars lost to estate taxes. Supercharge an installment sale by contributing part of the business to an IDGT to eliminate the income tax consequences on the note payments. Put a commercial property into an FLLC, and take advantage of valuation discounts when gifting an interest in the FLLC to a GST trust to stretch your GST exemption amount. But above all, see a qualified attorney to help you put your plan together.

12

Fiduciaries
The Linchpin to Making Your Plan Work

You can create the best, most personalized, and undeniably awesome estate plan in the world, but if you don't name the right people to carry out the plan, it's unlikely to meet your goals. Remember, your estate plan at the end of the day is a sheaf of papers. The individuals you select as your fiduciaries are the ones who breathe life into that plan and bridge the gap between your intentions and reality. There are laws that govern the fiduciaries' job description and some practical questions you should ask before you hire them.

■ **Chapter Brief**   You won't be here to carry out your estate plan. An *executor* has the temporary job of making sure your wishes under your will are followed and moving your estate from open to closed. A *trustee* has the long-term job of managing the assets and distributing them to the beneficiaries. The *guardian* is in charge of the person, but not necessarily the property, of any children under 18. Your *attorney-in-fact* will make financial decisions for you while you're alive. Your *health care representative* makes medical decisions for you. Considering *co-fiduciaries* and *successor fiduciaries* is just as important as naming the first person to act.

Who Is a Fiduciary?

In the simplest terms, a *fiduciary* is somebody who has the specific job of acting in your best interest, or your beneficiary's best interest, but not in their own. It's a relationship of trust. It's your money, not theirs. If the fiduciary violates that trust, they're personally responsible for any damages they might cause. In a practical sense, you need to trust in the people you name as the fiduciaries or the process you create to name them.

Your fiduciaries can be individuals, institutions, or combination of individuals and institutions. Individuals can be family members but don't need to be. In some states, the individuals can be the beneficiaries. An individual fiduciary can be one of your advisors, such as your attorney or accountant, but there is never a requirement that you name them as a fiduciary. If you're naming an institution, it needs to be a bank or trust company that has so-called *trust powers*. This means it's authorized to act as a trustee by a governing statute in the state in which it's operating.

▓ **Let's Get Real**   If you're married, you're likely to name your spouse as your fiduciary, regardless of what I tell you about the jobs in this chapter. However, I'm not worried about what happens if your spouse acts, or whoever else is your no-brainer go-to fiduciary. Presumably you and your spouse share the same values and have a joint economic interest. The hard question is, who will act if your spouse (or other no-brainer fiduciary) can't act? Who is the successor executor, trustee, guardian, attorney-in-fact, or health care representative? This is where you need to stretch your mind and think, "Who is the best person, or combination of persons, in that role today?" Bear in mind that as long as you (or your spouse, in a well-written document) are still here, you can change those successor fiduciaries as the people in your life change. But don't write off this chapter as unimportant because your spouse or other no-brainer fiduciary will act. Instead, think about who is in charge if they can't be.

Executor, Administrator, or Personal Representative

When you die, someone will be charged with the process of opening your estate, dealing with your assets and liabilities, paying any taxes, distributing assets to the beneficiaries or trusts for their benefit, and eventually closing the estate. Depending on the type of estate plan you have and the state you live in, that person may go by a different name:

Executor. If you've created a will, this is a person whom you've named under the will to carry out its terms.

Administrator. If you don't create an estate plan and instead rely on the one that your state creates for you, an administrator will be named. You won't select this person, because you didn't create an estate plan. Instead, they will be selected based on state statute. They will also normally need to post a bond as security that they won't run off with your assets. The expense for this of course will come out of your estate. (It's cheaper just to create an estate plan in the first place.)

Personal representative. The words *executor, executrix, administrator,* and *administratrix* are undeniably confusing and unwieldy. Some states have modernized the language so that whoever acts in this fiduciary role is referred

to as a *personal representative*. Although the title has changed, the job is the
ame.

r the rest of this section I'll use the word *executor*, but you can replace it
h *administrator* or *personal representative*.

---

the Attorney "Deirdre, my lawyer said I should name him as my executor. Should I?" For
ople, I honestly don't think so. Your attorney doesn't know your family and isn't intimately
vith your assets. I tell clients to search for a person in their family who can hire and
an attorney to do what the attorney needs to do. Or name the attorney as a co-executor.
on a secret. If your attorney is your executor, they will receive a commission from your
you die, in addition to legal fees. Most family members, although entitled to a
don't take it. I think attorneys should be paid for legal services they perform, not a
sed on the wealth you accumulated during your lifetime. Having said that, I'll act for
r considering their family, still want me to be the executor. However, I enter into an
hem about how I'm paid.

---

aid
gy.
is a
vhat
rida
ea of

on

the president of the mini-business that is your estate. The
nominated to their position by you in your will, or by state
't create a will. Once a person is nominated, they need to
position, which is done by the probate court or surrogate
of formality in the court's approval process depends on

approved for the job, they're given *letters testamentary*.
o your assets. The executor needs to produce letters
behalf of your estate. For example, the bank will say,
w you're authorized to act on behalf of the estate?"
vill reply "Aha! I have letters testamentary." And the
s our command."

be heady with all the power that comes with the
that with great power comes great responsibility.
of the following:

quirements of the probate court or

g all of your assets, and maintaining
until they can be distributed to the

- Identifying and paying any creditors

- Preparing and filing any estate, inheritance, or income tax returns

- Paying any expenses of the estate, including funeral expenses, probate court costs, and professional fees

- Allocating the assets among the beneficiaries in the manner set forth in the estate plan

- Transferring title of the assets to the beneficiaries or to any fiduciary on behalf of the beneficiaries

- Closing the estate with the probate court or surrogate court and the IRS

- Maintaining communication with the beneficiaries while the estate is open and dealing with their myriad issues

Compensation

The executor (and most any fiduciary, for that matter) is entitled to be paid for what they're doing. It's a real job—one that takes time, effort, and energy. In most states, the executor is entitled by law to a commission, which is a percentage of the assets the executor controls. To give you a sense of what the commission might be, consider how New York, California, and Florida compensate the executor. Table 12-1 lists these rates and gives you an idea of the commission on a $3 million estate.

Table 12-1a, b, c. Executor Compensation Rates in New York, California, and Florida

New York		
From	**To**	**Rate**
$ -	$ 100,000.00	5.0%
$ 100,001.00	$ 300,000.00	4.0%
$ 300,001.00	$ 1,000,000.00	3.0%
$ 1,000,001.00	$ 5,000,000.00	2.5%
$ 5,000,001.00		2.0%
Commission $3 million probate estate: $84,000		

California		
From	**To**	**Rate**
$ -	$ 100,000.00	4.0%
$ 100,001.00	$ 200,000.00	3.0%
$ 200,001.00	$ 1,000,000.00	2.0%
$ 1,000,001.00	$ 10,000,000.00	1.0%
$ 10,000,001.00	$ 25,000,000.00	0.5%
Commission $3 million probate estate: $43,000		

Florida		
From	**To**	**Rate**
$ -	$ 1,000,000.00	3%
$ 1,000,001.00	$ 5,000,000.00	2.5%
$ 5,000,001.00	$ 10,000,000.00	2%
$ 10,000,001.00		1.5%
Commission $3 million probate estate: $80,000		

Some caveats:

- Executor commissions are only paid on probate assets. These are assets in your own name, not joint, not with a beneficiary designation, and not in a revocable trust. So, if you had a $3 million estate but 100 percent of it was in joint name with your daughter, there would be no executor commission because nothing would come under the executor's control.

- In some states, if an asset is specifically given to someone ("I give you my house"), the value of that asset is excluded from the calculation of commissions.

- More executors means more commissions. In some states, the commission is increased and then the executors split it. In others, each executor is entitled to a full commission.

- If you think the commission is too rich, you can set an alternative fee in your will. However, your executor isn't

always bound to accept it. They can either turn down the job
or, if they didn't agree to the reduced compensation, in some
states they can ignore it and get the statutory amount anyway.

Hiring Considerations

Who is the best person for the job? Your spouse, son, cousin, friend, or
lawyer? The answer will be unique to you, but here are some things to think
about:

- *Some people are naturals.* These include your spouse, your
  two adult kids, or your dad. If it's a no-brainer that this person
  should be your executor, then put the plan in place.

- *Communication is the key job requirement.* Failure to
  communicate leads to resentment, suspicion, and, in extreme
  cases, litigation. The beneficiaries are devastated, money is
  involved, and the estate-administration process always takes
  longer than you expect. A person who won't communicate
  with beneficiaries, or won't make communication a priority,
  will be a detriment to your estate.

- *The executor doesn't need to be a financial, accounting, or legal
  wiz.* Their job is to hire the experts to do anything they feel
  they can't. In my experience, it's more important to select
  someone who knows the family than a relative stranger with
  a head for numbers.

- *Is the executor like you?* Do they have similar values or come
  from a similar background? Unexpected decisions come up in
  an estate. The more similar a person is to you, the more
  likely they will make the choices you would have made.

- *An executor or personal representative is a temp job.* It will last
  one to three years. Consider someone who has the skills
  now, not someone who has to grow into the job.

- *You can always change the executor as long as you're still here.*
  Choose who would do a good job today. Revisit your
  documents in three to five years and change the executor if
  they're no longer a good fit.

- *Go with your gut.* If, after reading all this, your friend Eileen
  keeps coming to mind, then name her.

Ask the Attorney "Deirdre, why is a revocable trust used so much in some states?" Well, it's not just the probate costs. In some states, the attorney who represents the estate is entitled to a percentage of the estate assets as their fee. This means a $3 million estate with three assets generates the same attorney's fee as a $3 million estate with 33 assets. Trust me when I say that there is a lot more work involved in dealing with 33 assets than just 3. In Florida and California, the attorney working on the estate would be entitled to $80,000 and $43,000, respectively, on that $3 million estate. And if they were both the personal representative and the attorney on the file, they would be entitled to both fees! You're free to change the arrangement, so you can consider a different way of paying the attorney. The key thing is that these fees are based on the amount of probate assets (there are separate fees for assets within a trust), so if the assets are held in a revocable trust, some of these fees can be avoided.

Trustee

Being a trustee is a long-term gig. Unlike acting as an executor, where the role is to get the assets into the hands of the creditors, the tax authorities, and eventually the beneficiaries, the trustee's job is to use the wealth for the benefit of the beneficiaries in a way that carries out your values. When you set up a trust, you have certain goals in mind. If you didn't, you wouldn't bother to establish a trust in the first place. These goals might include assisting your spouse with finances, caring for a special-needs child, providing your children with the skills to manage money and secure a head start in life, protecting wealth from your sister's lazy husband, or whatever other risks you want to minimize or values you want to pass along.

Job Function

All trusts, whether inter-vivos or testamentary, whether revocable or irrevocable, must have a trustee. The trustee is the person who's in charge of the assets in the trust. The trust itself describes the extent of the trustee's powers. The trustee may have total discretion, meaning they can use the money in the trust for the benefit of the beneficiaries in any manner they see fit. Or the trustee may have limited discretion to make distributions or investments, and have instructions as to when assets must be distributed from the trust to the beneficiaries. (For example, the trustee must give my niece Wendy all the income generated by the trust on a quarterly basis when she turns 25, and half the assets of the trust at 30 and the remaining half at 35.)

Full or Limited Discretion?

The benefit of giving the trustee the broadest possible discretion over investments and distributions is that they then have the flexibility to deal with an unknown future. You don't have a crystal ball (if you do, reach out to me—it would make estate planning infinitely simpler!) You may think your children will go to college, get married, have successful careers, and have kids of their own. But you've also been around long enough to know that not everybody sticks with college, marriages fail, careers sometimes never quite get off the ground or fall apart, and beneficiaries may have unanticipated needs. If the trustee has total discretion about how to make distributions, they can match the distributions to what you would've done had you been there at the time.

When giving the trustee such unfettered discretion, you really must—for lack of a better word—trust them. The beneficiary won't have a right to demand money from the trustee. If the trustee gets into a fight with the beneficiary, they can abuse their discretion by withholding money or acting in a punitive manner. Or the beneficiary might make a lifestyle choice that the trustee disagrees with, so the trustee decides not to support that choice, notwithstanding that you would've supported the beneficiary's choice no matter what.

The benefit of giving the trustee more limited discretion, by indicating ages or dates at which they must make distributions, is that you know the supervision of the money will end at a certain time. This reduces or eliminates the issue that the beneficiary and trustee may not get along, and the trustee might try to use their control over the money to either bully or punish the beneficiary. There's also inherent value in having an end date in sight. After all, if your kids aren't responsible by age 35, when will they be?

I've gone over the downside of mandatory distributions before. Without that crystal ball, you have no way of knowing what position your beneficiary will be in on the magic distribution date. After all, you're not picking a date based on some success or maturity factor in your child's life; you're picking a date based on some arbitrary number that was probably suggested to you by your attorney.

Disinterested or Interested Trustee?

I told you that you can consider one of your beneficiaries to be the trustee of the trust. However, there are some restrictions on a beneficiary who acts as the trustee.

A *disinterested trustee* is one who isn't also a beneficiary of the trust. Let's say you create a common pot trust for your two daughters, Lauren and Emma, and name your brother Anthony as the trustee. Because Anthony isn't a beneficiary of the trust, he can use the money for the benefit of Lauren and Emma distribute it to them equally or unequally—in any manner that he sees fit.

An *interested trustee* is a person who is both the beneficiary of the trust and a trustee. Let's say you create a family trust for the benefit of your husband, Eric, and your two boys, Alexander and Zachary. Eric has the total discretion to make distributions to Alexander and Zachary or for their benefit. However, when Eric makes distributions for his own benefit, he is limited to something called *ascertainable standards*, which means Eric can only make distributions to himself for his own health, education, maintenance, and support. Now, maintenance and support are pretty broad standards; it's the amount of money Eric would use to support and maintain his actual lifestyle, not some theoretical standard. However, a three-week trip to Aruba definitely wouldn't fall within these ascertainable standards.

Why is there a distinction? If Eric had an unlimited control over and access to the assets in the trust, they would be deemed his for purposes of estate taxes, as well as for asset protection purposes. The family trust is generally established to give the beneficiaries access to the funds through the trustee but exclude the assets from the beneficiaries' taxable estates. It's important that you don't give so much control to a beneficiary who is acting as a trustee that you defeat the overall planning purpose of having the trust in the first place.

Investment or Administrative Trustee?

Trustees aren't one-size-fits-all. You may have someone you rely on for all financial decisions, and perhaps you want to name that person to work with your spouse or with another trustee. You may have in mind a trustee whose only job is to make distributions, but you don't want them to manage the investments. You may even want a trustee who only performs recordkeeping functions but is in a state, such as Nevada or Delaware, that doesn't have income taxes, in order to keep down the costs of the trust[1].

The role of the trustee is only limited by your needs. You can carve out within the document a specific role for a specific trustee. This allows multiple people to act together, not by having joint decision-making responsibilities, but so that each is the decision maker within the sphere of influence you give them.

---

[1] If you have a trustee in one of these states the trust can be a "resident" of the state and get the benefit of not having to pay state income tax.

What Is a Trust Protector?

What happens if after all the work and effort you put into creating the trust, the trustee just isn't good at the job? This is unlike an executor, who will be out of a job in a few years anyway. The trustee's position could last for life.

One way of dealing with the situation is to name a *trust protector*. The purpose of the trust protector is to have a person or a group of people whose sole job is to monitor how well the trustee is doing at their job. After all, we often lament the tenure system, because people appointed for life aren't motivated to continually strive to improve. The trust protector doesn't make investment or distribution decisions; their function is to determine whether the trustee is doing a good job. If they're not, the trust protector can be authorized to remove the trustee and replace them with somebody else (not related to the trust protector, so you don't end up with favoritism issues).

Not every trust needs a trust protector. However, it's important that a mechanism exists for reviewing whether the trustee is doing a good job and essentially firing them if they're not. By naming a trust protector, you create checks and balances between your desire to have discretion for the trustee and your concerns that the trustee might not be doing their best at any point in the future.

Compensation

Because being a trustee is a long-term job, trustees are paid differently than executors or personal representatives. Again, the method and rate of payment depend on the state you're in. To get an idea of what you might pay for trustee services, let's look at New York, California, and Florida again:

- *New York.* Each year, the trustee is entitled to 1 percent of the income, plus an additional 1.05 percent to .3 percent of the principal depending on the amount of assets, plus whatever work your attorney does if you've named your attorney as the trustee.

- *California.* If the trustee fees are listed in the trust agreement, then the trustee receives those fees. Otherwise, they get reasonable compensation. There is no fixed guide to what is "reasonable", although 1% of the principal is often suggested on attorney websites. If an attorney is a trustee, they can get their trustee commission or their attorney fees, but not both without court order.

- *Florida.* Trustee compensation is a hybrid of that in New York and California. Like California, the trustee is entitled to reasonable compensation, if not otherwise set in the agreement. However, like New York, an attorney can be paid for legal services and a trustee fee.

What should you take away from this? That an attorney is a lousy choice for trustee? No. The point I'm making is that there is a huge difference in how a trustee is paid. The method of payment should figure into your selection. Whatever fees are paid are coming out of the trust you created for your loved ones.

But what if you do want your attorney to serve as a co-trustee, but you don't want to fund their retirement? Are you stuck with two bad choices: not having the attorney involved as trustee, or paying fees not based on work performed? No. You're always free to make an agreement with whoever's acting as a fiduciary regarding how they're paid (such as an hourly rate). If they choose to act as a fiduciary, then they accept the method of payment. If they find the method of payment to be unfair, they won't act as the trustee.

What happens if you name a bank or trust company as the trustee? In that case, the bank is likely to have its own fee schedule for acting as a trustee, which has nothing to do with the state commission schedule. In addition, the bank will be investing your assets. In their fee agreement, there'll be a provision that they can be paid for investment management of the assets as well as acting as a trustee. This can make a bank an expensive choice. However, you need to compare the fee to the fact that with a bank, you're getting professional management, and that if the bank does mismanage the funds, it has deep pockets to recoup any losses (which don't exist if Uncle Harry runs off to Bermuda with your kids' inheritance).

▧ **Ask the Attorney**   "Deirdre, does the trustee have to take a commission and get paid?" No. Most family trustees don't take the commission they're otherwise entitled to. First, whatever amount a trustee takes as their commission must be included in their taxable income. For an individual who is a trustee and a beneficiary of the trust, it might be less expensive to have an additional distribution from the trust instead of taking a commission. Also, individuals are more likely to be looking after the trust out of love and affection, rather than based on a financial arrangement with you. But you get what you pay for, and a professional trustee brings experienced management to the table.

Hiring Considerations

You may have the exact same people acting as both executor and trustee. However, because the jobs are different, there are some other considerations you should take into account when naming a trustee.

Consider naming co-trustees. There are lots of reasons to think about more than one person acting as trustee. Here are a few:

- With reference to minor children, you may want both families involved. If you name one person from each parent's family, you know that both parents' history and values will be accounted for.

- There may not be one perfect trustee in your life. Perhaps one person you're considering has great financial skills but doesn't know your beneficiaries well, and another loves and adores your beneficiaries but isn't in the same financial position as you. By having them act together, you could have the best of both worlds.

- A disinterested trustee has more flexibility than an interested trustee. By naming a disinterested trustee to act together with an interested trustee, you maintain this flexibility, and control remains in the family. In some states, a disinterested trustee is required.

- Sometimes people are concerned about mismanagement by the trustee. If two people are named as trustees, they would have to conspire together to mismanage the trust, which is much less likely than an individual exercising poor judgment.

- Consider allowing a younger beneficiary to slide into the role of co-trustee at some future point (such as a set age of 25 or 30, or upon life experience such as three years after college graduation).

Real Stories from Around My Conference Table   Imagine an estate administration with six children, where three are co-executors. Or, imagine a trust using three people as trustees. When two executors are named, they must act unanimously. This forces people to communicate and resolve issues. When three people are named, any two of the three can act. This can lead to resentment, distrust, and a total breakdown of communication. In most every situation I've seen where there have been three fiduciaries acting together, conflict has arisen. In many situations, the conflict could only be resolved in court, costing the beneficiaries in some instances hundreds of thousands of dollars. Being an executor or trustee isn't a job that lends itself to working well by committee. Select one person or two. Consider ways of oversight. But please don't let your concern about "making someone feel bad about not being named" cost your estate and your family.

Guardian

The guardian is in charge of the *person* of any minor child, as opposed to the money.

In case you missed my rant before, here it is again. The only place to name a guardian for your minor child is in your will. If you fail to create a will, you're leaving the decision as to who will raise your child to a judge you've never met, who can't understand why you couldn't do something as basic as make out a will. Get a will! If having an entire estate plan is something you don't feel ready for because you believe there are too many questions, I totally appreciate that position. *Please* go to LegalZoom.com and put something together for now so your child is protected in case, God forbid, something happens to you. OK—rant over.

Job Function

The guardian is charged with looking after the well-being of any child who is under the age of 18. They make decisions for the child regarding their housing and education, clothing them, feeding them, and making medical decisions. The guardian is in all instances the surrogate parent. Whatever you do now, they will do for your child in the future.

Compensation

You need to consider two types of compensation when naming the guardian. The first is direct compensation, where the guardian is paid an annual fee, similar to a trustee commission.

The second and less straightforward form of compensation is the indirect benefit the guardian receives by virtue of taking care of your children, who have independent funds set aside for them in a trust. For example, the guardian may move into your house, which is much larger than the one they were living in, and they and their children benefit from the house. You may indicate that travel is important to you, and the guardian is given an indirect benefit from being the person traveling with your child. There's nothing wrong with these indirect benefits, but you should consider that they provide additional compensation to your guardian as part of the selection process.

Hiring Considerations

The guardian has the most difficult job of all. Your fiduciaries are pretty much dealing with money; the guardian is raising your child. What should you look for in a guardian?

Your guardian and trustee can be the same person. The benefit is that because the dollars are being used for the person in their care, by naming the guardian as trustee, you put them in the best position to make decisions about the money for the benefit of the child. The drawback is that it's very tempting, not intentionally, to use the money to support the overall family and not just your child. When clients are concerned about this conflict of interest, I suggest that they may want to consider a solution that gives them the best of both worlds: having the guardian act as co-trustee with another person.

If you're considering naming a couple as the guardian, make sure you really mean that either of them can act. If you name your sister Kathleen and her husband, Stan, as the guardians of your kids, do you really mean Kathleen *and* Stan? If they get divorced, should they still be acting as co-guardians? What if Kathleen died? Would you still name Stan as the guardian? Or would you select your spouse's sister, Joni?

Think about your proposed guardian's lifestyle and your own. How do they approach education, religion, finances, work ethic, and diversity? Do their values mesh with yours?

Although an adult child is legally allowed to be a guardian for their siblings, it's a big job responsibility you're asking them to take on at the same time the child, adult or not, is reeling from your loss. You may want to look at their position in life, not just the fact that they're north of 18.

Attorney-in-Fact

OK, enough dying already. Let's look instead at what happens if you get hit by a bus and are unconscious in the hospital. (Fun thought, right?) Who will pay your credit card bills or mortgage? Who is going to convert stocks to cash? Your *attorney-in-fact* under the power of attorney does these things.

The job function and compensation of your attorney-in-fact are similar to those of a trustee. The key difference is that you're still around, so this fiduciary is acting for *you*, not your beneficiaries. Your attorney-in-fact also needs to be able to make quick decisions. In this case there is definite value to naming someone who might be more familiar with your finances and family and will have a shorter learning curve.

Health Care Proxy

Your health care representative is in a different position than all your other fiduciaries because they aren't dealing with money. Their sole job is to examine all the medical options and make the medical decision for you that you would have made in the same situation. In real life, medical situations tend to be emergencies. For that reason, I often suggest that you consider geography and location in naming your health care representative.

Also, this isn't a job for a committee. Although you may want all your sisters to discuss what treatment you would desire, you should name one person to be the final decision-maker. This person is whom the hospital will turn to as your voice. The worst situation is when the family is fighting over what to do instead of making a decision about how to move forward.

Ask the Attorney "Deirdre, you don't understand. There is *nobody* in my life who can act as my fiduciary." Really? No one? I would suggest that it isn't that you can't think of anyone to act for you, but that you can't think of anyone you *want* to act for you. Well, if there isn't one perfect person, consider naming two people to act together. There are banks and trust companies whose sole function is to be a fiduciary. Your attorney is a viable choice (now that you are educated about the role). Also, people get hung up on the third successor fiduciary—don't. Name two fiduciaries, and create a mechanism for naming a third (such as the last acting fiduciary names their own successor, your oldest beneficiary names a successor, the group of your beneficiaries names successors). What you shouldn't do is put off making your estate plan because of this decision. Name someone for today, and know you can change the fiduciary at any time in the future. Yes, it's hard. But the position your beneficiaries will be in if you don't make your estate plan is much harder.

13

Planning Guide for Kids

Whether you're married or single, or if your children are 8 or 58, parents are concerned about "what is the best way to leave assets to my kids." Bearing in mind that what is "best" for your family is unique to you, there is a spectrum of ways you can design an inheritance for your kids and questions you should ask yourself about where your family fits along that spectrum.

■ **Chapter Brief** There is a hard line between under and over 18 when it comes to inheritances. Beyond that, you have a mix-'n'-match menu of choices to think about when structuring your inheritance. You need to give careful consideration to unequal inheritances and disinheriting a child.

There Is No Right or Wrong

How do you leave your assets to your children? Well, it depends. This is one area where there truly is no "right" answer. Let me turn the question around and ask, "How do you want your kids to benefit from the wealth you're leaving them?" Are you concerned about your kids (or grandkids, for that matter) having security, money for a rainy day, money to spend now to have fun, the ability to retire at a reasonable age, money to fall back on, the chance to take their lives in a new direction, or the opportunity to reach a dream? Once you have an end in mind, you can plan an inheritance to meet that goal.

My first rule for designing an inheritance? It doesn't matter what the Joneses are doing, or the Smiths, or your in-laws, your siblings, or your neighbors.

This is your family and your money, and what is important to you is the only thing that matters.

My second rule? Although you don't have a crystal ball, always keep in mind that as long as you (or your spouse, if you plan it that way) are alive, you can change how your children inherit money. You may not know today what your 8-year-old will be like in 20 years, but if you're still here in 20 years, you can redesign an inheritance for a 28-year-old. Plan for today, with an eye toward a possible future.

The process of estate planning is to translate goals into a workable vehicle by taking advantage of the law. I'll give you some examples of what you could do so you can determine what you want to do. These are the same suggestions I give to clients in my conference room. Just like at the conference table, these suggestions are starting points, not an end-all and be-all. But my suggestions are colored by years of experience with what works best in certain situations. I suggest that you think of this chapter as being like browsing in a department store for that special dress or suit—you may not know exactly what you want, but you'll know what it is when you see it.

18: The Great Divide

If you have minor children, they legally can't own assets in their own name. For those children, the question isn't whether or not to leave assets in trust; it's what the trust should say.

■ **Ask the Attorney** "Deirdre, what would happen if I didn't set up a trust for my 7- and 10-year-olds?" Well, because they can't hold legal title to assets, someone needs to hold it for them. In most states, that person is the surrogate or probate court. The funds are deposited into an account for the benefit of the minor child. The funds are invested very conservatively (think certificates of deposit conservative). In order to use the funds for the benefit of the minor child, an application must be made to the court. It's then up to the court (a judge you've never met and whose values you don't know) to decide whether the distribution is appropriate. If that's not undesirable enough, when the child turns 18, whatever assets are sitting in the account are turned over to the 18-year-old to do with what they wish, with the infinite wisdom of a teenager. Not an ideal situation.

Once the child turns 18, you can leave an inheritance directly to them. The question now becomes whether you should give them unfettered access to money—and if so, how much.

Spectrum of Inheritance Design

When I meet with clients, I talk about the *spectrum of inheritance* (Figure 13-1). The options range from giving assets to the child outright at 18, to leaving the assets in trust for their lifetime with a bank or other third party as trustee. For most families, the best solution is somewhere in between. Let's take a look at the spectrum and build on it as we go.

A quick note: If you're reading this and have older kids, and it never occurred to you *not* to leave assets to them outright, don't think this chapter isn't for you. The hybrid lifetime trust I recommend later may be the best way to leave assets to your kids.

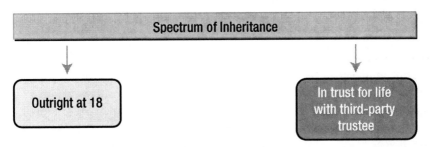

Figure 13-1. The spectrum of inheritance shows the range of options for leaving assets to children.

Outright at 18

On one side of the spectrum is leaving everything outright to your kids at age 18. Here's a question for you: would you have made good decisions about what to do with $100,000 at 18? No? If you don't think you would have made good decisions at that age, why risk your kids looking back five years later and saying, "I wish I hadn't done that"?

In my totally unscientific opinion, the age of maturity is rising. Many kids go to college and then come back home either because they can't find jobs or because entry-level jobs don't necessarily provide sufficient dollars. They may be burdened with debt from their education, so they're focused on paying it off instead of investing for their future. Even if they're looking forward, many 20- and even 30-year-olds may still be relying on their parents' wisdom and expertise in terms of making good financial decisions. People are getting married later, having children later, and generally becoming independent later and later. Just look around at your family and friends.

▓ **Let's Get Real** In my experience, the minimum age of inheritance is 25. For some people (a lot more than you would imagine), that's still too young. On one side, I see those who are finding themselves and trying out different paths. On the other is a child who has an extensive education but hasn't held down a real job prior to age 25 (a real job being one sufficient to support their lifestyle). The thing about money is, once it's gone, it's gone. Look back to the assets you listed. Remember that what to you is your house, retirement account, and rainy-day fund is a pile of cash to your kids. What would you do if somebody handed you a check for $500,000 or more? I urge deferred gratification.

Sometimes I hear, "I want my kids to have something now." That's great. Create a joint account with some amount of money that will go straight to the child the moment you pass away. Or create the trust but direct that a minimum amount be distributed upon your death.

Or your kids may be set, so you want to leave assets to them outright—but what about your grandkids? If your estate plan only provides for an outright distribution, and a child predeceases you, then their children could share in the child's inheritance. Although an outright distribution may make a lot of sense for your 38-year-old daughter, a distribution at 18 may not make sense for your 5-year-old grandson. To address this contingency, many parents leave assets to their adult children outright but create a trust to hold any assets that may go to their grandchildren if a child predeceases them.

Trust for Life with Third-Party Control

All the way on the other end of the spectrum of inheritance is leaving assets to a trust for the child for their lifetime and naming a third party as trustee, so the child has no control whatsoever over the assets. For most families, this solution doesn't fit any better than leaving the money outright at 18.[1]

First, you're trusting the trustee to always do the right thing as you would have. That may be fine when your sister is trustee, but what happens when she is older and can't act? Also, with a third-party trustee, you deny your children control over the money you're leaving them, ever. It may be that this is your desire. However, I find that most families don't want to prevent their children from ever having control over their inheritance; they just want to

---

[1] In some situations it makes sense to put an inheritance in a lifetime trust with somebody else as the trustee. One case that immediately comes to mind is a special-needs trust. Another is a child with a history of being unable to manage money, or perhaps one who has been facing addiction issues or bankruptcy. It could be that you're concerned about a child's spouse's influence or some other history that makes you think the child is unlikely to utilize an inheritance in their own best interest.

provide guidelines or protect the inheritance from the children's spouses. With such a restrictive trust, you also deny your children the chance to use the wealth to support their values for their kids, because they always have to go through the trustee in order to have a distribution made.

The big issue I see with having a third-party trustee for life is that if the child disagrees with the trustee, their only real recourse is to seek modification of the trust by the court. Be aware that a court will give great weight to exactly what is in the trust, including your selection of trustee, because these are truly your last wishes. A court will remove a trustee in the case of mismanagement or gross negligence, but the dispute between the trustee and your child may not rise to that point. Finally, the assets of the trust will be used to support the trustee's position, so in litigating against the trust, the child is essentially spending their own money twice: once for their own attorney and also from the trust to defend the trustee's position.

Real Stories from Around My Conference Table   I have married clients in their early 70s who are beneficiaries of a trust. It was set up by the husband's parents and provides that the couple gets all the income for their lives, with the principal to go to their children (the grandchildren) upon their deaths. At the time the trust was set up in 1988, interest rates were running between 8 percent and 10 percent. Fast-forward to 2012, and the couple can barely get 2 percent out of the trust. Additionally, they have a lot of health care expenses that they can't cover out of their own assets. The couple and all their children came to me because they wanted to use the trust for the couple's care—but it couldn't be done because the trust terms were clear. Don't forget that when you design a trust, you're doing it for tomorrow, not just for today. Flexibility should be a guiding principle.

Distribution at a Certain Age

If neither end of the spectrum of inheritance appeals to you, what are your options for something in between? One popular choice is to have a distribution from the trust at a fixed age. The language creating this distribution looks something like this:

Example 1. "I direct that my residuary estate be divided into equal shares for my children. Until a child attains the age of 25, the assets shall be held in trust for the child's benefit. The trustee shall distribute the net income and principal of the trust to the child for the child's health, education, maintenance, and support. Upon age 25, the remaining balance shall be distributed to the child, and the trust shall terminate."

Example 2. "I direct that my residuary estate be distributed to my issue, *per stirpes*. If any person shall be under the age of 25, their share shall be held in trust for person's benefit. The trustee shall distribute the net income and principal of the trust to the person for their benefit, in the trustee's sole and absolute discretion. Upon age 25, the entire remaining balance of the trust shall be distributed to the person, outright and free from trust, and the trust shall then terminate."

■ **Let's Get Real**   Did you note some of the key differences in the sample language? You need to read to distribution language in your will or trust very carefully to make sure the language really reflects your wishes. (I'm not being theoretical—get out those documents and read them now.)

• Example 1 distributes the residuary estate only to the "then living children." If a child predeceases the parent, then that child's share goes to the other living children, not the deceased child's children. In example 2, the trust estate is distributed among the descendants *per stirpes*, which means the predeceased child's share is divided among their children. More than 90 percent of my clients choose to divide their assets *per stirpes* and not just leave them to their living children.

• In Example 1, the trustee can only make distributions for certain standards of health, education, maintenance, and support. If the beneficiary has a desire outside of the standards (backpacking through Europe as a graduation present), the trustee doesn't have the discretion to make that distribution, even if it would've been the parent's intention. In example 2, the trustee has total discretion, but the beneficiary doesn't have the right to demand a distribution for their health, education, maintenance, and support, in the event there is an issue.

What are the benefits of having a distribution at a certain age? First, it's simple. The person turns 25, and they get the money. Second, you know the trust will end at some point, so you don't need to be concerned about expenses and fees eating into the trust principal year after year.

What are the drawbacks of mandating a distribution at a fixed age? I've mentioned this before, so don't be surprised that my question back to you is, "How do you know your beneficiaries will be mature at 25?" Maybe their age of financial maturity is 23, or 33, or never. What if they have an addiction, or are getting a divorce, or are facing bankruptcy, or just don't have the life experience to make long-term decisions about the money? Some parents say "that's life," and it's up to the kids to do as they wish. Other parents want to take a wait-and-see approach and use a safety valve to give the kids (or grandkids) a chance to use the inheritance well. Remember, there's no right or wrong answer.

Layer in Some Custom Elements

OK, so maybe you aren't happy with a one-size-fits-all approach. Let's go over some details you can use to tailor your estate plan to your family:

- *Multiple age distributions.* If you agree that picking a single age to make a mandatory distribution might not be right, but you like the simplicity of the approach, how about multiple ages? Instead of mandating a single distribution at 25, you might say, "I direct my trustee to distribute one third of the balance of the trust outright at age 25, one half of the remaining balance at age 30, and all of the remaining balance age 35." Here, you're breaking up the distribution among multiple ages. If the child doesn't do so well with the first distribution, there is the security of knowing that additional distributions are coming. Also, it's a form of forced savings for the future, so there will be funds available for goals that come with age, such as paying for education, buying a house, or starting a business. Using this option doesn't mean the funds aren't available to the kids prior to the mandatory distribution ages. Most parents indicate that the trustee has the discretion to make distributions for the child's benefit prior to the mandatory distribution ages.

- *Dividing income and principal.* Trust income consists of interest and dividends. Depending on the investment environment, the trust might give 2 percent to 8 percent of its value in interest and dividends (yes—investments used to actually pay interest). The language might read, "Starting at age 25, my trustee shall distribute all of the net income to the child on a quarterly basis." This is an attractive option because at a certain age the child gets an amount of money from the trust to do with as they wish, without having to speak to the trustee. The child will build life experience with that income stream. You could combine this option with making distributions at certain ages, such as starting an income stream at 22 and then calling for mandatory distributions at 27 and 30. I like this approach because it diffuses possible tensions between the child and trustee by giving the child some control.

- *Grant a right of withdrawal instead of an outright distribution.* Maybe one of your children won't be ready to manage the money at age 25. After all, some people just don't like having to manage money. Instead of creating a headache by mandating a distribution of assets to the child at a fixed age, you could instead shift the design by giving the child the right to withdraw the money at a fixed age. This language might read, "Once my child attains the age of 25 years, my child shall have the ongoing right to demand some or all of the trust." If the child doesn't withdraw the money, then the trustee continues to manage it. If the child withdraws money, then it becomes the child's responsibility. One very important caveat: Because the child has a right of withdrawal, the trust no longer provides asset protection. If the child has the right to demand money from the trust, so do any of their creditors.

Hybrid: Lifetime Trust with Child as Trustee

What if you want the best of both worlds? You see the value of asset protection that the trust provides, but you don't necessarily want to prevent your children from having control over their inheritance at some point in time. Or your children may be old enough now that you aren't concerned about their ability to manage money. You may, however, be concerned about their spouse's ability to *spend* money.

When I'm finished with this conversation about the spectrum of inheritance (Figure 13-2), the most-often-recommended solution is to leave the assets in trust for the benefit of the child and their children during their lifetimes, but have the child be the trustee (a subtle but importance design element).

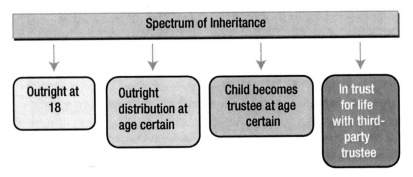

Figure 13-2. The Spectrum of Inheritance with additional, middle-of-the-road options

If your children are older, this hybrid approach allows you to combine the gift of asset protection with immediate control of their inheritance. If your kids are younger, and you don't know when they will reach financial maturity, you can create a wait-and-see approach: for a period of time you name the child as a co-trustee with another trustee, so they have an opportunity to learn the skills of managing money.

What does this look like? Let's take Phil and Colleen as an example. They have three kids: Aaron, Jeremy, and Christian, ages 20, 16, and 12. They're proud that Aaron seems to have a good idea of where he wants to go in life, but they're concerned about Jeremy because he's their "artist," and Christian is too young to make any sort of judgment. They know right now that they want Phil's sister, Molly, to be the trustee. After going through the spectrum of inheritance and evaluating other questions, we arrived at the following solution:

- When the second spouse passes away, three separate trusts will be established, one for each son.[2]

- Each child and their children will be the beneficiaries of the separate trust created for the child.

- Molly will be named as the trustee.

- When each child turns 25, they will be named a co-trustee to make all decisions with Molly. This means Aaron and Molly will jointly make all investment decisions over his trust, and so forth. Aaron and Molly will also jointly make all distribution decisions, as long as they're for Aaron's health, education, maintenance, and support. Molly will retain the flexibility to make distributions to Aaron for any reason whatsoever.[3]

- When the child turns 30, he will be named sole trustee of his trust. There doesn't have to be a fixed age at which the child becomes sole trustee. Instead, Phil and Colleen could name the child a co-trustee and leave it up to Molly to make the decision about when it would be appropriate for her to step down as a co-trustee.[4]

---

[2] There is no requirement to create a separate trust for each child. Back in Chapter 6, "Trust in Trusts," I described a *common-pot trust*, which is a sprinkle trust among siblings. Until a certain event happens (such as the youngest sibling turning 22), the trustee uses the money as they see a need among all the beneficiaries. With a common-pot trust more can be distributed to or for the benefit of one sibling than the others based on their needs. Only once a defined event occurs (the youngest turning 22, for example) is whatever is left in the trust divided into separate shares for each sibling.

[3] I mentioned before that, when a person is the beneficiary and trustee of the trust for their benefit, they're an *interested trustee*. As an interested trustee, the person is limited to making distributions for their own health, education, maintenance, and support (known as *standards*). These restrictions don't apply if they're (1) acting as trustee making distributions to other beneficiaries, such their children, or (2) if they're a non-beneficiary trustee (Aunt Molly in this example).

[4] In some states, the trust will collapse if there isn't a co-trustee involved. You need to discuss this with your local estate-planning attorney to see if having a sole trustee is an available option for you.

- If Phil and Colleen's children were already established adults (in their 40s, for example), they might simply divide the assets into thirds, leave them in trust for the benefit of each child and their children, and name the child directly as the trustee. By identifying the beneficiaries of each trust as the child and their children, Phil and Colleen are giving each child the flexibility to determine how to use the assets for the benefit of their own children, although not including any spouses in the inheritance.

When building a lifetime trust, you can layer in your own design elements to create a structure for your children that truly fits your family goals:

- You can indicate that the child will receive all of the income generated by the trust on a quarterly basis. This makes annual accounting simpler and allows the child to separate the trust principal from its income.

- If you want to make sure the child will receive a certain amount of money from the trust each year, you can indicate that there should be a minimum monthly distribution amount (and even tie that amount to inflation so the monthly distribution amount goes up over time). This language might read, "The trustee shall distribute $2,000 a month to the beneficiary. The distribution amount shall be adjusted each year in accordance with the consumer price index."

- Provide for a fixed rate of return for the child from the assets. This is called a *unitrust*. The unitrust might provide that the child will receive each year an amount equal to 5 percent of the principal of the trust.[5]

- Mandate fixed distributions for certain life events that are important to you, such as getting married, the birth of the child, a bar mitzvah, a quinceañera, college graduation, and so on.

Treating Kids Differently

If you have more than one child, you know that you don't treat your children identically. It's not that you play favorites, but you're also not keeping a ledger

---

[5] I go over the benefits and drawbacks of a unitrust in more detail in Chapter 17, "Planning Guide for Second Marriages."

that says if you gave this child a $35 shirt and the other one a shirt that you found on sale for $10, you somehow owe the second child $25.

However, when it comes to estate planning, many parents are very concerned that they do treat their children exactly the same. In many instances, this is appropriate: you don't see your children with different needs or abilities, and you believe they should have equal inheritances. In other situations, this cookie-cutter approach might not seem fair to you. Maybe one child is caring for you and has forgone life opportunities to do so. Perhaps you've lost contact with one of your children and don't wish to benefit them. Or your children are at different stages in their lives, and you're more concerned about supporting the younger ones than the older ones who are more established.

I suggest you stop right here and really think about it: for you, does it make sense to treat all your kids the same? Does one child have a need that is much greater than another's? When I advise people who don't have children, I find that they determine their beneficiaries based on the strength of their relationship with them. Do you have the same relationship with all of your children? Are there any behaviors or activities that you wish to encourage or reward? After going through this thought process, most people honestly say, "No, I want to treat my children the same." However, because you're planning for you and not for "most people," you should close the book for a minute and consider this carefully.

Non-Probate Assets

Although it's perfectly OK to treat your children differently, in order to avoid both hurt feelings and incredibly expensive *will contests*, you need to be very up front about your plans.[6] I mentioned earlier in the book that non-probate assets can create a huge problem when they go to one child at death but the will provides that everything should be divided equally among all the children. Did you or didn't you intend the child who received the non-probate assets to get more than the other children?[7]

---

[6] Will contests are a lot more prevalent on TV than in real life—probably because the facts that lead to them can be juicy and scandalous. (I even got a call once from a production company that wanted to do a reality series about will contests.) When will contests do happen, they can ravage an estate and a family. Fortunately, the grounds to successfully challenge a will are limited. Curious? I go over them in Chapter 15, "Planning Guide for Singles."

[7] For a more thorough discussion, look back at Chapter 5, "Will Alternatives and Avoiding Probate." The key is to remember that how an asset is titled determines the method of its distribution upon your death, whether by will or by operation of law to a joint owner or beneficiary.

Instead of leaving it up in the air, discuss it in your will. You can say, "I acknowledge that I've named my daughter Amy as the beneficiary of certain accounts that will be distributed outside of this will. I don't intend for there to be any adjustment in the distribution of my residuary estate based on this." Or, if that isn't your intent: "In the event that any child of mine receives any assets as a result of my death passing outside of his will, the amount of the assets so received shall be deducted from their share of my residuary estate." It doesn't matter which way you go; it's up to you. What matters is that you're clear about your intentions.

Specific Bequests

Making a specific bequest before dividing the balance of your estate equally is a terrific way to tweak your estate plan to meet your family's situation. It allows you to generally treat your kids the same but make appropriate adjustments either with specific assets or to meet specific goals. Here are some design elements to consider:

- Sarah is the only child of four who uses the family lake house. Anne says in her will, "I give the lake house to my daughter, Sarah, and, if she isn't living, to her issue *per stirpes*, to be held in trust." What should the next question be? Is Sarah receiving the lake house before the rest of the assets are divided, or does the bequest to her reduce Sarah's share of the residuary estate? It doesn't matter how Anne answers the question, but the answer needs to be clear in the will.

- Peter's parents loaned him $100,000, and they want to forgive the debt upon their deaths. They can make a specific bequest of the promissory note to Peter upon their death, effectively canceling it.[8]

- Ron and Gina want to make sure each of their kids has the same opportunity for education. They indicate that for any year of college a child hasn't completed, $50,000 will be added to their trust; and for any year of high school a child hasn't completed, $30,000 will be added to their trust. If all the children are out of school when Ron and Gina pass away, then the bequests will lapse.

---

[8] Many people overlook that the promissory note from Peter to his parents is an asset in his parent's taxable estate. Prior to the time they passed away, Peter's parents were owed a certain amount of money, which was an asset of theirs. By forgiving the money at death, they're distributing value to Peter.

The specific bequest can be an amount of money or a thing. It can be taken off the top before the division of the residuary estate, or you can adjust the recipient's share of the residuary estate. The bequest can be permanent and automatic at the time you pass away, or it can be contingent on things either happening or not happening. It's a fantastic tool for addressing the feeling of "We wanted to treat the kids equally, except ..." because you can deal very simply and easily with whatever that exception is.

Equalization

At times, families come to me with the problem that one of their children has already received a pre-inheritance. Maybe the parents provided a down-payment for a house, or they gave or plan to give the family business to one child, or they lent one child money. In any event, the parents want to make everybody equal in their estate plan.

The key to equalization is being able to very clearly define the thing that is being equalized. If you gave your daughter Tabitha $50,000 as a down-payment for a house, you can say in your will that your son Tyler gets $50,000 before the residuary estate is divided. Another question, though: does the $50,000 grow over time? For example, if 10 years have gone by, does Tyler still get $50,000, or is the amount increased 5 percent each year? There's no right or wrong answer, but you need to go through the thought process of what to you is fair.

Using another example, Ted transfers the family business to his son Carson, who works in the business. Ted's other two children, Lucy and Kyle, don't work in the business. If the business is worth $500,000 dollars at the time he gives it to Carson, Ted might provide that $500,000 passes to each of Lucy and Kyle at his death before any other assets are distributed. What if Ted doesn't have $1 million sitting around at the time of his death? Carson still has the $500,000 business. This is a situation where it might be appropriate for Ted to purchase life insurance (in an irrevocable life insurance trust [ILIT], of course) so he knows that no matter what, Lucy and Kyle will end up with the same amount of money as the value of the business he gave to Carson.

▓ **Let's Get Real** If you're not planning to treat your children equally, you need to be up front with them about it before you die. We've all seen TV shows with a big surprise during the reading of the will. It doesn't work that way in real life. There is no formal reading of the will. The executor for the most part mails it to the beneficiaries. Death and money don't make good bedfellows. If Lucy is surprised at what she is getting in comparison to Carson, her initial response may be, "I'm calling my lawyer." As soon as lawyers are involved, your chances for continued family harmony rapidly decrease. Let your children work through the situation while you're still alive. Or, if you don't want to create drama with the children who aren't benefiting, at least give reasons upon your death, whether in a separate letter or otherwise. Foster communication, not hurt and resentment.

Disinheriting a Child

Unfortunately, sometimes parents don't have a relationship with one of their children, and they don't wish to benefit the child in their estate plan. Children don't have a right to your assets.[9] If you choose not to give them anything, then that is up to you. The important thing is to be unambiguous in that choice, so you don't create a will contest after death under the auspices of "Dad didn't mean to disinherit me."

Clarity is key. Sometimes I see language along the lines of, "I leave my son Seth the sum of one dollar for reasons that are known to him." Beyond the obvious and immediate question of "What are those reasons?"—we humans are a naturally curious species, after all—you haven't fully conveyed what you're intending to do. If your intention is to leave no benefit to Seth, say so. "It's my intention to not leave any assets upon my death to my son Seth." What about Seth's children? Is it your intention to disinherit them as well? If it is, add to your statement "or any of his descendants." If it's not, provide for your grand-children in your will.

After you do this, you need to be very careful with the boilerplate in the will. We attorneys often throw around the terms *issue, children,* and *descendants.* If your intention is to exclude Seth and his children, you need to better define exactly who they are to you. You may want to add, for example, "For all pur-poses under my will, in defining the words *issue, children,* and *descendants,* my son Seth, and any of his descendants, shall be deemed to predecease me." What you don't want to do is have any confusion whatsoever about your in-tentions with reference to Seth and his descendants. Remember, you won't be here to say what you intended. You need to rely on the documents to speak for you.[10]

 ▌ **Let's Get Real**   I find it ironic that parents put so much effort into making sure Johnny makes the travel baseball team, or Susie aces her SATs, or Patty has the coolest graduation party ever, but they don't spend a lot of time thinking about how to provide for their kids beyond the money, when

---

[9] That is, unless you live in Louisiana, where children under 24 and incapacitated children can qualify as *forced heirs* and demand a share of the estate.

[10] What if the document doesn't do a good job of laying out your wishes and Seth contests the will. Can he? If he does, will you be successful? Look to Chapter 15 ("Planning Guide for Singles"), where I go over will contests in more detail.

they are no longer here. I get that the topic of death sucks—I don't much like thinking about it myself. But then I think about my son and all the hopes and dreams I have for him, and I remember that if I don't share those hopes and dreams with other people nobody will ever know what they were—including my son. I'm going to bring up something I already suggested: each year, write a letter to your guardian, trustee, or child—or all of the above—about what you would like to have done if you weren't here. You might talk about education, camp, travel, using your engagement ring, experiencing the family's roots, or anything that comes to mind. You might also look back on the year and tell your child how proud you are about something, how it made you think about who your child might be in the future, and how the inheritance could help. I guarantee you that this letter will be infinitely more valuable than anything else you do as a result of reading this book.

14

Planning Guide for Marrieds

Tax law favors the married. You may not feel that way on April 15 of each year, but a variety of exemptions and deferrals from taxes are only available to married couples. The ticket to this tax-haven nirvana is that you have to plan to have your estate take advantage of most of them *before* you die—once you're no longer here, it's too late.

▨ **Chapter Brief** What do you value in your estate plan? Simplicity? Flexibility? Tax savings? Control? Tax laws might outline the skeleton of your estate plan, but your goals build the body. A family trust creates tax savings; a marital trust gives you control beyond the grave. The best-laid plans fall apart if there aren't assets that will flow under the plan. For many, a wait-and-see approach is best.

Marital Deduction Math

The single best way to save taxes when you die is to be married. Although saving taxes certainly shouldn't be the sole reason to tie the knot, if you've been hesitant, avoiding a tax rate up to 55 percent owed to the US government might be enough to push you down the aisle.

As long as your spouse is a US citizen,[1] any assets you leave to them, whether it's $100 or $100 million, will pass to them estate tax free. The timing of the

---

[1] Spouse not a citizen? You can flip to Chapter 19, "Planning Guide for Noncitizens," to find out about leaving assets to your spouse.

estate tax is when the assets pass to the next generation or to anyone other than your spouse.

The kicker is that the marital deduction doesn't *eliminate* estate taxes: it merely *defers* them. The government *wants* you to leave all your assets to your spouse; it will end up collecting more tax dollars that way. "What?" I hear you thinking. "She just told me that any assets I leave my spouse pass tax-free. How could that possibly increase my tax bill?" Well, it's all about the exemptions.

You and your spouse each have a federal estate tax exemption amount of $1 million starting in 2013.[2] However, if you leave all your assets to your spouse, you won't be taking advantage of your $1 million exemption. When your spouse dies, they will be left with only their $1 million exemption, yours having vanished into the wind.[3] Clearly, sheltering $2 million from estate taxes (if both you and your spouse use your exemption amounts) will save more estate tax dollars than merely sheltering $1 million from estate taxes (the single remaining exemption of the surviving spouse). Sneaky, sneaky, sneaky government.

Here's the math:

- *All to spouse.* Frank and Lindsay have $3 million between them. Frank dies, leaving everything to Lindsay. Lindsay unfortunately passes away six months later. The estate tax bill when she dies is about $930,000.

- *Exemption amount to trust; balance to spouse.* Frank and Lindsay met with me before Frank died. Frank's estate plan provides that an amount equal to his exemption from federal estate taxes ($1 million starting in 2013) passes into a family trust. Lindsay still unfortunately passes away six months later. Guess how much lower the estate tax bill is? How about if I told you the amount due the IRS went down to around $435,000? That's right. Creating a trust reduced taxes by $500,000. (I have to say, I really don't get why people aren't just high-fiving us estate planning attorneys on the street.)

What should your takeaway be? Estate tax savings come from the planning done in the estate of the *first* spouse to die. This is why you need to sit down and make up your estate plan now, while you're both still here to do it and

---

[2] Which, of course, may and probably will change. Stay tuned or go to my website, www.deirdrewheatleyliss.com.

[3] A new estate tax law could mean that your exemption won't necessarily vanish. I talk about the idea of "portability" of your estate tax exemption at the end of this chapter.

take advantage of the tax exemptions the government gives you. It's giving you *free money*—run out and grab it!

Grabbing the Marital Deduction

How do you make sure the assets you're leaving to your spouse will qualify for the marital deduction? You need to give assets to your spouse in one of two ways. Each method is designed so that whatever assets you leave your spouse will be included in your spouse's taxable estate when they die (deferral, not elimination, remember?):

- *Outright.* If you leave your assets to your spouse outright, with no restrictions whatsoever, the government is assured that if your spouse hasn't spent the assets before they die, it will have an opportunity to tax them.

- *QTIP trust.* I really don't make up these names. QTIP stands for *qualified terminable interest property.* (That clears everything up, doesn't it?) Essentially, one way for a trust to qualify for the marital deduction is to provide that (1) the spouse receives all the income from the trust at least annually, (2) nobody else can benefit from the trust during the spouse's lifetime, and (3) the executor of the estate of the first spouse to die makes an election that whatever balance remains in the QTIP trust upon the death of the second spouse is included in that spouse's taxable estate. The spouse creating the QTIP trust directs to whom the assets will go when the second spouse passes away. The QTIP trust also enjoys the asset protection of a trust created by a third party with their own money.

Ask the Attorney "So Deirdre, how did they come up with the QTIP trust?" The story I got in law school is that back in the 1980s, senators wanted to figure out a way to leave money for their wives and get a marital deduction, but not have to worry from the grave that their wife would lavish their wealth on the pool boy, the chauffer, or some other undesirable. (So much for the "my spouse is my partner" spiel that politicians give.) Can you imagine, a woman in control of money?! The senators thought it be great to leave their money to their wives in a trust, give them an income stream (which is a lot like an allowance, which is all the little woman really needs, after all, to keep her in hairpins and such), and let somebody else make all the decisions about the money so the little woman wouldn't have to strain her feeble mind. I may be going a bit overboard, but you get the gist. I'm a huge proponent of the QTIP trust, but remember that my philosophy is that the spouse can be the trustee of their own trust.

Designing the Skeleton of Your Plan

Taxes, or rather tax minimization, is the force that molds the skeleton structure of the estate plan. You build the body and soul of the plan by adding instructions and options to the skeleton to flesh out your goals and values.

Outright

Certainly the easiest way to design your estate plan is to leave everything to your spouse outright. We even have a name for a will that does this: an "I love you" will. The benefit of this approach is that it's straightforward and simple: whatever you own when you die goes your spouse. It's up to your spouse to make the decisions about how the assets are invested or spent and who gets the money when they die. The downside of this approach are that (1) you're giving up the opportunity to save estate taxes at the second spouse's death, (2) the assets your spouse is inheriting are available to creditors and predators, and (3) your spouse could choose to ultimately leave your assets to someone other than your children or family.

If none of the downsides is a concern for you, then an outright distribution scheme is the way to go. It looks something like Figure 14-1.

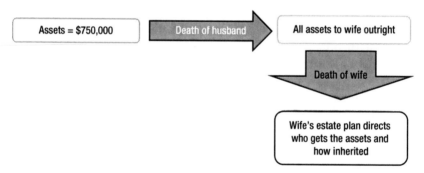

Figure 14-1. "I Love You" distribution scheme, outright to spouse

Family Trust and Outright

What if you want to capture the estate tax savings? In that case, you need to direct an amount equal to your federal estate tax exemption amount (or potentially your state estate tax exemption amount) to someone *other than* your spouse. When I say "other than your spouse," that doesn't mean you need to exclude your spouse. If you leave the assets to a trust of which your spouse is a beneficiary, you get the benefit of the estate tax savings because the trust is someone "other than your spouse," and your spouse will get the benefit of the trust. On the other side of the coin, you could leave your estate tax exemption amount to anyone you want to, outright or in a trust for them.[4]

Moving on, let's further assume you want your spouse to be the beneficiary of this trust, which I'll refer to as the *family trust*. If you do, the skeleton of your estate plan will look something like Figure 14-2 (notice that the size of the estate is increased because you need to have an estate tax problem to be looking to avoid estate taxes).

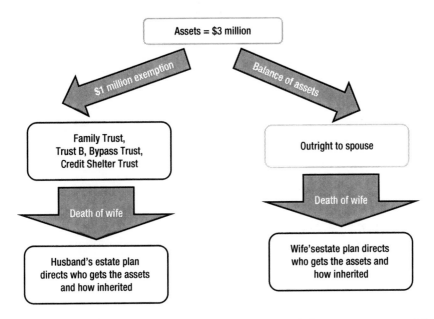

Figure 14-2. Leaving your assets to a family trust with the balance to a spouse outright

You may have noticed in my diagrams that the husband always dies first. Well, statistically men have a shorter life expectancy. And it's my book, so I get to set up the fact patterns as I like! Or think of it as my small part to balance the history of the QTIP trust.

---

[4] It could be that you're not planning to leave all your assets to your spouse because this is a second marriage, or you have other family members you want to benefit. If that's the case, I suggest you look at Chapter 17, "Planning Guide for Second Marriages," for some thoughts on how you can tailor an inheritance when you want to benefit your spouse and your family other than your spouse.

■ **Ask the Attorney** "Deirdre: I'm looking at your chart and wondering what the difference is between a *family trust*, a *bypass trust*, a *credit shelter trust*, and *Trust B*." Not a darn thing. All of these are names for the same thing—a trust is designed to capture your exemption from estate taxes. The name used depends on what resource you're looking at, be it a book, online, or the attorney you're talking to. I like to use the term *family trust* because I think it best captures the purpose of the trust so the name is more meaningful to you.

Options for the Family Trust Structure

Now that the skeleton is in place, it's time to build up the body of the family trust. The distribution scheme can be as lean and straightforward or bulked-up and detailed as you like. My questions to you: How much benefit and control do you want your spouse to have over the family trust? Is your spouse your sole beneficiary, or are you adding the children or other family members too? Are distributions mandatory or discretionary? Is your spouse the only trustee, or is control shared with anyone else?

■ **Let's Get Real** If you're thinking of doing your estate planning online, studying these options and the rest of the chapter is a "must do" for you. I'm not reciting the standard provisions here. Instead, I'm describing the various constructions I consider for my clients based on the world of options available. It's like 15 years of experience boiled down to 20 pages. Take the education you're getting through this book and apply it to the design element choices you're given online. This will put you in the best position to customize a plan that works for you at a lower cost than hiring an estate planning attorney.

Because it's hard to make a decision in a vacuum, let me sketch out some options you can consider for how the family trust is structured:

- *Spouse is the sole beneficiary with mandatory income.* This design comes closest to mimicking the outright-distribution scheme. Your spouse is the sole beneficiary of the family trust. Any income generated by the family trust goes directly to your spouse. The downside to consider with this structure is that if the trust mandates that the income goes to your spouse, and your spouse doesn't need to spend the income, then you're giving up the opportunity to shelter that income from estate taxes. You need to consider how much income will be generated by the assets likely to fund the trust in the context of what your spouse will need in the way of income to run the household.

- *Spouse is the sole beneficiary with discretionary principal and income distributions.* This is similar to the previous distribution scheme but addresses the fact that a mandatory income distribution to the spouse from the family trust is inefficient from an estate tax perspective.

- *Spouse and family members are possible beneficiaries; mandatory income to spouse.* In real life, the spouse will probably use the inherited dollars to continue to support the household, which may include children, stepchildren, grandchildren, parents, or whoever else makes up your family. Because this is a family trust, all of those people can be potential beneficiaries of the trust. The benefit of this structure is that the trustee has the ability to look at all the assets available to the family (the spouse's individual assets, other inherited assets, and the beneficiaries' assets) and make an informed decision about where dollars should come from to provide for a beneficiary. In short, having other family members as beneficiaries creates more flexibility. In this design, those other family members are only beneficiaries as to the principal; you can continue to direct that all the income is payable to your spouse.

- *Spouse and family members all possible income and principal beneficiaries.* This is the most flexible arrangement. The trustee, be it your spouse or somebody else, has the ability to sprinkle the income or principal among any of the beneficiaries.

- *One or more people other than your spouse are the beneficiaries.* I never said your spouse had to be a beneficiary of the family trust.[5] Although the spouse is most commonly included as a beneficiary, your exemption amount is the amount of money you could pass to anybody *other than* your spouse estate tax free. You could name your children, your parents, your siblings, your grandchildren, or even your dog, if it's allowed,

---

[5] Remember, just because you're married to each other doesn't mean you have to leave all your assets to each other or for each other's benefit. There will be a minimum your spouse must receive based on state law, but you're free to leave the balance to whomever else you like. Just bear in mind that if the balance exceeds your federal or state estate tax exemption amount, then taxes will have to be paid when you die, even though your spouse is still alive.

as the beneficiary of the family trust. You don't even have to put your exemption amount into the trust; you could leave it outright to those beneficiaries (other than your dog). There would be no estate tax on the dollars that are passing to non-spousal beneficiaries because it's within your federal estate tax exemption amount.

Add-Ins to the Family Trust Structure

You've got the skeleton, you've built up the body, but there are a few last tweaks to consider in fine-tuning the family trust so it has all the elements in place to work for your family. (Again, if you're going the online route, look at these carefully.)

Trustee

Will your spouse be the sole trustee, a co-trustee, or not a trustee at all? This has a huge impact on how appropriate the family trust will be for your family. Forget tax savings; if you have to involve someone else in your affairs, it may not be worthwhile to you to plan for taxes. Also, you need to find out if, in your state, your spouse can act as sole trustee.

Whether your spouse is acting as the sole trustee or the co-trustee, you need to bear in mind that when the spouse is both trustee and beneficiary, they can only make distributions to themselves for their own health, education, maintenance, and support.[6] The terms *maintenance* and *support* aren't subject to some standard set by the government. Instead, it's the level of maintenance and support needed to keep your spouse in the lifestyle to which they've become accustomed. However, it's a real restriction on the flexibility your spouse has to withdraw assets from the family trust. A cruise through the Panama Canal won't fall under the standard of health, education, maintenance, and support. But, to be practical, why would your spouse want to use the assets sheltered from estate taxes for such a thing, instead of using their own assets, which will be subject to estate taxes?

Another note of caution: If your spouse is acting as a sole trustee, this may also jeopardize the value of the asset protection. There is a bit of a disconnect

---

[6] The restriction on self-distributions applies to any person who is both a trustee and a beneficiary of the trust. If a trustee/beneficiary has total discretion over the trust assets, then all the assets in the trust will be considered "theirs" for estate tax and asset-protection purposes. The standards of "health, education, maintenance, and support" create a wall between the trustee/beneficiary's own assets and the assets in the trust.

between saying "The spouse's creditors can't access the trust assets because it's in the trust" and "The spouse as trustee can use the money."[7]

▒ **Let's Get Real**   Is it tax savings or asset protection that's motivating you to create a family trust? If it's tax savings, and you want to maximize flexibility, you may not want to involve another person as trustee. If it's asset protection, then you'll at a minimum want a co-trustee to act with your spouse, if the spouse is acting at all. If you're concerned that your motivation may change in the future, why not leave the decision-making to your spouse? Give your spouse the right to name a co-trustee or successor trustee in the future. Who knows how the tax laws or asset-protection laws may change? Because the trustee is the linchpin to a successful estate plan, giving your spouse the right to control who is in that role can keep the plan relevant in changing future circumstances.

If your spouse is acting as a co-trustee, carefully think about the practicalities of who your spouse will be working with as the other co-trustee. Does this person need investment knowledge and experience? Will your spouse feel comfortable going to that person to request distributions from the trust, or is that not an issue for you? Sometimes it's not the person you first name as a co-trustee, but who the successor will be that is the most challenging. (Can't decide? Leave it to your spouse or a trust protector to name successor trustees in the future.)

Power of Appointment

One of the major benefits of the family trust is that you—the person creating the family trust and the person who's dying first—get to say who the ultimate beneficiaries of the family trust are when your spouse dies. So, you could structure the family trust to be available for your spouse and children during your spouse's lifetime, but direct that upon your spouse's death whatever is left over must pass to your children (*not* your spouse's new loser of a husband, *not* to any kids that aren't yours, and *not* your husband's good-for-nothing sister who can't get her act together). This is all great if you assume the facts that exist today will continue forever in the future, but that's not how life works. It could be that one of your children suffers addiction issues in the future or has a falling out with your spouse, or one child's needs are much greater than another's. If you would have changed your estate plan to account

---

[7] The same advice applies to any person who is acting as a trustee of the trust for which they're also a beneficiary. If the driving concern in creating the trust is asset protection, the beneficiary should be a co-trustee at the most and restricted from participating in distributions to themselves.

for those facts if you knew them today, doesn't it make sense for your spouse to have the power to modify the plan in the future?

I've described the limited power of appointment as the *out clause*. It allows your spouse to change the ultimate beneficiaries of the family trust.[8] Your spouse can exercise the power either during their lifetime or in their will. You can give your spouse the right to leave the assets to anybody in the world, or limit the power to appoint to a group of people, such as your descendants. Question: Are you only setting up the family trust for tax-planning purposes? If it weren't for taxes, would everything pass to your spouse? If this is the case, the power of appointment puts your spouse in close to the same position as if they inherited all the assets outright. Your spouse will be able to make the final decision as to who gets what, how, and when, based on future circumstances. In almost every estate plan I prepare for married couples, I create a power of appointment that the spouse can exercise either during their lifetime or at death. My goal is to build in as much flexibility as possible while maintaining a structure that will produce estate tax savings.

If, on the other hand, you want to be sure the people you name as beneficiaries will in fact be the ultimate beneficiaries of the family trust, make sure there isn't a power of appointment in the family trust. I would also suggest making sure there's a co-trustee acting with your spouse at a minimum so assets remain in the trust to pass to the beneficiaries.

Family Trust and Marital Trust (the A/B plan)

I've been pretty clear that the estate tax savings come from creating the family trust within the estate plan of the first spouse to die. I've also mentioned that you can leave assets to your spouse either outright or in a marital trust. So if there are no estate tax savings from having a marital trust, why would you want to create one?

- *Asset protection.* A trust provides asset protection; an outright distribution doesn't. If your spouse is a professional or a business owner, or your wealth puts you at higher risk for a lawsuit, why not leave the assets in the trust to your spouse so they're protected?

- *Control of remainder beneficiaries.* If you leave assets in a marital trust instead of outright, then whatever remains in the marital

---

[8] The power of appointment can be granted to anyone, not just your spouse. The person could be a beneficiary or not, as your family circumstances dictate. I go over this in more detail in Chapter 6, "Trust in Trusts."

trust upon the death of the spouse passes to the beneficiaries you designated. This means if your spouse were to get married again, the assets of the marital trust wouldn't eventually end up with their new spouse, or any new family members. The spouse is obviously free to leave their own assets to those people.

- *Financial control.* You might have particularly complicated assets (family business, investment in private entities, or significant wealth) and be reasonably concerned that your spouse doesn't have the skills to manage those investments. Or you could have a complicated family situation (children from another relationship, people you want to prevent from inheriting, or a charity you're passionate about). Or your spouse may not have strong financial skills, because that is your role in your marriage. In these situations, you might want somebody other than your spouse to be the sole or co-trustee.

- *GST election.* Fair warning—I'm delving into the tax code here, and this reason is likely to apply to people with larger estates. If you're looking to pass assets tax-efficiently to successive generations, you may be interested in having a generation sharing trust (see Chapter 11, "Advanced Tax Strategies") in your estate plan. The amount that the generation sharing trust can be funded at death is equal to your exemption from generation-skipping taxes (GST taxes). Similar to the federal estate tax exemption amount, if you don't use your generation-skipping tax exemption amount at death, it's wasted. For this reason, at times a marital trust equal to the first spouse's generation skipping tax exemption amount is created to ensure that those assets will pass GST tax free into a generation sharing trust upon the death of the second spouse.

- *Different state and federal estate tax exemption amounts.* Eighteen states and the District of Columbia have their own estate tax. If the state exemption amount is different than the federal exemption amount, you may limit the amount you put into the family trust to avoid paying any state estate taxes when the first spouse dies. It may be appropriate to put the difference between the federal exemption amount and the state estate tax exemption amount into a marital trust so the trustee can make one estate tax exemption election for state estate tax purposes and another for federal estate tax purposes. If you're in one of these states, and you have a taxable estate for state estate tax purposes, you really need to see an estate planning attorney.

"OK. It sounds like a marital trust might make sense. Let's say I incorporate this into my estate plan. What would it look like?" See Figure 14-3.

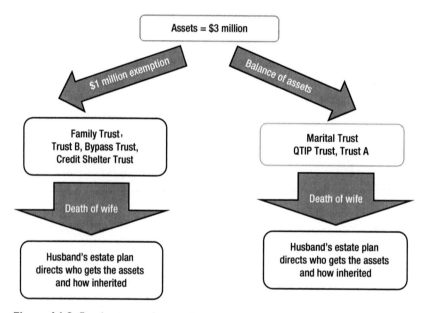

Figure 14-3. Family trust with marital trust (A/B plan)

■ **Ask the Attorney** "Deirdre: What is an A/B plan?" Some estate-planning textbooks refer to an estate plan with a marital trust and a family trust as an *A/B trust plan*. The A trust is the marital trust, and the B trust is the family trust. Because that's the nomenclature the lawyers learned in law school, that's the nomenclature they use with their clients. Here's my problem: if I, who do this for a living, can't always remember which is the A trust and which is the B trust, I can't expect these letters to have any meaning for you. This is why I use descriptive terms when talking about different types of trusts instead of academic language.

Options for the Marital Trust

The skeleton of your estate plan, whether you make an outright distribution to your spouse or make the distribution via a marital trust, looks similar. But the devil is always in the details; the rules for building up the body of the marital trust are very different from family trusts.

Marital Trust "Musts"

If you want the trust to qualify for the marital deduction from estate taxes, it must have certain minimum characteristics:

- *Spouse sole beneficiary.* No other person can be the beneficiary of a marital trust during the spouse's lifetime. If anyone else is a possible beneficiary, no marital deduction will be allowed.

- *Mandatory income.* The spouse must receive all the income generated by the trust at least annually. In my documents, I normally provide for quarterly distributions of income to the spouse.

- *Right to make income-producing.* Having an income right wouldn't be very valuable to the spouse if nothing was invested in income-producing assets. Therefore, the spouse has the right to demand that all the assets be income-producing. This means if you leave your spouse a piece of unproductive real estate or the family business, they can demand that the trustee sell it and invest it in something that produces income, like bonds.

Marital Trusts "Mights"

You don't really have any options when it comes to the income of the marital trust, but what about the principal? I'm going to ask the same question I did about the family trust: how much benefit and control do you want your spouse to have over the marital trust?

- *Spouse as trustee can make distributions to themselves for health, education, maintenance, and support.* This is the most control over the marital trust that you can give to your spouse. If your goal is asset protection, you'll probably want to consider another distribution scheme where the assets are more sheltered, through discretionary distributions or by having another trustee involved in making distributions.

- *Discretionary distributions to spouse.* A third-party trustee may, but doesn't have to, make distributions to the spouse. I often combine this with the first option so that if the spouse is acting as sole trustee, their ability to make distributions is limited to health, education, maintenance, and support; but if any co-trustee is serving, that person can make distributions to the spouse for any reason. Obviously, if the spouse steps down as co-trustee, then distributions can only be made in the discretion of the trustee. This provides an increased level of asset protection.

- *Limited principal distributions.* It may be that you believe your spouse should be spending their own money on their own future care and maintenance (this often happens in second marriages or later in life) and wish to limit the possibility for principal distributions to be made from the marital trust to very specific circumstances, such as health or only if the spouse has exhausted all other assets.

- *Percentage of the principal to the spouse each year.* If you don't think the income is enough, but you're afraid the principal will be totally spent and nothing left for your remainder beneficiaries, you might make a distribution of only part of the principal each year, such as a percentage of the value as of December 31 of the prior year. This is also referred to as a *unitrust* or *total return trust* approach. [9]

- *No distributions to spouse.* No law says you have to make the principal of the marital trust available to your spouse. Instead, you could say that no distributions of principal can be made to the spouse. It's not likely to make your spouse very happy, but it could be the right plan for you.

Add-Ins to the Marital Trust

Just as with the family trust, after you've built the body of the marital trust, you can make small adjustments to bolster your values and goals.

Trustee

Who will be the trustee? If you're looking to give your spouse as much control and flexibility as possible, you may want to consider naming them as the sole trustee but giving them the right to name a co-trustee in the future. If you're trying to protect the assets for your remainder beneficiaries, you may want to name a co-trustee to act with your spouse to make sure the spouse's assets are taken into account before distributions are made to the spouse. If you're concerned that your spouse can't manage the assets, you should name somebody else as the trustee or co-trustee just to avoid waste. If your spouse

---

[9] The best way to set up this type of arrangement is through a unitrust. I discuss unitrusts in detail in Chapter 17, where I talk about planning for second marriages, because this is a situation in which I find a unitrust can solve a lot of problems.

isn't a beneficiary of the principal of the marital trust, they shouldn't be a trustee.

Power of Appointment

I'm sure you understand by now that the power of appointment is the key to making sure the marital trust you set up today has the flexibility to be changed to deal with the unforeseen future. But remember the rule that no other person can be a beneficiary of the marital trust during the spouse's lifetime. This means you can't give your spouse (or anyone else, for that matter) a power of appointment over the marital trust during the spouse's lifetime. However, you can grant a *testamentary* power of appointment that can be exercised in the spouse's will. If you and your spouse have the same beneficiaries after the death of the second spouse (your children, for example), then I strongly encourage you to demand that the marital trust include a power of appointment so your spouse, who is in possession of all the facts, will have the ability to make any necessary changes as future events unfold.

5x5 Power

In addition to distributions that can be made at the discretion of the trustee, you can also give your spouse the ability to demand that a certain amount of the principal be paid from the trust each year. You can give your spouse (separate from any powers as trustee) the ability to demand the greater of (1) $5,000 or (2) 5 percent of the principal of the trust, regardless of any other distributions made by the trustee. We refer to this as a *5x5 power* (pronounced "five and five power").

This is most often used when there is a third-party trustee, so the spouse can access some of the money without the trustee's consent. Although you can have a 5x5 power in any type of trust, you don't often see it in a trust designed to minimize estate tax consequences. That's because the existence of the power means 5 percent of the principal of the trust is included in the power holder's taxable estate upon their death.

Dividing Assets to Fund the Trust

You now know just about everything there is to know about how you plan by utilizing the federal estate tax exemption and the unlimited marital deduction (and you didn't even have to spend several semesters in law school to get there!). You can draw the skeleton of your estate plan and have a toolbag of options to build out a family trust, and possibly a marital trust, that reflects your goals and family situation. But if you don't absorb this section of the chapter, everything else is irrelevant.

If all your assets are held in joint name, no tax savings will be achieved. If all your assets name each other as beneficiary, no tax savings will be achieved. If one spouse has all the money and the other spouse has nothing in their own name, and the less wealthy spouse dies, no tax savings will be achieved.

So how do you get the tax savings? Each spouse must either (1) have probate assets or (2) have funded assets into their revocable trust. Look back at Figure 14–3: see that $3 million? If it's all in joint names, it won't exist in the box to flow into either the family trust or the marital trust. There was a reason I spent so much time talking about titling your assets and probate. You can have the most customized and most expensive estate plan in the world, but if you don't hold title to your assets in a way that allows them to flow through that estate plan, it's literally not worth the paper it's written on.

How do you make sure your assets are divided to take advantage of the estate plan you put into place? Look at Chapter 23, "Action Guide: Completing Your Plan."

Disclaimer: Wait-and-See Approach

What if you don't know right now if you want a family trust or marital trust? After all, the family trust only makes sense if you have a taxable estate, and who knows what the federal government is going to do with the estate tax? You may not have the assets you feel would warrant a marital trust, but you're on an upward track, and you hope to have more at some point in the future. How do you decide now about something that will only come into being in the future?

Well, one option is that you don't. Don't make a decision today about whether the family trust or the marital trust is created. Instead, put an estate plan in place that defers the decision until you die and allows your spouse to decide whether to create the family trust or the marital trust.

To Disclaim in the Eyes of the Law

Just because a will or trust says you're supposed to inherit assets doesn't mean you have to take them. You can *disclaim* your inheritance, essentially saying, "I don't want it." The effect of a disclaimer is as if you predeceased the person who passed away; the will or trust is read as if you had died right before they did. So, if the will reads, "I give 50 percent of my estate to my sister Beth, and if she isn't living, to her children" and Beth disclaims the bequest, then the 50 percent you left to Beth would instead pass to her children, as if she predeceased you.

If anybody other than your spouse disclaims any inheritance, they can't benefit from the disclaimed assets in any way. After all, the legal fiction that's created is "as if you had predeceased the decedent." If you had in fact predeceased the decedent, you wouldn't be around to inherit anything under their will.

Spousal Disclaimer

However, when a spouse disclaims an asset, that asset is permitted to pass into a trust for the benefit of the spouse. This means you could leave your entire estate to your spouse, and your spouse could still do estate tax planning upon your death. Your spouse could look at all the facts and circumstances that existed at the time of your death and make a decision then to do estate tax planning. Your spouse would execute a disclaimer saying, "I don't want some of the assets," in which case they fall into the family trust you've already created to catch any disclaimed assets.

Your will or revocable trust would read, "I give 100 percent of my estate to my spouse. If my spouse disclaims any interest in my estate, I direct that the amount disclaimed will pass to the family trust."

Disclaimer Estate Plan Pros and Cons

"This is great," you may be saying to yourself. "Why would we set up anything more complicated if we can just figure it out later?" Maybe this is the absolute best plan for you, but let me point out some of the advantages and disadvantages before you come to a final decision.

Advantages

The huge advantage is that your spouse will know three things when you die that you can only guess about today:

- *How much money you have.* There is no way you can tell me today to the penny what your total net worth will be in 17 years. Nor can you tell me the composition of that net worth in the future (retirement plans, insurance policies, real estate, investments). When you die, your spouse will know exactly what you own then.

- *What the tax laws are.* In September 2012, I couldn't tell you exactly what the tax laws would be in January. I could have told you what would happen if Congress took no action with reference to the estate tax, but I couldn't know if they were going to pass a retroactive law sometime in 2013. Even if they were to do, I couldn't say it would be the same in 2015, 2021, or 2030. The reality is, I'm just guessing what the tax code will be in the future (an educated guess, but a guess nonetheless). When you die, your spouse will know exactly what tax laws apply to your estate.

- *What your family is like.* If your kids are little now, you may have great hopes for who they will become as adults, but you don't know. If your kids are young adults, you've seen them grow, but you may not know what kind of parents they will be. If your kids are grown with kids of their own, they may go through life changes you can't anticipate, like a divorce, a career shift, or a health situation. At the time you die, your spouse will know what the future in fact held.

Disadvantages

With all those advantages, why isn't every single estate plan set up as a disclaimer? Well, because there are disadvantages too:

- *Nine months.* Your spouse has only nine months from the time you pass away to elect to disclaim assets. If they don't, they lose the opportunity forever. This means on top of dealing with the devastation of your loss, trying to rebuild their life, and being a leader for your other family members, they need to see a lawyer, educate themselves about all this stuff, make a decision about what assets should be disclaimed, and carry out that plan. Quite frankly, it's a lot to ask. Nine months may seem like a long time, but it isn't when dealing with these issues. With many clients I see who have a disclaimer plan set up, the spouse doesn't carry out the plan because they feel very insecure about finances and emotionally don't want to give up money within that nine-month period.

- *Accepting assets.* The spouse can only disclaim assets that they haven't already accepted. If your spouse shares the news of your passing at the bank, the bank manager might innocently offer to convert a joint account into the spouse's sole name. Although doing so is logical, if they accept the asset by putting it in their name, they can't do any estate tax planning with that asset. It's not that the spouse doesn't *want* to do tax planning; it's that they didn't get any advice before they started trying to deal with your estate. The result is that they end up putting themselves in a position where they can't do the tax planning. You've looked at the numbers before. Failure to do estate tax planning can lead to hundreds of thousands of dollars in unnecessary taxes on the assets eventually passing to your children.

- *Asset protection lost.* I already told you that except in very limited circumstances, you can't set up a trust for your own benefit and have it be protected from your own creditors. If your spouse is given the money outright but then says, "I don't want it," which causes the assets to go into a trust, is that any different than your spouse setting up a trust for their own money? This isn't a settled area of the law. Logically, though, does one situation really differ from the other? If asset protection is important to you, you need to set up the family trust and mandate its funding—not leave it up to a disclaimer by your spouse.

- *Powers of appointment lost.* I harped on the value of the powers of appointment. The ability to change is unquantifiably important in your estate plan. When you set up a trust, it could last for decades. If you don't give your spouse the ability to adjust the trust as family circumstances change, the trust may not fit in the distant future. Any trust established through a disclaimer can't have powers of appointment. This is so important in my practice that, except for married couples with minimal estates, I always design an estate plan so the family trust is created without disclaimer. I do this to keep powers of appointment in the plan. I can't tell you how many estates I've administered where, if only there had been a power of appointment, all sorts of issues would've been avoided.

Portability

The 2010 Tax Act (scheduled to expire at the end of 2012) added one new twist to estate tax planning that could be very valuable for spouses. Whether Congress extended the law was unknown at the time of publication. In the event that they did, I want to take a moment to introduce you to the concept of *portability*.

The idea behind portability is that if one spouse fails to effectively use their entire estate tax exemption amount, they shouldn't lose it. Instead, the unused portion of the estate tax exemption amount should pass to the surviving spouse. This would make planning a heck of a lot easier. It would also make people who failed to put an estate plan into place a heck of a lot happier. Unfortunately, it's scheduled right now to go by the wayside, but it's a good enough idea that it may be resurrected in future estate tax laws.

Ask the Attorney "Deirdre: I think I know what I want. How do I make sure my estate plan includes it?" I suggest that you do what I do: literally sketch the structure of your plan. Add bullet points under the box for each trust with the instructions you're giving your trustee: Who gets the principal, the income, and so on? Who are the trustees? What about powers of appointment? Then, when you're reviewing the draft of your estate plan, go back to each bullet point and see if you find language in the plan that lets you check it off. If you don't find your bullet points in your draft documents, go back to the source until what your plan says matches your design.

15

Planning Guide for Singles

Sometimes it's hard to be single. Tax laws are harsher for singles than for marrieds. In addition, you may need to decide whom you want to benefit because you don't feel you have obvious heirs. Your blood heirs may be disappointed with your choices, and because they have standing under the law, this increases the chance of a will contest. All this means your estate plan may need to be more thoughtful than that of your married friends.

A quick note before you read too far: If the goal of your estate plan is to pass your assets to your children and then grandchildren, I set out lots of ideas for you in Chapter 13, "Planning Guide for Kids." Most of the ideas in this chapter revolve around a single individual who may be considering a large group of people as beneficiaries and who perhaps wants to benefit different people in different manners.

▨ **Chapter Brief**   People don't deserve to share in your estate just because they're related to you. Who do you want to benefit when you go? Family? Friends? Charity? Pets? Leaving a percentage of assets can be attractive, but you need to anticipate challenges in carrying out the plan. The lowly tax-allocation clause can be the difference between a successful plan and a failed one. By understanding the grounds for a will contest, you can use practical preventions to keep your plan intact.

Who Gets Your Assets

When a married couple comes to see me, there is a customary order to their estate plan: they want to benefit each other and then their kids; or, they want to benefit each other and their respective kids. They may throw in some bequests to other family members or charities, but for most married couples, this is what their distribution scheme looks like.

When I meet with a single client, the universe of "who's going to get my assets" expands exponentially. If clients have children, they tend to give them the bulk of the estate, but there may be other people they're very close to whom they don't want to forget. Clients without children might be looking at family members such as parents, siblings, or nieces and nephews, but they're just as likely to have other people in their lives whom they're closer to than blood relatives. I have a number of clients whose closest companions are their pets, and they want to make sure they're cared for. Finally, a number of my single clients are very involved in charities and would like to see those organizations benefit instead of their family.

What kind of questions should you be asking yourself in narrowing down your list of beneficiaries? Let me share with you some conversations I've had with clients over the years:

- *Family.* The questions of family tend to revolve around whether you're leaving assets to a group of people (my siblings and then their issue) or specific family members. I've had clients come in and say, "I want to leave my assets to my nieces and nephews"—but in the course of conversation, only one niece's name keeps coming up over and over again. My question is, are your relationships with all these people on the same level? If you're closer to one versus the others, do you want to benefit that person more than your other family members? Just because somebody's related to you, it doesn't mean they're entitled to a share of your estate. Just because they share the same degree of relationship with you that another person does, that doesn't mean you have the same relationship with them. If you're closer to your niece Hillary, for example, then consider leaving her a specific bequest before your residuary is divided up equally, or giving her a greater percentage of your residuary estate. Don't feel bad about benefiting the person you're closest to, if that's what you really want to do.

- *Friends.* The great thing about friends is that you can select them, unlike family, who come as part of the package. Your friends may be the people with whom you enjoy life, so they're the people you want to benefit in the event of your death. A lack of blood relationship doesn't mean they're not important to you. However, you may not want to involve your friends in your estate if the balance of it is going to your family; after all, they may have no relationship with each other. This is where will alternatives can really come in handy. For example, you could name your best friend Ruth as the beneficiary of one of your bank accounts, with a note that she should take that trip she's always wanted, and then have everything else pass to your siblings under your will. Or, you could divide your entire estate equally among certain friends and not leave anything to any family members. If you choose that approach, be clear in the drafting about your intention to exclude family members.

- *Charity.* You may believe there are many more deserving people out there than your family and friends and want to benefit them through charities you admire. You could do this by leaving a specific amount to charities and then the balance of your residuary to friends and family, or the flip circumstance, where friends and family receive specific amounts and the residuary goes to charity. You should be aware that whenever charity is a beneficiary of an estate, the attorney general of your state gets involved to make sure the charity's interests are protected. If your charity is receiving a specific bequest, the attorney general's involvement is very straightforward—the will says the charity was supposed to get $50,000; did they in fact receive $50,000? If the charity is a residuary beneficiary, it becomes more complicated. The attorney general is likely to audit the expenses of the estate to make sure all the expenses were appropriate for the estate and none were personal expenses of the individual beneficiaries the charity shouldn't have to share in. Because of the expenses this might generate, I strongly recommend considering specific bequests to charities.

- *Pets.* You love your pets and want to make sure they're cared for in the same manner you provided for them during your lifetime. In some states, you're permitted to set up a trust for the benefit of your pet. Obviously, pets can't inherit money directly—how would they sign checks? By creating a trust for the benefit of the pet, you can not only leave money to care for the pet, but also identify a person to provide the care and a committee to oversee the person who's providing for the care to make sure they aren't abusing the money you've designated for Kitty, Fido, Mr. Ed, or Alex the talking parrot. If you can't set up a trust for your pet in your state, consider finding an organization you can contract with to provide care for your pet for the rest of its life in return for receiving a fixed amount under your estate plan. Believe it or not, there are rest homes for all sorts of animals. I would try to build in protections so somebody checks in to be sure your pet is receiving the care that was promised (sort of the same way you want to frequently and unexpectedly stop by the nursing home were Grandma lives).[1]

How to Give Assets

As a single person, there generally won't be any tax benefits in your estate to setting up a trust for your beneficiaries unless you're looking at the generation-skipping tax. You only have one federal estate tax exemption, and it will be applied before the assets are distributed to the beneficiaries. However, you should still consider how you can structure an inheritance to maximize your goals within your estate plan.

If your primary beneficiaries are your children or grandchildren, I suggest you look at Chapter 13 to go through the options for planning an inheritance. For other beneficiaries, consider the following:

- *Outright.* Clearly, the simplest method to leave a bequest, whether specific or residuary, is outright to your beneficiary. However, depending on who your beneficiary is, you may want to carefully consider who will receive the asset in the event that the beneficiary predeceases you. Would you want it to go to their children, with whom you may not have as strong a relationship, or be redistributed among your other beneficiaries? You may want to pick a new contingent beneficiary.

---

[1] There is a fabulous resource, www.pettrustlawblog.com, where attorney Dennis Meek blogs about everything to do with pet law. As an animal lover, I enjoy following this blog, and I've gotten a lot of great ideas over the years about how to structure an inheritance to benefit pets.

- *Family trust.* Just because there are no estate tax savings, it doesn't mean a family trust structure, where the trust assets are sprinkled among a group of people, wouldn't best fit your goals. Think about leaving your assets in a sprinkle trust for the benefit of each of your siblings and their children. This way, if your siblings don't need or use the assets during their lifetimes, the assets will pass outside of their taxable estate to their children. If you left the same assets to your siblings outright, and they had a taxable estate, the inheritance would end up being taxed once in your estate when you died and then again when they passed away. Also, an outright bequest runs the risk that the inheritance will pass to that brother-in-law you can't stand.[2]

- *Single-beneficiary trust.* If your beneficiaries are younger, you may want to consider leaving assets to them in trust until they reach an age of maturity. Chapter 13 discusses how to leave assets to kids and presents some ideas about how to structure this type of trust.

- *Generation-sharing trust.* For wealthier individuals, it may make sense to take the family trust a step further and structure an inheritance so that, to the extent the assets aren't used during a beneficiary's lifetime, they will flow to successive generations estate-tax-free. Although your estate would pay estate taxes upon your death, further taxes would be avoided on the deaths of subsequent generations.

How to Divide Assets among a Group

Let's say you want to divide your assets among a group of people. Does it make a difference whether you leave a fixed amount as a specific bequest to four people and whatever is left over to a fifth residuary beneficiary? Or should you give everybody 20 percent? There are pros and cons to making a specific bequest of a fixed amount of money versus creating a percentage allocation among beneficiaries.

---

[2] If your beneficiaries are in their retirement years, you may want to consider the impact of an inheritance on long-term care needs. See Chapter 20, "Planning Guide for Your Parents," for ideas of how to prevent an inheritance from having an unintended negative impact on seniors.

Percentage Bequests

If you set aside a percentage of assets to all your beneficiaries, their inheritance will grow or shrink depending on the size of your estate. If each of five people is supposed to receive 20 percent, everybody will get 20 percent. If one person passes away and the percentages are to be reallocated, the four surviving beneficiaries will each receive 25 percent. The potential downside to dividing everything in percentages is how administrative expenses are allocated.

Let's say there are five equal beneficiaries to your estate, and you name your nephew Al as the executor. As executor, Al needs to spend lots of time with the attorney to make sure the estate is being properly administered. Assume that part of your inheritance consists of a retirement plan, and Al is a 20 percent beneficiary. Al has lots of questions about the retirement plan and poses them to the attorney, who answers them and incorporates them into the bill for the estate. The bill for the estate is shared among all five beneficiaries. Al's sister, Abigail, thinks Al is wasting a lot of the estate's money with the attorney (Abigail is one of those people who is always looking to find the worst in others). Abigail is sure she's found the smoking gun when she sees that the attorney gave Al what she feels is personal advice and charged the consultation to the estate. Abigail gets her own attorney to challenge every step Al has made as executor, your estate dwindles, and only the attorneys benefit from it.

A percentage allocation gives rise to these types of disputes regarding the allocation of expenses. I bring this to your attention so you can take into account the relationships, if any, among the parties you name as beneficiaries.

Specific Bequests, then Residuary Bequest

Let's use Al and Abigail as examples again, but add to the mix the fact that you named Al as the executor because he's been the one helping you as you age. After meeting with me, you want your estate plan to take into consideration that Al and Abigail never got along. I suggest you leave Abigail (and perhaps some of your other four beneficiaries) a specific bequest of a fixed amount of money instead of using percentages.

The benefit of the fixed amount is that the person receiving the bequest gets what the bequest says; the expenses of the administration are charged against the residuary estate, so they have no impact on a specific bequest. Al could then be the residuary beneficiary.

The downside of this structure is what happens if the value of your assets goes down. Because specific bequests are satisfied before the residuary bequest, Al could end up with less than everybody else, even though you intended him to receive the bulk of your estate. This situation can be solved by indicating that the total of the specific bequests can't exceed more than a fixed percent of your estate (say 50 percent), thus setting a minimum amount that Al will receive.

Don't forget that specific bequests don't need to be created *inside* your will or revocable trust. You could use a will alternative, such as the beneficiary designation on a retirement account or life insurance policy, or a joint account or a transfer-on-death account, to pass a specific bequest to a person outside of your overall estate plan. This is a good technique to keep in mind if some of the people you're benefiting have no relationship to the other people (specific bequests to friends, a will or revocable trust to the family).

Special Tax Issues

Taxes are, well, more taxing when you're single individual. I already mentioned that you have one exemption from estate taxes, not two as with a married couple.

The tax-allocation clause becomes a very important element of your estate plan when you're single. If you only have residuary beneficiaries (you don't make any specific bequests, and no beneficiaries receive assets as a result of will alternatives), then the standard tax-allocation clause that pays taxes out of the residuary will work for you.

However, if you've made specific bequests to some individuals or are using will alternatives as part of your estate plan, a tax allocation that provides for the residuary estate to pay all the taxes could shortchange, or even bankrupt, your residuary beneficiaries.

I'm going to use the example of your nephew Al again. Let's say your estate is $1.5 million and you pass away in 2013. In your will, you provide that $250,000 goes to each of four other nephews and nieces, but Al is the residuary beneficiary. You don't look at your tax-allocation clause, and it's the standard one that says all taxes are paid from the residuary. Your federal estate tax bill is $210,000. Because that comes out of the residuary, instead of Al getting $500,000 as you intended, he only receives $290,000.

For single individuals with disparate beneficiaries, a better tax-allocation clause is to say that each beneficiary pays their proportionate share of the taxes. If you used that tax-allocation clause in the example, each beneficiary who received a $250,000 specific bequest would be responsible for 16.67 percent of the estate tax bill, or $35,000. At the end of the day, the four would each receive a specific bequest of $215,000. Al would also be partially responsible for the estate tax. Because his share of the estate represents 33.3 percent, he would pay $70,000. Al would end up with $430,000, which is less than the $500,000 you intended but reflects the fair allocation of the estate taxes.

Now, if you really wanted to make sure Al received a minimum of $500,000, you should've first made a specific bequest to him of the $500,000, next made bequests of $250,000 among the other four beneficiaries, and finally left any residue to Al as well.

Here's one more little reminder. Eight states collect inheritance tax: Indiana, Iowa, Kentucky, Maryland, Nebraska, New Jersey, Pennsylvania, and Tennessee. If you live in one of these states, different tax rates may apply to different beneficiaries depending on their relationship to you. These taxes need to be accounted for in terms of whether they'll be paid out of the residuary estate or allocated to the beneficiaries who receive the assets.

Risk of a Will Contest

One problem with having all these choices is that somebody might be very peeved about the decisions you make. It's amazing how many people believe an inheritance is "owed" to them merely by virtue of sharing some DNA characteristics with you. Here's the crux of the issue: if you die without a will, then the law leaves your assets to your relatives based on how closely they're related to you. If a cousin can successfully overturn your will, the intestacy statute may provide that this person inherits your entire estate, *even if you've never met them!* This bias in the law in favor of blood relationships, combined with the money left in your estate, can be a fertile breeding ground for a will contest.

Four Reasons to Contest a Will

The good news is that, despite what you see on TV, there are only four limited grounds on which to contest a will:

- *The will wasn't signed in accordance with state law.* All the way back at the beginning of this book, I harped on how important it is to have a will properly executed under state law. If a will fails to meet the very stringent execution standards, then it won't be deemed to be a will. If it's not a will, it can't transfer your property at death. This is one of the biggest areas of concern I have with using an online service or do-it-yourself estate planning—if you don't get the signature section right, you don't have a valid estate plan. This has led to many a person believing that they have a perfectly valid estate plan— but instead leaving their heirs in for a very nasty surprise because the will wasn't executed properly.

- *Lack of testamentary capacity.* This invalidates a will on the grounds that the person executing the will was incompetent to do so at the time they did it. You most often see this issue raised regarding an older person who modifies their will and removes some people who were beneficiaries under a prior will. The fact of the matter is that the level of capacity required to execute a will isn't very high; it's actually lower than the level of capacity needed to execute a contract. In essence, in order to be competent to execute a will, a person needs to know (1) the nature and value of their assets, (2) who would receive their assets if they didn't have a will, and (3) the legal effect of signing the will. Someone would have a long road ahead of them to prove you didn't have the capacity to execute your will. It's hard to come by historic evidence of lack of capacity.

- *Undue influence.* This is the biggie when it comes to will contests. The issue is that if a person is in a *confidential relationship* with you, then the person might be able to cause you such duress about your will that you lose your independence of thought process. What if you rely on one of your daughters to cook and clean for you, and she hints that unless she gets the house, she won't be able to continue helping you? Or, what if a hired caregiver threatens to withhold your medication unless you change your will to benefit them? Or, perhaps your nephew helpfully drives you to his attorney to create a new will, which just happens to leave everything to him. When a will has unequal distributions, or distributions to non-family members, a court is reasonably concerned that the will was created out of fear that the favored beneficiary would cease caring for or even harm the person making out the will. Nine months before you died, were you threatened into changing your will to name your caregiver as the primary beneficiary? Or has your caregiver helped you for eight years, you don't see your relatives, and you just got around to making out your will nine months before you died? This is such a fact-based inquiry that, again, undue influence is very hard to prove.

- *Fraud.* You give a person a contract to sign, and it turns out someone slipped a will into the document and the person didn't know they were signing a will. The will is invalid because it clearly isn't an expression of the person's intent. Another fraudulent situation is where somebody slips pages into the middle of the will. This is why I have the person making out a will or revocable trust initial each and every page.

Who Can Contest

If you're still concerned about someone contesting the will, who has legal grounds to bring a suit? Three categories of people can do so. The first are people who are named under a prior will but aren't named under the current will. This is most likely to come up when somebody is potentially claiming a situation of undue influence, or the will was changed under suspicious circumstances prior to your death.

The second category is one I alluded to before: people who would be your heirs if you had no will. Because of the possibility of disgruntled relatives with unreasonable expectations, you need to be very clear in your will about whom you're benefiting and why. You should also be clear about whom you're not benefiting, so they can't raise the issue that you "forgot about them." It goes a long way if you say, "I know Bill is my nephew, but it's my specific intention to exclude him under this document."

The third situation involves a promise to pay upon death. This is really a contract claim from a creditor rather than a will contest. The facts could be, "Mr. Smith told me I would get $50,000 at his death if I ran all his errands for him." Again, this is difficult to prove. So if you're Mr. Smith, and you want your neighbor to receive the $50,000, you need to write it down, either in your will or as a contract the neighbor can enforce against your estate.

Practical Prevention

How do you avoid a will contest? Another falsity of movies and TV is the value of the *no-contest clause.* You state in your will that if anybody contests it, they get nothing. There are a bunch of problems with this. First, if you don't like the person you think might contest the will, it's unlikely that you provided much, if anything, for them in the will, so where is their financial incentive to not contest it? The second problem is that courts are reasonably very concerned about the issue of undue influence. If the person who got you to create the new will under undue influence could be protected merely by putting a clause in the will saying that nobody else could contest the will, then your intentions would be thwarted at every turn. You can't rely on a no-contest clause, and in some states, they're absolutely unenforceable by law.

The bad news about will contests is that no matter what precautions you take, people may contest the will as a "nuisance suit" type of situation. They may understand from the outset that they don't have the proof to demonstrate undue influence or lack of competency, but they're not worried about winning the case. Their goal is to get your estate to give them some money merely to go away. If you're concerned about these types of nuisances from a specific person, you should lay out in your will what the issues are, direct your executors to vigorously defend any lawsuit, and be clear about your intention not to benefit the nuisance party. The entire purpose is to give your executor grounds to seek damages from the party for bringing the suit, including repayment of attorney's fees.

▒ **Let's Get Real**   If I were to sum up this chapter in one word, it would be *clarity*. For a single person, it's even more important for your desires and motivations to be transparent and clear in your documents. You may want to include an introduction in your will or revocable trust that identifies not only whom you want to benefit but also why, as well as whom you don't want to benefit. If you're using a will alternative, make a statement in your will if the assets passing to a person outside of your will are in addition to or in lieu of any assets the person receives under your will. If you're worried about a will contest, tell your attorney so they can make extra efforts to document your competency and intentions at the time of the will execution.

16

Planning Guide for Unmarried and Same-Sex Couples

Same-sex couples are in an estate planning no-man's land. If your legal status is recognized under your state's law, it isn't under federal law. If you move, your legal status may change.

Unmarried couples can be a common family and economic unit. But without the benefit of a marriage certificate, you don't get the benefit of a variety of tax breaks or legal standing. All of this leads to the need for some creative planning to put your family on footing similar to that of a married couple.

▓ Chapter Brief Under state tax and intestacy law, partners in a same-sex relationship are treated as being single unless they're in a same-sex marriage or civil union in a state that recognizes it. Under federal tax law, you're treated as being single. You're empowered to name your partner as a beneficiary and fiduciary, but if you don't act, they won't benefit or have a right to act for you. Unmarried couples are, of course, treated as single under both state and federal law.

Disconnect of State and Federal Law

In the eyes of the law, unmarried couples, same-sex or otherwise, have no legal relationship with each other. This disconnect creates both obstacles and gaps in creating a coherent estate plan. Unless you live in a state that recognizes same-sex marriages or civil unions, when you die you'll be treated as a single individual. If you don't have a will or revocable trust in place, your assets will pass via the intestacy laws. This means all your assets will pass to your family members, and none to your partner.

Even in states that do recognize same-sex marriages or civil unions, that recognition is only valid in that state or in other states that have similar recognition. It has no effect when it comes to federal law. This means you don't get the benefit of the marital deduction from estate taxes, the benefit of the marital deduction from gift taxes, or any other benefits of being a spouse.

Same-sex couples who are legally recognized in their state can benefit from state level income and estate tax breaks but not from the federal income or estate tax. To say that this makes planning more complicated is a huge understatement.

To further complicate matters, remember that some states have their own estate tax or inheritance tax. A same-sex couple might be exempt from state estate tax but subject to federal estate tax. Unmarried couples—even those who share a joint economic unit and have children together—could be hit with the federal estate tax, state estate tax, and, if they're in New Jersey or Maryland, potentially an inheritance tax as well. The end result is all that money going to the government instead of continuing to be available to support your family.

Form of Estate Plan

You'll have to be creative with your estate plan, because the law just isn't designed right now to accommodate your relationship.

Is a Will the Way?

Fact: Some people, inside your family and outside, may not be thrilled with your lifestyle choice, either as a same-sex couple or as an unmarried couple. Bear in mind that a will is a public document. As such, it's subject to scrutiny by anybody with the money to pay the photocopying fee. In comparison, in the majority of states, a revocable trust isn't a public document. Thus, in order to maintain your privacy, you may want to consider carrying out your desired distribution provisions in a revocable trust rather than just a will.

Also, there seems to be disproportionate number of will contests involving same-sex and unmarried couples. Your blood family are the people who would benefit in the event your estate plan was determined to be ineffective; they're your intestate heirs under state law if your will is declared invalid. Sometimes this is a sad incentive for them to contest the will in order to benefit from your estate. To be frank, they may try to contest the will just to harass your partner and get some settlement from that person. Your partner might agree to a settlement "just to make them go away." This risk of a will contest makes it even more important that your estate plan be created with the guidance and input of an experienced attorney, and not created using the do-it-yourself approach.[1]

You may also want to consider a divided estate plan, where you leave some assets to your partner and some assets to other members of your family. This could be done in a will where you left specific bequests to certain people and the residuary to your partner, or vice versa. You could also accomplish this by passing non-probate assets to your partner and using your will to benefit other family members.

Non-Probate Assets to the Rescue?

For same-sex and unmarried couples, non-probate assets that pass outside of your will are potentially your best bet. First, those assets are immediately available to your partner; all they need is your death certificate. Remember, here are the options:

- *Joint tenants with rights of survivorship.* Consider this form of ownership for your real estate and bank accounts. Upon death, the assets pass directly to the joint owner. Both owners have access to the asset during life. Be aware that naming your partner as the joint owner has drawbacks. First, you may be making a taxable gift (remember, there is no unlimited deduction for gifts between non-spouses). Second, if the relationship ends, the partner has actual ownership of 50 percent of the asset. They also have the right to withdraw 100 percent of the asset. In a particularly nasty situation, you

---

[1] Although there are limited grounds for a will contest, the issue isn't always whether a person could be successful in a contest; it's the ability to bring a contest in the first place. If you're concerned about will contests and what to do about them, look back at Chapter 15, "Planning Guide for Singles."

could find yourself with no money because your partner has stripped the accounts. Due to these downsides, some couples choose to limit the joint assets to those they jointly contribute to (potentially the house and a joint bank account).

- *Pay-on-death accounts.* These name the person to receive the account in the event of your death, outside of your will. The beneficiary doesn't have any control over the asset during your lifetime. This is a neat way to sidestep a will and the probate process; at death, your partner has almost immediate access to that asset. One problem is that this form of ownership tends be limited to bank accounts and investment assets. And if the relationship ends, you must remember to change the pay-on-death beneficiary!

- *Retirement accounts.* You have the right to name a beneficiary of any retirement account. If you name your partner, that account will pass to them. Be aware that your partner doesn't qualify for the spousal rollover of a retirement account, because those rules are governed by federal law, which doesn't recognize your relationship. This means no matter what your age, your partner must begin taking required minimum distributions and paying income tax on them.

■ **Ask the Attorney** "Deirdre, if I name my partner as the beneficiary of some non-probate assets, have I successfully avoided all the issues with a will?" Not necessarily. Remember when I gave you an example of a convenience account, and there was a factual issue of whether the father meant for the account to pass to the daughter co-owner on his death? That same question can be raised regarding naming partners on non-probate assets. The better practice is to use non-probate assets *and* make a statement in your will that it's your intention that the non-probate assets (identify them) pass to your partner.

What About When You're Still Alive?

It's already a complicated situation, but there's more: your planning can't be limited to what happens if you die. It also needs to consider what happens if you get sick. Your partner (unless you're in a state that recognizes same-sex marriage or civil unions) has absolutely no legal right to make financial decisions or medical decisions for you while you're alive. You have the power to give them that right by executing a power of attorney, a living will, or an advance directive. However, if you fail to do so, the person who knows you best, or with whom you share your life, won't be able to act for you in the event of your disability. Heck, they may not even be able to visit you in the hospital. So, study Chapter 7, "Rounding Out the Plan," to learn about other documents that will round out your estate plan and put the decision making authority in your partner's hands.

Tax-Minimization Strategies

You don't get the tax benefits of being a married couple, but you want 100 percent of your assets to be available to each other in the event of death. How can these differences be reconciled?

- *Federal estate tax exemption amount.* Don't forget that each partner has the ability to leave the federal estate tax exemption amount ($1 million in 2013) to the other partner without any estate tax. This in and of itself may mean taxes aren't an issue. If one partner has more than $1 million and the other has less, consider gifting from one partner to the other to try to balance out the assets. Of course, this means the person who received the assets now owns them, and you run the risk of them taking the assets elsewhere in the event the relationship ends. Also, gifts are limited to the $13,000 annual exclusion, unless the lifetime exemption amount is applied.

- *Irrevocable life insurance trust (ILIT).* There was a reason I devoted an entire chapter (Chapter 10, "Insurance Trust") to the ILIT. If you look at your planning and believe you'll lose $350,000 through estate taxes upon the death of one or the other of you, each partner can purchase a $350,000 life insurance policy, hold it in a trust, and replace estate tax dollars through insurance premiums. Yes, it's more expensive because you have to pay the premium, but it puts you in a situation similar to that of a married couple, where 100 percent of the assets pass tax-free to the surviving spouse.

- *Advanced gifting strategies.* Given the limitations of the annual exclusion amount and the lifetime exemption amount, it may be appropriate to attempt to leverage the assets passed to the other partner during your lifetime. The grantor retained annuity trust (GRAT) might be especially effective because the partner creating the GRAT receives back the initial contribution plus a rate of return, and any excess passes to the other partner gift tax-free.[2]

Guardian of Minor Children

I feel as though I'm beginning to sound like a broken record (or scratched CD) about how same-sex and unmarried couples have no legal rights. In most states, your partner has no legal authority to act as guardian for your minor children. Generally speaking, only one partner is legally recognized as the parent of your minor children. It could be that your children are from a prior relationship and have another surviving parent (who will be the default guardian). Other times, there was a birth or adoption by only one partner in a couple.

Because the noncustodial partner doesn't have any legal relationship to the child, this can leave you in a situation where you have no recourse whatsoever in the event of the death of the custodial parent to continue to parent that child. Even if you name your partner as guardian in your will, that nomination is subject to being overturned by a judge on a variety of grounds, including what is "in the best interest of the children." To be quite frank, the judge may find that your untraditional relationship isn't in the child's best interest no matter what.

The first plan of action is always to name the partner as the guardian. I even insert language describing why they should be the guardian, including what the family relationship is like. The second step is to leave assets to your children and name your partner as trustee of that trust. Although giving your partner control of money isn't nearly the same as your partner acting as guardian, this step at least provides a continuing legal relationship between your partner and your children. Finally, take action during your life to head off any objections from your family to the guardianship arrangement. If possible, make sure everybody's aware up front of what your wishes and desires are; it's better for you to be the person having the conversation about why you made the selection, instead of your partner facing angry people who feel left in the dark.

Funeral Arrangements

Unless you're in a state that recognizes same-sex marriages or civil unions, your partner has absolutely no legal standing to claim your body and/or plan a funeral. This can be the ultimate slap in the face. Unfortunately, although you may plan in your will and living will that your partner can make decisions for

---

[2] If you're looking for a refresher on the GRAT, see Chapter 11, "Advanced Tax Strategies."

you, the fact of the matter is that these things are done very quickly and, because your partner has no legal standing to claim your body, a family member may override your wishes. The practical solution? Talk to your entire family about what your wishes are, and try to make sure everybody's on the same page while you're still here to discuss it.

17

Planning Guide for Second Marriages

Blended families give rise to lots of challenges, estate planning among them. There is an inherent tension between providing for your spouse, your children from a prior relationship, your spouse's children, and joint children. Often added to the mix are other agreements you've made, such as a separation agreement or prenuptial agreement. Finally, you don't want your plan to create such confusion or discord that the lawyers are called in. Careful thought is needed to defuse a potential family explosion.

Chapter Brief Create an estate plan based first on who gets what and second on tax considerations. A marital trust may be the best vehicle for leaving assets to your spouse. A unitrust could perfect a marital trust by eliminating the investment tension between your spouse as the current beneficiary and your children as the eventual beneficiaries. Consider differentiating between the beneficiaries with retirement accounts and life insurance.

Tension Between Children and Spouse

When families blend, they create their own unique interwoven tapestry. The texture of this tapestry changes depending on the length of the marriage, the ages of the individuals, the stage of development of the children, and interactions with former spouses. Your estate plan won't be as easy as just saying, "I want to provide for my spouse and my children." You need to focus on the details of how much you're setting aside and for whom.

Let me talk about the pink elephant in the room. You and your spouse might agree that you'll leave everything to your spouse (and vice versa) but you'll provide for each other's children in your will. You don't want to say it, but you're thinking, "What if they change their mind and cut my kids out?" It's OK to admit you're thinking this—everybody does. This is the core problem: you have two (or more) sets of people to provide for, but they don't have the bond with each other that you have with them.

You also need to do a gut check. First, look at the rapport between your spouse and your other family members right now. Do they have a relationship? Is it close, cordial, or tolerated? Dying is truly hard only on the living. Be honest with yourself about the strength of the relationship today, because that will determine the probability of those bonds remaining strong in the future. Next, accept that their relationship will change when you're no longer here as the binding force. Some relationships stay the same or grow closer, but most people drift apart. Worse, it could be that years of resentment come to the surface regarding who gets what following your demise; and then the lawyers are called in.

Don't forget about your spouse's children. Are you treating them as your own, choosing not to benefit them, or doing something in between? Will benefiting your stepchildren exacerbate issues with your children and other family members, and how do you plan to defuse that? Are you sure you and your spouse are on the same page about how the stepchildren should be treated? You need to actually speak to each other about it—this isn't a good time to assume.

Real Stories from Around My Conference Table   Jerry and Rebecca had been married 10+ years, and each brought two kids to the marriage (now in their 20s and 30s). They came to do estate planning, and I asked, "Forget about anything else. If you were to get hit by a bus tomorrow, where would you want your assets to go?" Jerry said, "I want to make sure Rebecca is provided for, and then the kids." Rebecca said, "I want Jerry to have the money, then my sons." Silence. Jerry said, "I thought we were treating the kids equally." Rebecca said, "I need to provide for my kids." Chilly silence ensued. I was looking for a hole in the ground. Needless to say, the meeting didn't progress further. I'm guessing it was a very long and cold ride home for them.

Start with the End in Mind

I've described estate planning as a process in which tax issues create the skeleton plan structure, and then you build on that by designing an inheritance that works best for your family. Well, it's time to stop and flip that around.

Forget about taxes for now (can't believe I just said that, can you?). With blended families, you need to invert the formula. The first question is, how do you intend to provide for your (1) spouse, (2) children, (3) stepchildren, and (4) other family members? The emphasis is on the "and" because it isn't necessarily a collective solution. The answer to this question can range from "I'm going to leave everything to my spouse and trust her to take care of my children," to "I'm not leaving anything to my spouse," to something in the middle. There is no right or wrong answer, because the best solution for you draws from the bonds and relationships of your unique family. However, there are some common thought processes to consider:

- If a spouse has been widowed, there's often a sense of giving "what the other parent left me" directly to the children from that marriage. Dennis dies and leaves everything to his wife Jennifer, including a life insurance policy. Jennifer remarries and keeps separate the account funded by the insurance. She may direct in her estate plan that that account go to her children because "it's from their father."

- Leave a fixed amount to the children and the balance to the spouse. This may come across as, "I give $100,000 to each of my children and direct that my residuary estate be distributed to my spouse." When taking this approach, you need to revisit the amount you're leaving the children every couple of years. It might have been reasonable to leave each child $100,000 when you had a $1.2 million estate, but that same plan may no longer fit your goals if your total estate is reduced to $750,000 as you fund a long and lively retirement.

- Take the tax-free approach by saying you leave the federal estate tax exemption equivalent to your children and anything else to your spouse. Although this certainly minimizes taxes, remember that the federal estate exemption amount has been jumping around for the past decade or so. A $5 million exemption might mean everything goes to your children and nothing to your spouse, which may not be your intention. If using the tax-free approach, you might want to say, "I leave my children an amount equal to the lesser of my estate tax exemption amount or $1 million."

- Give the spouse the minimum amount required by law, and leave the balance to the children. In most states, the spouse is entitled to approximately one third of your estate. Note that if you don't leave a minimum amount to your spouse, they can go to court and successfully demand that their minimum share of the estate be distributed to them (unless you have a prenuptial agreement in which your spouse waived that right).

- Treat your children and stepchildren alike and provide first for your spouse until they die and then equally among all the children. When taking this approach, you need to look very carefully at the boilerplate of the will or trust. Often, the words *children*, *descendants*, and *issue* are defined in a way that excludes stepchildren and their descendants. Because so much language in a will relies on its definitions, make sure your documents are consistent throughout in including stepchildren in the group of beneficiaries.

Tax Considerations

OK. You've determined who is going to get what. Now you need to look at the tax impact of your distribution scheme. Any assets passing to your spouse or a marital trust for the benefit of your spouse won't be subject to estate tax upon your death. Conversely, any assets passing to your children or other family members in excess of your estate tax exemption amount will be subject to estate tax. Also, you need to consider that if you live in one of the states that have a state estate tax or inheritance tax, there may be an additional cost upon your death.[1]

If your intended distribution scheme will create estate taxes upon your death, you need to very carefully consider the tax-allocation clause in your will (which is likely to be buried somewhere toward the back).

Let's take the example of Richard and Melissa. The marriage is Richard's second, and he has two children, Noah and Chloe, from his first marriage. He and Melissa don't have any children together. Richard has a little over $3 million of assets he wants to divide equally between Melissa, Noah, and Chloe.

---

[1] In New Jersey, an inheritance passing to step-grandchildren, but not grandchildren, is subject to an inheritance tax. If your state has an inheritance tax, make sure you find out how it applies to your spouse's descendants.

His idea is to leave Noah and Chloe $1 million each, with the balance passing to Melissa. Here are the options:

- *Taxes are paid from the residuary.* This tends to be the default tax-allocation scheme when no real attention is given to how the taxes will be paid. In Richard's case, assume the $2 million bequest to Noah and Chloe generates $430,000 in estate taxes (because any amount over $1 million passing to someone other than a spouse or charity generates an estate tax). Specific bequests are paid first, so Noah and Chloe each receive $1 million. However, Melissa receives the residuary only after the tax payment, so her share is $570,000. Strike one. This doesn't achieve Richards's goal of each of them receiving the same amount of money.

- *Tax is allocated to the distributions giving rise to the tax.* This seems fair. The tax is paid by the beneficiary whose bequest created the tax. But wait. Anything passing to Melissa qualifies for the marital deduction, so her inheritance doesn't generate an estate tax. Accordingly, the only place for the taxes to come from is the $2 million being set aside for Noah and Chloe. Assuming the same $430,000 in estate tax, Noah and Chloe receive only $785,000 each, whereas Melissa receives $1 million. Strike two.

- *Tax is allocated to the beneficiaries in proportion to their share of the estate.* This will probably come closest to achieving Richard's goal. Here, the $430,000 is allocated among Melissa, Chloe, and Noah in proportion to what they're receiving from the estate. If they receive the same amount of money, then they're each charged one third of the tax.

Marital Trust

It's very common in second marriages for the philosophy to be, "I want my spouse to have the benefit of my assets while they're alive. But upon their death, to the extent they haven't spent the assets, I want them to go back to my kids." In this situation, a marital trust is ideal.

A quick refresher on the marital trust: It's a trust created for the sole benefit of the surviving spouse and qualifies for the marital deduction from estate taxes. The surviving spouse must at a minimum receive all the income generated by the marital trust each year. You can permit, but don't have to, principal distributions. If they're allowed, they could be at the discretion of the trustee, for fixed amounts, or for specified needs.

Using Richard and Melissa again as an example, Richard can leave some or all of his assets to Melissa in a marital trust. If the trust isn't exhausted when Melissa passes away, any remaining balance is distributed back to Noah and Chloe (or trusts for them, because Richard has read this book!).

Income

Income for trust purposes is interest and dividends. For the marital trust to qualify for the marital deduction from estate taxes, the spouse must have the right to make the trust income-producing. This means Melissa could demand that the trustee invest everything in income-producing assets.

The problem with differentiating between income and principal is that it exacerbates tensions between the spouse and the children. Melissa as the income beneficiary wants everything invested for interest and dividends (bonds and dividend-producing stocks). Noah and Chloe, on the other hand, want the trust invested for growth, because they get anything that is left over. These are opposite investment goals. And whoever is the trustee has the responsibility to consider both groups in designing an investment portfolio and to try to avoid being sued by favoring one over the other.

An additional downside to the "payment of income" approach has been starkly illuminated in recent years because we're in an interest-rate environment close to 0 percent. In reality, it's nearly impossible for the spouse to find a low-risk investment that will generate income in excess of inflation. Also, when Richard was formulating a plan for Melissa to receive the income each year, he probably didn't think it would be at 2 percent.

Principal

You aren't required to make any distributions of principal from the trust to your spouse. However, I find that the Richards of this world usually want to provide for the Melissas, but they're concerned about the money being used for Melissa's own children or next husband instead of going back to Richard's own children.

So how might Richard want to provide principal to Melissa?

- *No principal distributions.* I most often see this with second marriages that happen later in life, when both spouses are already financially established and each spouse's children are adults. With this option, each spouse essentially has an annuity from the assets of the first spouse to die; if the second spouse needs any other money, they have to spend their own assets.

- *Distributions for health only.* Even in marriages later in life, spouses recognize that health care costs can leave a person entirely vulnerable. In this case, one spouse may create a marital trust from which the surviving spouse receives all the income, and the principal can be used in very limited circumstances, such as to support a health need.

- *Distributions for health, maintenance, and support.* The inquiry becomes, "What is needed to maintain the spouse's standard of living?" A corollary question is, "Does the spouse need to exhaust their own assets before the assets in a marital trust are available?" You'll generally find language in a will that indicates that the trustee "must," "may," or "may not" take into consideration the spouse's other assets in making a distribution. You can start to see more possible disagreements. Melissa may believe that her maintenance and support require a $200,000 yearly household budget. Noah and Chloe may disagree, arguing that their father always lived frugally. This difference in what the trustee can and can't use funds for might bring the spouse and children to court.

- *Distributions in the discretion of the trustee.* Here, the trustee is free to use assets in the trust for the spouse's benefit as the trustee sees fit. Expansive language can be added, such as, "I direct my trustee to provide for my spouse for any need she may have, even to the extent of exhausting the principal of the trust." From the spouse's perspective, though, what happens if the trustee doesn't exercise the discretion to make distributions, and the spouse needs the money? Are they then being placed in a situation where they have to take the trustee to court to demand distributions?

Let's Get Real   My suggestions aren't exhaustive. As long as spouses receive the income, you can distribute principal in practically any way you can imagine. Want your spouse to have an allowance each month? Not a problem; add it in. Want to encourage your spouse to keep the family home? Give financial incentives in the trust. Want to end the trust if the spouse remarries? *Buzz.* That one won't work; your spouse must get the income for life. Other than that, think about what feels right to you, and talk to your estate-planning attorney.

Trustee

The success or failure of making the marital trust work for both the spouse today, and the children as ultimate beneficiaries, revolves around who is acting as the trustee. You could name your spouse the sole trustee of the marital trust. However, if your intention is that the trust only be used after the spouse's assets are exhausted, or only to bolster the spouse's assets as needed, this may be a bit like asking the fox to guard the henhouse. What if in our example Melissa had other children from a prior marriage? If Melissa is the sole trustee of the marital trust, she could use the marital trust for her needs, even to the point of exhausting it, while saving and investing her individual assets to pass to her children.

You could name one of your adult children as the trustee of the marital trust. They would then be making all the investment decisions in order to generate the income for the spouse as well as the distribution decisions to the spouse. However, this situation can be equally tense: if the child is an eventual beneficiary of the trust, they may, consciously or unconsciously, try to keep the money in the trust because it will benefit them in the end.

The best solution might be to name the spouse and an adult child as co-trustees of the trust, or name a third party. Both foster an environment where competing points of view—the spouse's and the children's—are considered in any investment or distribution decisions.

Unitrust: The Total Return Approach

The unitrust is a sorely underutilized tool (so much so that you may never have heard about it before reading this book). It's an excellent solution to the tension between spouses and children when it comes to how a marital trust is invested and distributed.

Accept for a moment my assertion that if you invest for income, you're limiting growth, and if you invest for growth, you're limiting income. It's a stalemate. How can you satisfy both the current beneficiary spouse and the eventual beneficiary children? The unitrust breaks that stalemate with the principle (punny, yes?) that the total return matters, not the income or principal.[2]

A marital trust designed as a unitrust tosses the distinction between income and principal out the window. Instead, the unitrust provides that that the spouse is entitled to a percentage of the December 31 balance of the trust

---

[2] A unitrust can also be an excellent way to structure an inheritance for children so they can receive a consistent stream of money from the assets. The bulk of the inheritance remains in trust for long-term growth, with all the asset-protection benefits.

each year (typically 3–5 percent). Let's say Richard sets up Melissa's marital trust as a unitrust with a 5 percent payout. Each year, Melissa will be entitled to the greater of (1) the actual income generated by the marital trust or (2) 5 percent of the marital trust. We've changed the paradigm. Now, the more there is, the more everybody gets. With a unitrust, the trustee can look at the market as it exists at that time and make the best overall investment allocation without being constricted by an artificial divide of trust income and trust principal.

If Richard structures the marital trust as a unitrust, Melissa, Noah, and Chloe will all benefit from the same thing: a greater amount of principal in the trust. To the extent the balance grows, Melissa receives 5 percent of a larger number, and Noah and Chloe will receive more money upon Melissa's death. If the balance goes down, all three share in the loss. The unitrust bridges the divide.

You could also layer into the unitrust the ability for the trustee to make additional distributions of principal to the spouse in the same ways described earlier.

Other Governing Documents

When it comes to second marriages and estate planning, you might be limited by more than the tax laws, the amount of your assets, and your imagination. Your plan may need to satisfy contractual obligations.

Do you have a separation or divorce agreement with any prior spouse? If so, you could have guaranteed your children or former spouse a certain amount of money to backstop child support or alimony in the event of your death. This could have been addressed through a requirement to purchase life insurance. You might also have agreed as to who could be named as guardian, and so on. You need to ask your estate planning attorney to review any separation or divorce agreement to see if any items in that agreement restrict your ability to design your estate plan.

Do you have a prenuptial agreement? Such an agreement can break the right of one spouse to inherit the assets of the other spouse upon death. In this case, you would be free to exclude your spouse from your estate plan. Other times, prenuptial agreements are drafted to guarantee the less-wealthy spouse a certain interest in the estate of the wealthier spouse. That minimum needs to be reflected in the estate plan. A failure to provide for that minimum will lead to litigation in which the spouse is sure to prevail because you have a contractual obligation to provide them with the assets.[3]

---

[3] Unmarried and same-sex couples might have a cohabitation agreement. If this is case, add it to the list of documents your estate-planning attorney needs to review.

▓ **Let's Get Real**   Any action you take after the prenuptial agreement is signed is likely to stand regardless of what the prenuptial agreement says. I had a client who entered into a "she gets nothing" type of prenuptial agreement. However, during the marriage, the husband added the wife as a joint owner on bank accounts, beneficiary on some IRAs, and eventually as tenants by the entireties on their residence. The children, who were beneficiaries under the will, challenged the assets passing to the spouse by operation of law, arguing that under the prenuptial agreement she was to get nothing. The children lost because the husband's actions after the agreement was made had priority.

Finally, were trusts previously created for the benefit of either spouse? This might be the case if one spouse had been widowed and a trust was created for their benefit from their prior spouse. That trust could provide that significant assets will pass directly to the children from that marriage, which means you may feel confident leaving more assets to your spouse.

Retirement Accounts

When you're trying to figure out which assets will go to your spouse versus your children, don't forget that retirement accounts are special. I've talked about this before, but the fact of the matter is that inheriting a retirement account is more attractive for a spouse than it is for children. The spouse can roll the account into their own IRA and defer distributions until their retirement age of $70\frac{1}{2}$. In contrast, if your kids inherit the account, they must start taking minimum distributions right away. If you're thinking, "OK, I'll name my spouse as my IRA beneficiary and give my brokerage account to the kids," bear in mind that retirement accounts are a constantly shifting asset. During the accumulation phase, they tend to grow larger and larger because you add, invest, and don't spend. During the distribution phase, because you're required to take out more each year after $70\frac{1}{2}$, the account could be entirely depleted. You may want to keep an eye on the retirement account in proportion to the rest of your assets to make sure your spouse and children continue to receive the "right amount."

As a non-probate asset, a retirement plan calls for careful coordination with the rest of your estate plan. If you name your spouse as beneficiary of the retirement plan and indicate that they're to receive 50 percent of the assets passing under your will, then your spouse will end up with *more* than 50 percent of your entire estate. This may be OK with you. But if it's not, you need to make sure your estate plan indicates that whatever amount your spouse receives under your will is adjusted based on the retirement account (or any other non-probate asset they might be receiving).

One other issue is whether the retirement account will go to your spouse outright or be held in trust. If it passes outright to your spouse, then your spouse has the right to direct who gets any remaining balance of the retirement account upon their later death. If your retirement account is one of your largest assets, and your intention is for any unused assets to pass to your children, this may not be an attractive solution. As an alternative, it's possible to name a trust as the beneficiary of a retirement account. *Caution!* This must be very carefully done. Only certain specially drafted types of trusts can be beneficiaries of a retirement account without triggering income taxes.[4] Here are two options:

- *Conduit trust.* Here, any retirement account distribution received by the marital trust is simply paid out directly to the spouse. If a $1000 required minimum distribution from a retirement account is paid into a marital trust designed as a conduit trust, the marital trust in turn automatically distributes that $1000 to the spouse. This is the most straightforward way of dealing with having a retirement account in trust for the spouse. Any required minimum distribution or other distribution from the retirement account passes to your spouse; but any amount remaining in the retirement account upon your spouse's death passes to your children.

- *Accumulation trust.* In this type of trust, the amount of the required minimum distribution (except for any portion of attributed income) is held in the marital trust. Recall that trusts pay more income tax than individuals do. Because 100 percent of the retirement account is likely to be subject to income tax, more income taxes are paid with this methodology than with a conduit trust. However, the dollars (other than any income element) stay in the trust, to be eventually transferred to your children.

---

[4] Most any trust can be the beneficiary of retirement assets. The concept isn't limited to a marital trust. In fact, I often layer these provisions into trusts for children. For many couples, the retirement plan is one of their largest assets. It makes no sense to design a great inheritance structure in the will but then leave the largest asset to the kids outright. I use the accumulation trust approach in the children's trust and leave it up to the trustee to determine how much of a retirement account distribution to pass to a child.

▦ **Let's Get Real**   Naming a trust as the beneficiary of a retirement account isn't DIY planning. It's not even something you can fully rely on your financial advisor to handle. I often find that financial advisors haven't been educated on the nuances of trusts as beneficiaries of retirement plans. If a retirement plan makes up a large portion of your estate, you need to speak to an experienced estate planning attorney in your state.

Is There Enough to Go Around?

The fact of the matter is that there may not be enough money in your estate to make everybody happy. You could be concerned that if you leave anything to your children upon your death, your spouse may not have sufficient assets to live on. Conversely, you may feel that your children are entitled to a minimum amount because of promises you made to them.

The solution? Consider the irrevocable life insurance trust (ILIT). I know I keep going back to this, but being able to add tax-free dollars to your estate can solve a lot of problems. First, you can create new dollars to allow you to meet your goals for both your children and your spouse. Second, in the event that your children and your spouse don't get along, you can separate their interests in your estate. You can name the children the sole beneficiaries of the ILIT and your spouse the sole beneficiary under the will. The kids get their money in trust under the terms of the trust; your spouse gets everything else in a marital trust.

▦ **Let's Get Real**   When you have a blended family, you have very different histories and relationships with your spouse versus your children. Even if it's your intention to leave everything to one or the other, bear in mind that you have a relationship with each. I always encourage my clients who are leaving everything to their spouse to at least make some token bequest to their children at their death to recognize them in their estate plan, so the children feel special and important during a time of loss and confusion.

18

Planning Guide for the Family Business

When you own your own business and you meet your demise, not only has your family lost you, but your business has lost its leader. Can your business be liquidated or continued in a manner that maximizes its value to your family? Have you created a situation where someone has the know-how and skill to replace you? If that's not possible, can the business be sold? On the upside, tax laws love a family business, so your tax burden might be deferred or reduced.

Chapter Brief   Understand what your business is worth and how you can turn that value into cash for your family. During the time before the business is cashed out, who can operate it? When you're leaving your business to one of your children, don't forget to address the others. Estate tax laws favor family businesses and will allow you to reduce taxes and get a low-interest loan to pay them.

When I talk about the *family business* in this chapter, I'm using the term to embrace a bunch of different types of business interest. One is a small business, which you and maybe your spouse own and operate. A second is a closely held business, where you're an active participant, you may have one or more partners, and you earn some or all of your living from the business. For my purposes, *family business* also includes any passive investment you have in a closely held business, because the liquidation and tax issues may be similar. The *family business* also encompasses real property, such as a farm, ranch, or rental property from which you make money.

The family business can be structured as a sole proprietorship, corporation, partnership, or limited liability company (LLC). If it's real property, it could be held in one name, joint names with rights of survivorship, or joint names as tenants in common. Whatever form it takes, the family business is a unique asset that can't just be lumped into everything else passing through your estate plan.

Liquidating the Business

Whether your financial statement says on paper that your business is worth $100,000 or $10 million, my question is, "How do you translate the 'worth' of your business to cash upon your death?" Consider that, as a result of your death, your business may just have lost 30 percent or more of its value, given your key role in operating it. If business operations can continue, does your spouse or beneficiary really want to be involved in running your business? And even if they do, do they have the skill set to do so?

The first step is knowing what your family could get *in cash* from your business. The degree of business succession planning you've done directly affects the value:

- *Liquidation value.* If you don't have a plan for who would buy your business, this is what your family will get. Ask your accountant to ballpark the net dollars you would receive if you liquidated everything. Be prepared to say, "Ouch." Depending on the type of assets the business has and how leveraged you are, your business liquidation value could be close to zero. This is what your family would receive if you were hit by a bus. If you don't like the number, keep reading.

- *Buy-sell agreement.* If you have partners, then you're all in the same situation. Your partner may be able to continue the business without you, but they don't want to be partners with your beneficiaries any more than your beneficiaries want to be partners with them. A good buy-sell agreement provides a formula to determine the value of the business and the payout schedule of that value. It also offers some security for your family so your partner can't just go out and leverage the whole business or run it into the ground, leaving your family with nothing.

- *Employee purchase.* You may have one or more key employees who would be interested in purchasing the business in the event of your death. After all, they're in the best position to develop value from continued operations.[1]

- *Friendly competitor or key customer.* Unlike the liquidation value, with these types of purchasers your business may have a going-concern value, which will increase the bottom line dollars to your family.

- *Family succession planning.* It may be that you don't plan to sell the business, but instead plan to have one of your children take it over. If that's the case, what's available for the rest of your family while this child is learning the ropes and reinvesting in the business to keep it on firm financial ground?

■ **Let's Get Real** Have an exit strategy in mind for your business? Great. Have you put it on paper? Probably not. Let me paint a picture for you. When you die, your family is feeling insecure and wants cash to avoid their assets being tied up with your partners. Your business partners are concerned about how they can continue, and they want to keep dollars in the business for a rainy day. Add a lack of communication between these polar-opposite positions because everyone is looking inward at their issues. Stir in grief and anger, and then ask everyone to agree on a value and who gets paid what and when. Watch the explosion take place. It's not fair to your business or to your family to put them in this situation, which can be totally avoided if you invest the time entering into a buy-sell agreement or other arrangement in advance. Call your business attorney today to put your exit strategy on paper.

Insuring the Business's Estate Value

Let's say you go through all of the scenarios I've described, and none of them will give you enough dollars to replace the income or value your family is losing if you're no longer here to operate the business. Consider replacing the lost value with life insurance:

- *Family-owned life insurance.* If you're a sole proprietor or your partners aren't on board with prioritizing estate-planning issues, then you need to do it yourself. In that case, think about creating an irrevocable life insurance trust (ILIT) and

---

[1] If you have a group of employees interested in purchasing the business, they may be able to do so on a tax-advantaged basis through an employee stock option plan (ESOP). Reach out to your business attorney if this seems like a possible exit strategy for you.

funding it with a life insurance policy sufficient to replace the anticipated shortfall from the business value in the event of your death. If the business ends up being liquidated for more than you thought, it's gravy to your family. If not, you know the minimum you're providing them.

- *Business- or partner-owned life insurance.* If you have a buy-sell agreement, you may make the business decision to insure the agreement by either (1) the business purchasing insurance on the owners or (2) the partners purchasing insurance on each other. Mechanically, you're agreeing to sell your business interest to the party that has the insurance. That party will pay your estate some or all of the insurance and then the balance of the value over time. This is attractive because your business partners get your share of the business (which your family likely doesn't want anyway), and your family gets cash immediately, thus reducing their risk of not receiving the full value of the business if your partners aren't successful after your death.

Operating the Business

Now that you know what value your family might get out of your business, the next step is to look at how the business will operate if you get hit by a bus.

Legal Authority

Who has the legal authority to act on behalf of your business? If you have a business entity, such as a corporation, limited partnership, or LLC, rules govern who has the ability to act on behalf of the company. Some of these rules are statutory defaults (such as that a corporation will have both directors and officers), and others are set by agreements between the parties (such as what the members' relationship to each other is, as outlined in the operating agreement). If it's just you, your executor or trustee would be in charge.

You need to examine your business's governing documents (certificate of incorporation, certificate of formation, by-laws, operating agreement, partnership agreement, and so on) and determine who would have the ability to act on behalf of the entity if you weren't here. For example, if you named your HR person as an officer because the bank told you that you had to have more than one, but you know they could never deal with the financial end of the business, you should carefully consider each officer's role. Similarly, an LLC operating agreement may provide that in the event of your death your estate loses all management authority. In that case, are you comfortable with your partner making all the decisions? Or should the agreement be changed so your executor maintains voting and operational authority?

In certain situations, your fiduciaries will be able to step into an overarching managerial role. For example, your attorney-in-fact, executor, or trustee could exercise your rights to vote stock in a corporation for a slate of directors, or be involved with other "big picture" questions. You may want to consider naming somebody with experience with your business as a fiduciary or co-fiduciary over your business assets, and naming your spouse as the fiduciary over your other assets.

For a business where you're the only owner, you may want to take steps now to make sure your spouse or other family member will have legal authority to act. This might be accomplished by naming them as an officer or director of the business, or a manager of the entity. I would also suggest that you consider giving that person signatory authority at the bank in the event they may have to carry on the business at some point.

Practical Authority

Making sure somebody has the legal authority to act is only the first part of the question. The second is creating some kind of succession planning so whomever you name to act knows what they need to do. After all, how will your fiduciary maintain the value of the business if they have no idea how to operate it?

You should sit down with your fiduciary and any other key family members and educate them about what they need to know to operate the business on an interim basis. What are the immediate steps that need to be taken? Does payroll need to be addressed, or are there immediate orders to fulfill, or mortgage, rent, or other debt payments, in order to maintain the business?

Who are the key advisors of the business (your accountant, business attorney, banker, business consultant)? Does your fiduciary know who these people are and what their role is in your business and have their contact information? Your accountant is likely your best resource about how to move forward with maintaining the operation of the business in the face of your death. If you don't agree, you may want to evaluate your relationship with them.

Who are the key employees your fiduciary can rely on? Who could step up and handle the day-to-day operations of the company? What about a person who can maintain customer relations and continue to obtain sales? Are there limitations of your employees that your fiduciary should know about?

Who are your key vendors? Educate your fiduciary about their role in your business, the lead time needed, and their contact information. The ability to work with your top vendors may be the key to keeping the company afloat until new management can take over.

What liabilities exist? Your fiduciary needs to know whom the business owes, as well the payment terms. This would include a mortgage, a line of credit, rent, equipment leases, and loans to investors. Summarize whom each liability is owed to, the principal amount, interest, payment terms, any personal guarantees, and where the documents are stored.

What additional resources are needed long-term for the business to thrive? If the fiduciary should be looking to hire a new manager or president, what skills will that person need? What are your growth or expansion strategies? What have you considered in the past and found isn't a fit for your business to grow moving forward?

The essential point is that your fiduciary needs to be involved in understanding your business operations *now*. Once you die, it's too late for them to learn from you. Instead, you're leaving them scrambling and probably making a lot of really expensive bad decisions purely through lack of knowledge. This doesn't mean you need to bring the fiduciary into the business every single day and train them on every single job. Instead, as part of your estate plan, invest the time in giving your fiduciary the tools to maintain the business until whatever exit strategy you put in place is achieved.

■ **Let's Get Real** Does your business owe you money? For lots of owners, that's a big yes, because you've loaned dollars over the years and not taken them back out. It's sort of like a rainy-day savings fund: "I can always take it out when I need it." You need to paper these loans. First, if your family doesn't know about the loan, how will they know to collect it after you're gone? Second, when you make a loan to the company, you may have the opportunity to secure it with business assets. If a business fails, secured loans (like a mortgage and some equipment leases) are paid before all the other creditors. Again, make notes of these ideas, and call your business attorney.

Unequal Bequests to Children

If one or more of your children work in the family business, and your goal is to pass it to them, what are you going to do about your other kids?

The foundation of designing a plan to transfer your business to a child is having a real appraisal of the value of business in hand. By *real* I mean something you pay for, not what your balance sheet says or your best guess. Yes, this means you'll have to cough up a couple thousand dollars to get this done. Once you have a firm number, you can compare strategies to transfer the business to the children who are involved in it but potentially compensate the children who aren't. After looking at the appraisal, you might even decide to make a gift of some or all of the business now, or to do a part gift/part sale by selling the business to a child for discounted sale price.[2]

If you're earning your living from your business, it's likely to form the bulk of your estate. Join me as I sit down with Patrick, whose total estate is $4 million. His restaurant and its building make up $2.5 million of that. Of his three kids, Nathan is the executive chef and works hand in hand with Patrick. His other kids, Austin and Julia, aren't involved in the business. If Patrick just says "The restaurant and building go to Nathan," his remaining estate is only $1.5 million. Out of that, estate taxes (which could be up to $1,495,000) need to be paid. Presumably Patrick wants Julia and Austin to divide more than $5,000. Here's what I would talk to Patrick about:

- *The inequity may not be a problem.* If Nathan has contributed to the value of the business, it may be perfectly fair to Patrick that Nathan receives more of the estate than his other children. If this is the case, Patrick needs to be careful with the tax-allocation clause, so everybody pays their proportionate share of taxes (Nathan on $2.5 million of value and Julia and Austin on $750,000 each.)

- *Nathan purchases the business with a credit.* Leave each child an equal share of the estate, and Nathan can use his share as a credit toward the purchase of the business. For example, if each child's after-tax share of the estate was $835,000, then Nathan would be allowed to apply his share as a credit against the value of the business and purchase it for $1,665,000 instead of $2.5 million. The key to this type of planning is a solid valuation. Patrick should provide in his will exactly how the valuation will take place (an appraiser selected by the accountant, perhaps) so nobody is trying to sway the value of the business up or down. Also bear in mind that if the purchase is structured so that Nathan puts some money down but owes the balance of the purchase price to the estate to be paid over time pursuant to a promissory note, Julia and Austin are hostage to Nathan's success in running

---

[2] Looking for some ideas to leave the business to your kids as cheaply as possible? Go back to Chapter 11, "Advanced Tax Strategies." Then call your lawyer and accountant together for a meeting about your goals and ideas.

the business. If Nathan runs the business into the ground, Julia and Austin will also suffer because the promissory note will never be repaid to them.[3]

- *Divide the business from the real estate.* Although the restaurant needs the real estate because that is where it operates, the building has value regardless of the tenant. If the business is worth $1 million and the real estate $1.5 million, Patrick could leave the business to Nathan (whether he equalizes with the other kids or not) but have everyone share in the real estate. To protect the status quo, I would have Patrick put the real estate into a separate entity (an LLC perhaps) and have that entity enter into a long-term lease with the restaurant with a formula for adjusting the rent based on market conditions. As long as Nathan pays the rent, the restaurant stays in the building. If the business goes south, the LLC can evict the restaurant and bring in another tenant, so Julia's and Austin's interests are considered as well.

- *Gift the business to Nathan.* Take advantage of tax-minimization strategies to give the business to Nathan today at a lower cost than in the future. Patrick could provide a specific bequest in his will to Julia and Austin to equalize some or all of what Nathan received during life.

- *ILIT.* Take advantage of the ever-versatile ILIT and leave the business to Nathan, but purchase an insurance policy for approximately the same value as the business to pass to Julia and Austin. Nathan gets the business, the government gets its taxes, and Julia and Austin get an amount Patrick considers fair. I like this approach because Julia and Austin have no continuing interest in the successes of the business. If Nathan helps Patrick grow it more, then he inherits a more valuable asset. If he isn't a good manager, he inherits something worth less, but Julia and Austin aren't affected.

Real Stories from Around My Conference Table   Businesses involve risk. The child who gets the business at a discount or gets more of the estate is inheriting a double-edged sword. I have seen a daughter who maintained and grew the business to 10 times its worth. Why should her

---

[3] If Patrick wanted to reward Nathan for all his hard work over the years, he could layer into this approach the ability for Nathan to purchase the business for a discount from the appraised price.

siblings share in something they put no effort into (not that it stopped them from suing and saying dad was incompetent, notwithstanding the multimillion dollar empire he built)? I have met with a son who was in bankruptcy four years after the father died and then complained that the father should have left life insurance to him instead of his sisters. There go the holiday get-togethers. All this resentment because mom and dad weren't being "fair." It's OK to be unfair. The best way to defuse this situation is to be up front with all your children about to who will get what and why you created the estate plan you did. Surprises lead to hurt feelings, which can lead to lawyers and litigation.

Tax Laws Benefiting the Family Business or Land

I'm sure you've seen those ads about how estate tax laws ruin the family business or force the family to sell the farm. Fortunately, that's just not the case. First of all, only about 2 percent of American families are subject to the estate tax. As you can see from the hundreds of pages devoted to the topic in this book, there are lots of ways to reduce and/or minimize estate taxes. But even if you don't take any action to reduce or minimize taxes, the government provides tax breaks that allow the family business or farm to pass to the next generation in a tax advantaged manner.

Section 6166 Estate Tax Deferral

If your estate meets the requirements, it can pay part of your estate tax bill over time at incredibly favorable interest rates. Basically, this means the US government gives you a loan in the amount of the portion of the estate tax associated with the family business or farm. The whole purpose of this code section is to allow you to pay the tax over time and *not* be forced to sell the family business or farm. So what does the loan look like?

- To qualify, you need to be a US citizen, and the value of the family business or farm must be 35 percent or more of the value of your overall taxable estate.

- You can only defer the portion of the estate tax associated with the family business. If the family business makes up 60 percent of your estate, you can defer 60 percent of the tax. The deferred portion of the estate tax can be paid over 10 years. And get this: you can defer the first payment of principal for 5 years, giving you 15 years to pay the tax!

- A portion of the interest can be at the incredible rate of 2 percent (try getting that from your local bank branch). The rest of the interest will be at 45 percent of what the IRS is then charging on overdue taxes (another steal—the current interest rate for underpayment of tax is around 3 percent).

- If the business is sold outside the family before the estate taxes are paid, they become due upon the sale of the business.

Remember: the family business must account for 35 percent or more of your taxable estate to take advantage of section 6166. This might mean you don't want to give away too much of the business now.

Special-Use Valuation for Farms and Ranches

But wait—there's more! It's great to be able to defer the tax, but it's even better to value real estate at a lower number in the first place.

Generally speaking, when something is valued for estate tax purposes, it must be valued at its highest and best use. This is particularly problematic for farmers and ranchers, because your property might be much more valuable to a developer looking to raise the next Wal-Mart or McMansion development than to another farmer or rancher. If a developer would pay $2 million but another farmer or rancher only $1.2 million, then the general rule is that the property is valued at $2 million for estate tax purposes.

However, the government is trying really hard not to put family farms and ranches out of business just because somebody died. They know land isn't liquid. If certain requirements are met, under code section 2023A, real property (your real estate holdings) will be valued at its actual use, not at its highest and best use. Does your real estate qualify?

- The real estate must pass to a *qualified heir* via gift, inheritance, or a purchase from the estate. Qualified heirs include parents, descendants, and spouses of descendants.

- You or a family member needs to have worked on or with the real property in five of the eight years leading up to the transfer.

- The family business must make up at least 50 percent of your taxable estate, and the real estate included within that must make up at least 25 percent of your assets.

- The qualified heir needs to agree with the IRS that if the property is sold or transferred outside of the family within 10 years of when the property was transferred, or if the property ceases being used as a family business, farm, or ranch, they will pay the estate taxes based on the "highest and best use" value, not the special valuation they have been taking advantage of.

• The amount of the value by which the property can be reduced is limited by law. In 2012, the dollar limit is $1,040,000.

See? Even if you don't do any planning, the government gives family businesses a break. Not that I recommend that course of action!

19

Planning Guide for Noncitizens

Tax law favors married couples, except if your spouse isn't a US citizen. In that case, the United States is very concerned that your spouse, after your death, will run back to their home country, and it will lose its chance to tax your assets. Your planning needs to focus on understanding and complying with the rules as much as the exceptions and ways to avoid them.

▓ Chapter Brief The unlimited marital deduction from estate taxes and gift taxes doesn't apply to transfers made to a noncitizen spouse. Instead, you must take care in your planning to establish a qualified domestic trust (QDOT) and understand the gift tax limitations. Different planning techniques can be used in advance to minimize the negative tax consequences.

Remember all that stuff about how there's no tax between spouses when the first spouse dies? Well, if your spouse isn't a US citizen, ignore what I said earlier and read on.

Why? If your spouse is a US citizen, then from the government's perspective it's OK to defer the estate tax. After all, Uncle Sam will get his bite of the apple when the second spouse dies, and the estate might have even grown by then. However, if your spouse isn't a US citizen, they could take all the money you left them and flee back to wherever they came from, and the US government wouldn't get any tax dollars when they died. From the US Treasury perspective, this isn't an acceptable outcome.

What Can Go Estate-Tax-Free to a Noncitizen Spouse?

Now, it's not as if every dollar you leave your noncitizen spouse will be taxed. To illustrate the lay of the land, I'm going to introduce you to Joe and Marguerite. They met when Marguerite was visiting New York and are happily married with two children. Marguerite is proud to be a French citizen, is raising their children to be bilingual, and often visits her family in Europe. Their combined assets are about $2.5 million dollars.

When I first sit down with Joe and Marguerite, I tell them they need to pretty much throw out everything they might've heard about estate planning, because they have a unique situation. Anything Marguerite leaves to Joe will follow the customary rules, because she is US resident and as such subject to US estate tax rules. However, anything Joe leaves to Marguerite could be taxed upon his death, notwithstanding that he is survived by his spouse.

I start the conversation with what's not subject to tax: the federal estate tax exemption amount. This is the amount, scheduled to be $1 million in 2013, which you can leave to anyone and not pay estate tax. This remains true if Joe leaves this amount to Marguerite. Unfortunately, this still leaves $1.5 million subject to estate tax on Joe's death.

Qualified Domestic Trust (QDOT)

If Joe doesn't do anything, then the $1.5 million going to Marguerite after his death will be subject to estate tax. This would mean about $210,000 less will be available to support Marguerite and the children going forward (it might have been nice to put that toward college tuition instead of taxes).

All is not lost. The US tax code has a methodology to put Marguerite in a position similar to that of a US citizen spouse. This is done by Joe's leaving any assets in excess of the federal estate tax exemption amount to Marguerite in a qualified domestic trust (QDOT, pronounced "q-dot"). The QDOT is governed by code section 2056A. It's a marital trust with additional special requirements intended to ensure that the US government gets its estate tax dollars:

- The spouse must be the sole beneficiary of the QDOT, and all the income must be paid to them at least annually. This is the same as with any other marital trust.

- At least one trustee must be an individual US citizen or US trust company. This means Marguerite could be a co-trustee, but the other trustee must be US citizen or bank.

- If the QDOT is funded with more than $2 million of assets, then there must be a bank as at least one of the trustees. The alternative is funding a bond to secure the money in the QDOT. From a practical perspective, the expense of the bank as trustee will be less than that of the bond.

- The trust must be a taxpayer in a US state or the District of Columbia. No offshore trusts are allowed if you want the benefit of the marital deduction.

- The big requirement: Any distribution of principal must pay estate tax at the time the distribution is made. This means if Marguerite needs a $100,000 distribution from the trust, the trustee must pay the estate tax on that distribution. Remember, a marital trust merely defers the estate tax; it doesn't eliminate it. So, if the estate tax on the $100,000 distribution was $35,000, Marguerite would receive only $65,000. If she truly needed $100,000, she would have to have a distribution of approximately $154,000 to net $100,000.

- Exception to the big requirement: If the distribution is for *hardship*, the estate tax does *not* need to be paid on the distribution. A hardship distribution is one that is made for an immediate and substantial financial need of health, education, maintenance, or support for the surviving spouse or any person the surviving spouse is legally obligated to support (minor children). In making a hardship distribution, the trustee has to consider whether any other assets are reasonably available to the surviving spouse (such as marketable securities, certificates of deposit, cash, and so on).

Annual and Lifetime Gifts

"OK," say Joe and Marguerite. "That QDOT thing doesn't sound really attractive. How about we just put all our assets in Marguerite's name?" Well, the unlimited gift tax exemption between spouses doesn't apply to noncitizen spouses either. Whereas two US citizen spouses could happily transfer $100 million dollars to each other six times a year without a gift tax consequence, Joe is limited in the amount of money he can give Marguerite. Joe has an annual gift tax exclusion amount of $139,000 per year (adjusted for inflation) that he can transfer to Marguerite. Any amount over that would be a taxable gift, utilizing Joe's lifetime exemption amount.

Tax Treaties

Estate planning with noncitizen spouses is even more complicated by the fact that the United States has estate tax and gift tax treaties with certain other countries that change the rules.

Why are these tax treaties important? Let's say Joe dies and Marguerite continues to own real estate in France. When she dies, the real estate, together with all her other assets, will pass to her children. Remember, as a US resident, any assets Marguerite owns worldwide are subject to US estate tax. If France has an estate tax, and there is no tax treaty between the United States and France, then Marguerite's land could conceivably be subject to (1) a tax in France because she owns French real estate and is a French citizen and (2) a tax on the same assets in the United States because she's a US resident. Taxes are bad enough the first time around; can you imagine having to pay twice on the same property?

Tax treaties between countries are designed to eliminate this double taxation. The United States does have a tax treaty with France, but it doesn't have tax treaties with all countries in the world.

Also, tax treaties can give the nonresident spouse additional benefits. For example, in the tax treaty between the United States and France, a noncitizen spouse who is a French citizen is entitled to a limited marital deduction (so a certain amount of dollars in excess of the estate tax exemption amount can pass tax free to the French citizen surviving spouse), which may avoid the QDOT in a smaller estate.

Planning Alternatives

Most people don't find a QDOT something they want to do. So how can you minimize the consequences of the fact that a noncitizen spouse doesn't get preferential treatment under the US tax code?

- *Irrevocable life insurance trust (ILIT)*. Remember when I said that an ILIT can solve a lot of problems? This is a case in point. Continuing the earlier example, if Joe purchases insurance owned by an ILIT and names Marguerite as the beneficiary of the ILIT, then the death benefit can pass to Marguerite without the restrictions of the QDOT because the insurance proceeds aren't included in Joe's taxable estate. He can leave the death benefit to Marguerite outright or in trust.

- *US citizen.* Marguerite could become a US citizen. For some clients, the ability to get the benefit of US estate tax savings is enough to tip the scales in favor of US citizenship. Furthermore, the QDOT can provide that, should Marguerite become a US citizen before the estate tax return is filed, the QDOT restrictions will drop off.

- *Gifting.* Joe is allowed to make a gift of $139,000 tax-free to Marguerite each year. There are no restrictions on the assets Marguerite leaves to Joe. The more of their joint assets Marguerite has in her own name, the fewer assets are subject to the QDOT restrictions. However, there are practical problems with this method. What if the couple divorces? What if Joe wants to spend the money? Or what if most of Joe's assets are in a retirement plan?

- *Unitrust.* Instead of providing that Marguerite is entitled to all the income each year, design the QDOT as a unitrust that provides 3–5 percent of the principal amount each year. This would allow Marguerite to receive, potentially, a greater amount of return on investment because (1) there's not a bias toward investing in income-producing properties assets, which may have low growth potential, and (2) Marguerite isn't punished by a low interest-rate environment such as the one we've been dealing with.[1]

- *Illiquid assets.* The hardship exception to paying estate tax on principal distributions from the QDOT revolves around the spouse both having a need and not having other liquid assets reasonably available to satisfy that need. One plan might be for Marguerite to ensure that her assets are potentially invested in illiquid investments, whereas the assets in the QDOT are in more liquid investments.

---

[1] For more details on the unitrust, flip back to Chapter 17, "Planning Guide for Second Marriages," where I go over the elements of the unitrust and its benefits in detail.

Let's Get Real What does all this mean for bi-national couples from a practical perspective? If neither of you is a US citizen, you need to work with an estate planning attorney who not only has experience dealing with US estate planning but also has the expertise to address the international tax law issues. Ask the attorney about their experience with a QDOT during the interview process—their knowledge should be at least equal to yours after reading this!

20

Planning Guide for Your Parents

More and more families are finding their parents financially dependent on them with the economic downturn and the high costs of living and health care. Special care needs to be taken in leaving assets to parents so they get the benefit of those assets without any government claims.

Chapter Brief If your parents are financially well off, a straight gift of dollars may exacerbate their own estate tax issues. If your parents aren't financially well off, a straight gift of dollars may disqualify them from necessary long-term care benefits. Wrap any gifts to your parents in a trust to avoid unintended consequences.

Adding to the Tax Burden

For those of you reading this book who are younger and whose parents are healthy, vibrant, and, quite frankly, more financially secure than you are, I urge you to consider the tax results of leaving your assets to your parents. If your parents have a taxable estate and you name them as your primary beneficiaries, whatever assets you have will merely add to their taxable estate. Instead, I suggest you look at who your parents' beneficiaries are (after all, these are the people who will get the money anyway at the end of the day) and think about leaving your assets to those people instead of to your parents. Regardless, have a conversation with your parents if this is what you intend to do. You may find that your parents say, "No, Charlie, it doesn't make any sense for you to leave the assets to us. Instead, what about your nieces and nephews?" Or they may be grateful for your largess.

This chapter focuses on parents who are older and either not entirely independent now or may not be in independent the future. I'm targeting families who are concerned about providing financial support for their parents. Remember, the person you're concerned about doesn't have to be a parent. I've engaged in planning like this for the benefit of siblings who were not as financially well off, as well as for grandparents, aunts, and uncles.

Shifting Care Relationship

For most of this book I've talked about how to leave your assets to your spouse, partner, and members of younger generations. I've even touched on charities. What I haven't talked about is the growing portion of the American population where adult children are supporting their parents.

Why is this happening? This is my totally unscientific opinion, but here are the trends I see. First, people are living longer but not necessarily better. I have a large number of clients in their 80s and 90s who wouldn't be able to live independently without the assistance of their children. Second, nobody born in the 1920s or 1930s ever envisioned nursing homes costing $10,000 or more a month and eating into their assets. So, we end up with a situation where the Greatest Generation and their younger siblings did everything they were told to do (worked hard, saved, bought a house, sent their kids to college), but they just don't have enough money to provide for themselves. Third, and on the flipside, some of you may have parents who've become victim to the credit-card craze, and they simply live beyond their means. They may be aware that someday there will be a reckoning, but they keep putting it off until it becomes your problem.

All this has been brought to the forefront in recent years as downward pressure on Social Security has left the amount flat or growing slowly combined with astronomical increases in healthcare costs. Any seniors who were in the stock market could have lost between 20 percent and 40 percent of their assets in the market crash, and they may not have time within their life expectancy to make that up (especially if they sat out the 2011–12 run-up).

Whatever the reason, adult children who should be concerned about their own retirement are caring for their parents. Sometimes the costs of care are direct—payment to the health aide. Others are indirect but insidious. These include constant days off work or distractions that could lead to poor performance reviews at a time when your earnings should be their highest.

Obligations

Do you have to provide for your parents in your estate plan? No. However, you may be surprised to find that in 29 states, there are laws on the books that require children to support their parents while alive.[1] To be fair, many of these are antiquated laws that aren't often used. But in a very recent court case in Pennsylvania, the state successfully argued that the son should have to pay for his parents' care.

Regardless of the legal obligation, there may be a moral obligation. Your parents raised you, and one of the reasons they may not have a great nest egg is because they put you through college or financially assisted you in other ways. Family relationships are complicated, and there could be myriad reasons you're assisting your parents financially at this point in time. The question is, if you die, does your support die with you?

Financing Long-Term Care

Just setting aside some money for your parents isn't the best solution to provide for their care if you aren't here. To understand why, I need to give you a quick overview of the problems with financing long-term care.

Everyone is familiar with Medicare. You turn 65, and it provides health and hospitalization insurance for you. You can even buy supplemental policies that wrap around Medicare to pay for coverage it doesn't pay for. The key point is that Medicare is health and hospitalization insurance. It's intended to provide for you when you get sick and to assist you in recovering.

The issue is that with many diseases and symptoms associated with aging, you can't get better. I'm talking about Parkinson's, Alzheimer's, and dementia. I'm also talking about the fact that if you break a bone at a certain age, you may never be independent again. People in these situations may need assistance with what we call *activities of daily living*, including personal hygiene, dressing, eating, continence, moving in and out of bed, and walking. Medicare doesn't pay for help with these problems, which I'll refer to as *long-term care needs*.

There are three ways to pay for long-term care needs: your money, long-term care insurance, and Medicaid. Medicaid is available for people with limited assets to provide for the long-term care needs Medicare doesn't cover. Medic-

---

[1] Do you live in Alaska, Arkansas, California, Connecticut, Delaware, Georgia, Indiana, Iowa, Kentucky, Louisiana, Maryland, Massachusetts, Mississippi, Montana, Nevada, New Hampshire, New Jersey, North Carolina, North Dakota, Ohio, Oregon, Pennsylvania, Rhode Island, South Dakota, Tennessee, Utah, Vermont, Virginia, or West Virginia? If so, you may be responsible for supporting your parents under certain circumstances.

aid may provide for the cost of a nursing home, an assisted-living facility, or even in-home care in certain circumstances. However, Medicaid is needs-based, meaning if you have too much money, you aren't eligible for benefits. Right now, your parents may be able to qualify because their assets are limited. However, if you leave them an inheritance that isn't properly structured, it will destroy their Medicaid eligibility and go straight to the nursing home or assisted-living facility; and then, once it's all spent down, your parents will be back to square one and have to reapply for Medicaid.

Tax Considerations

Any distribution of assets to your parents upon your death reduces the amount of the estate tax exemption amount available to shelter assets passing to other people. For example, if you set aside $350,000 in a trust for your parents, then the maximum you could fund a family trust for your spouse and children (assuming a $1 million estate tax exemption amount) would be $650,000.

You should also consider the income tax consequences of transferring assets to your parents. Depending on the amount of their assets, they may currently be receiving some form of financial assistance (prescription drug relief, housing, health insurance, property tax rebate) based on their level of income. If you distribute assets to them in such a way that the income generated by those assets becomes your parent's income, you may void their ability to qualify for benefits they're currently relying on.

How to Give Assets to Your Parents

Now that you know why I'm concerned about how you're leaving assets to your parents, let's talk about some better ways of doing it.

First, what amount of money are you considering leaving to your parents? Is it a fixed amount (such as $250,000) or a percentage of your estate? I ask this because if you just want to make a small bequest (less than $25,000, for example), special planning isn't necessarily required because this isn't a large amount in the grand scheme of things. It probably won't affect your parents' ability to finance long-term care because it can be spent on things they need.

Next, do you leave the assets to your parents outright or in trust? If you leave the assets to them in a properly created trust, then the assets won't be deemed to be available assets for purposes of Medicaid qualification. This means your parents won't be forced to spend the assets on their care prior to their qualification for Medicaid. Instead, the inheritance could be used to supplement their care by paying for things Medicaid doesn't pay for, such as a single-room supplement, an electronic wheelchair, a special bed, or even a large, high-definition flat-screen TV to catch their favorite shows. If you're setting aside a substantial sum for your parents, my suggestion would be to make it payable to them in trust.

In designing the trust, consider the distribution terms of the trust:

- *Income.* You may provide that all the income generated by the trust will be payable to your parents on a quarterly basis. This would give them some money for things they need today, as well as create a nest egg for larger expenses they might have in the future. Beware of any income-based benefits they're currently receiving, though.

- *Principal.* Make sure principal distributions are totally discretionary. If you indicate that the trust is available for their health, maintenance, and support, or a combination thereof, it may be interpreted under the laws of the state your parents reside in that the trustee *must* expend the money on their health and support, thus converting the trust into an available asset for Medicaid purposes.

- *Trustee.* Carefully consider who should be the trustee. You may have named your spouse as the trustee of all other trusts created under your estate plan, but here it might be appropriate to name your sister or other family member who knows your parents well and whom your parents will feel comfortable asking when they need something.

- *Ultimate beneficiaries.* It's likely that any trust you create for your parents will have a balance remaining when they pass away. Recall that you need to use your estate tax exemption amount in order to fund any trust for your parents. As such, consider naming the ultimate beneficiaries of the trust as your children, the family trust you created, or some other party other than your spouse. If you give the assets to your spouse, they will simply be added back to their taxable estate, and the utilization of your exemption amount will be wasted.

▓ **Let's Get Real** When it comes to public benefits, the income qualification rules are set in stone with harsh results. I once had a client who didn't qualify for home-based care financially because his Social Security income exceeded the state's limits by $17 a month. The cost of that $17 month was about $3,000 in care services. Before putting your parents into your estate plan, make sure you absolutely understand the potential consequences of the inheritance to their financial landscape.

21

Planning Guide for Special- Needs Children

What if your child or grandchild has developmental challenges that will, or may, prevent them from being an independent adult? They could even be dependent on public resources for their care and living arrangements. A poorly planned, or unplanned, inheritance can disqualify vulnerable beneficiaries from the benefits they rely on to live. When one beneficiary may have more needs than another, how can you balance their different situations?

▒ **Chapter Brief**   The issue of ability to handle an inheritance goes beyond traditional special needs. When a person relies on public benefits, an outright transfer will void eligibility. Although some fixes exist, a planned inheritance will have greater flexibility.

Recognizing Special Needs

Although totally unscientific, my own experience indicates that special-needs planning is becoming more and more prevalent. I'd say I have a discussion about special-needs planning with about 20 percent of my clients. I always ask in a meeting, "Do you have any family members with special needs?" Some people answer, "I don't know. I have a grandson I'm concerned about because he's been diagnosed with ADHD" or some other issue identified by their school. Other people have come to me specifically because they're concerned about a child they know can't be independent due to either a mental or a physical challenge.

When I talk about a special-needs child, I'm referring to somebody who may never reach the level of being able to be independent, either financially or in their lifestyle. I want clients to tell me about beneficiaries who the clients are concerned may never develop the critical thinking skills necessary to be able to use their inheritance in their own best interest. My broad use of the term *special needs* encompasses both traditional special needs as well as beneficiaries for whom uncertainly exists about where life will take them.

When people speak of special needs in the traditional sense, they're referring to individuals who have mental and physical disabilities that prevent them from being able to independently care for themselves. Some of these beneficiaries may be institutionalized. More often, I find these are beneficiaries who will always require additional supervision. Universally, their care needs are extensive, and they may need to qualify for financial-based aid in future.

Under my expanded definition of special needs, I'm also referring to beneficiaries who may be able to live independently at some point but about whom you have a concern that they won't have the ability to use inherited assets in their own best interests. Perhaps they're on the high end of the autistic scale, or they have a history of addiction issues or mental illness, or for whatever reason they haven't demonstrated the ability to lead an independent life. These beneficiaries won't necessarily qualify for financial-based services in the future, but you might still be reasonably concerned about their ability to manage their own affairs for their own benefit.

Special-Needs Trust

A special-needs trust (SNT) is a trust that is designed to be available to be used for the benefit of the beneficiary but not deemed an *available asset* in the event they need to qualify for a public benefits.

Needs-Based Benefits

Public benefits are traditionally needs-based. This means in order to qualify for Medicaid or Supplemental Security Income (SSI), or other publicly funded programs, you must demonstrate that you have a financial need. In calculating that financial need, there is a question of whether you have any *available assets*. Available assets are those you could spend on your own care. Generally speaking, you need to spend your available assets down to next to nothing in order to qualify for these needs-based benefits.

You know by now that my first question in estate planning is, "What are your goals for your family?" When it comes to a special-needs beneficiary, I can sum up that goal in one word: *security*. If they receive an inheritance and have to spend it down to next to zero, they're totally insecure. They're forced to rely on the whims of the government to determine which of their needs will be met. A special-needs beneficiary receiving financial-based services literally has nothing: their bank account can contain a maximum of $2,000 to qualify for Medicaid. If the government cuts the program they're relying on, how will they to pay for their care? As with many questions in this book, the answer can be found in a thoughtfully designed trust.

Discretionary Special-Needs Trust

When a third party creates a trust for a special-needs beneficiary, there is broad latitude as to the distribution terms of that trust. Federal benefits law provides that, in the event the trust is purely discretionary (that is, the trustee has total discretion to make or not make a distribution), the trust won't be deemed to be an available asset for the special-needs beneficiary. Some states go further and provide that the SNT must specifically indicate that it's available to supplement the beneficiary but not to supplant the benefits the person otherwise qualifies for. That is to say, the trustee isn't authorized to pay for housing for the beneficiary if the beneficiary is receiving a benefit for housing.

During the life of the special-needs beneficiary, the trustee can be creative with the use of the assets in a discretionary SNT. For example, if there is a family wedding, the trustee can arrange for the transportation and care necessary for the beneficiary to attend the event. No public benefits will pay for that. Additionally, a decision can be made about whether applying for public benefits is in the beneficiary's best interest. It may be that when the trustee examines the beneficiary's needs and the assets sitting in the SNT, those needs can be better satisfied through the trust's assets than by relying on public benefits.

Upon the death of the special-needs beneficiary, the discretionary SNT allows the assets be distributed to someone else in the family, whether other children or as you desire.

Ask the Attorney "Deirdre, I live in Louisiana but my granddaughter with mental disabilities lives in Texas. Do I need an attorney in Texas?" Special-needs planning is an area where cross-jurisdiction issues come into play. Because you live in Louisiana, your estate plan is governed by Louisiana law and must be prepared in accordance with Louisiana law. However, because public benefits programs are generally funded by a combination of the federal government and the state government, your granddaughter's qualification for a public benefits program is subject to Texas law. I suggest that it would be well worth a telephone consultation with a Texas attorney to discuss the requirements for special-needs planning in Texas, and that you have your attorney work with that person to make sure the trust you set up in your Louisiana estate plan will carry out your goals and intentions when reviewed by the public benefits agency in Texas.

The SNT should be established under a separate article of your will or revocable trust. Not only does this specifically delineate your intention that these assets not be deemed available assets for public benefits purposes, but it also creates a logical area in your plan to give your trustee appropriate instructions for dealing with the SNT versus any other kind of trust. In a non-special-needs trust, you may be concerned about college funding or a distribution at a fixed age. Compare that to a SNT, where you might direct the trustee to plan to invest the money for the beneficiary's lifetime.

Also, the actual language governing a discretionary SNT must be different from that governing other trusts. For example, many beneficiary trusts call for distributions for the "health, education, maintenance, and support" of the beneficiary. However, if you use the word *support* in the SNT, that in and of itself may be sufficient to convert the trust's assets to available assets for public benefits purposes, thus defeating your goal. Details matter here: the seven little letters in s-u-p-p-o-r-t, can mean the protection is lost.

Statutory Special-Needs Trust

If I were you, I might be wondering, "What would happen if I didn't do any special-needs planning?" For example, Grandpa Lewis wants to provide some money for his granddaughter Devon's care, knowing she'll never be able to take care of herself. Unfortunately, Grandpa Lewis doesn't get good estate-planning advice before putting his excellent intentions into action. So, his will says, "I give $500,000 to my granddaughter, Devon."

Well, Devon is living in a group home and has significant medical bills that are currently being paid by Medicaid. The inheritance means she must start paying the group home out of her inheritance, which runs $10,000 per month. In addition, Devon loses her qualification for Medicaid, so she needs to pay all her medical bills, which could run upward of $50,000 per year. At this spend rate, Grandpa Lewis's generosity will disappear very shortly, and Devon won't get any benefit from it. Devon will receive the same services she was receiving previously, with the difference being that she needs to exhaust her new inheritance in order to pay for them. Not really what Grandpa Lewis intended, don't you think?

Once Grandpa Lewis has passed away, it's too late to create a *discretionary* SNT. However, Devon's parents can petition to have a *statutory* SNT created. This is a trust created under section 1396p(d)(4)(a) of the Medicaid statutes. Unlike a discretionary trust, there are significant restrictions on statutory SNTs:

- *Self-settled.* The trust is created with the beneficiary's own money. This is why it's used in the event of a poorly structured inheritance. It's also commonly used for a personal injury award.

- *Disabled.* The person must be deemed disabled under the standards of the Social Security administration. If they're receiving SSI or Social Security Disability (SSD), then they qualify under those standards. A statutory SNT isn't an option for a beneficiary if you aren't sure they can be independent but they haven't been classified as disabled.

- *Use of funds.* The income and principal should be used for goods and services not otherwise provided by government assistance. Common examples include more sophisticated medical treatment and therapies that aren't medically necessary, special bedding, wheelchairs, mobility aids, and so on. Statutory SNTs don't allow the total flexibility of the trustee's decision-making that is the hallmark of the discretionary SNT.

- *Payback provision.* This is the big one. A statutory SNT must provide that the state in which the beneficiary lives is the primary beneficiary of the trust upon the special-needs beneficiary's death, to the extent that funds were expended on the person's behalf. For example, if during Devon's lifetime Texas spends $450,000 on her care, then upon her death, the first $450,000 of the trust must be paid over to the state of Texas.

Planning Recommendations

In addition to creating and designing a discretionary SNT instead of relying on a statutory special-needs payback trust, there are some other points to consider when special-needs planning is part of your family situation:

- *Unequal distribution.* Here is a situation where you may not want to treat your children equally. If one child has needs that are greater than those of another child, you may want to provide more dollars for those needs. You could do this by taking a fixed amount of dollars and providing that they'll go directly to the SNT, or making an unequal-percentage distribution of your estate (such as 50 percent to the SNT and 25 percent to each of your other two children).

- *Irrevocable life insurance trust (ILIT).* This is yet another situation where an ILIT can work to your advantage. Let's say you want to leave your wealth equally between two children but create new dollars to be held for the benefit of a special-needs child. You can own a life insurance policy in an ILIT that also includes a discretionary SNT. Using this plan, you know exactly how much money will be available to your disabled child, instead of having the amount be determined on the basis of your estate's value at the time you pass away. Not sure what an appropriate death benefit might be? Retain a care manager to prepare a life-care plan for your child so you can estimate the care needs over their lifetime.

- *Guardianship.* When special-needs children turn 18, they become legal adults. They may not have the capacity to make their own decisions or even to nominate you to make decisions for them. In that case, as parents you may have to seek a legal guardianship over your now-adult special-needs child. In your estate plan, you need to consider who would be the successor guardian to the child. Note that you can merely nominate the person, not direct who the successor guardian is, because any successor must be approved by a judge.

■ **Let's Get Real** When you have a special-needs beneficiary or think you may have, I suggest you really consider the beneficiary's possible capabilities and needs before you see the attorney or go online. If you can share a clear picture of the beneficiary's needs, the attorney will be able to better tailor a trust to meet those needs. If the beneficiary can manage small amounts of money, maybe you want to incorporate a monthly allowance. Are there life experiences, such as travel, that you would like to see happen? Give instructions to the trustee on how to make that happen. Is there an ideal living arrangement if you're no longer here? Describe it and make sure you fund it. Your trustee may have no experience dealing with special needs. Bridge that gap by communicating to them, through conversations and in writing, your goals for your loved one.

22

Action Guide: Getting Started

You now know everything you ever wanted to know about estate planning (and more, I hope!). So, what is your next step? This is your guide to go from adding "get estate plan" to your to-do list to checking it off.

Chapter Brief Sit with me at my conference table (or as close as we can get on paper) as I take you through a client meeting. I'll share with you what I think about as I speak with a client to combine their family and goals with my knowledge into a recommended plan of action. I'll go through the information you need to prepare for a meeting with an attorney or to sit at your computer to create your estate plan online. What are the pros and cons of attorney versus online estate planning, and which might be right for you?

Meet Me in My Office

We're finally here! You've done all your homework and have ideas and questions about what will work best for you and your family. So, what are the steps of actually putting together an estate plan? Let's go through the process I share with my clients when they're sitting at my conference room table. I also want to give you some insight into what I'm thinking as I gather information during our conversation to develop a recommended strategy.

Grab a cup of coffee or tea, or your favorite beverage. Being that you're reading this at home, a glass of wine might be in order. Get comfortable so you can focus on yourself and your plan. Make sure you have a pad of paper and pen to take notes during your meeting with yourself.

Why Are You Doing Your Estate Plan Now?

I usually start my meetings with some small talk to try to get a sense of the person sitting across the table from me. Because you presumably already know yourself pretty well, you can skip this part.

The first question I always ask, in some form or other, is, "What is motivating you to do your estate plan now?" The majority of Americans don't have an estate plan. I get that doing pretty much anything else is more fun than talking about death, taxes, and disability (unless you're doing it with me, of course!). So, if it's such an unpleasant task, what motivated you to do it now? Did you see a situation happen to somebody else that you want to avoid? Have you been doing some reading and want to take advantage of certain things you've learned about? Has a loved one died, which brings the importance of this topic close to home? Has your accountant or financial advisor told you to do this every year, and you want to get it off your to-do list?

I ask this because if there is a specific motivation caused by something you want to either accomplish or avoid, you should make sure you incorporate it into your plan.

What Are Your Goals?

I don't come out and say, "What are your estate planning goals?" Presumably, clients come to see me partially because they don't know what their goals should be when it comes to developing an estate plan. What I do say is, "Forget about taxes and everything else. If you got hit by a bus tomorrow, whom would you want to get your stuff?" This question allows me to narrow down who's important to you and your family. My next question is something along the lines of, "Do you have any concerns about how they get your stuff?" This helps me to start get a sense of what you're looking to protect your assets against. Are you concerned about taxes, the age of your beneficiaries, their maturity, or having enough money to go around? What do you see as being risks to your family?

I quickly review the estate planning questionnaire you brought with you, and we talk about your biographical information. Your answers clue me in if this is a second marriage, or if you have a noncitizen spouse, or if your parents are still living and you might be responsible for them. I look at the ages of your children and where they live, whether you have grandchildren, and whether your children are married or divorced. By asking about your children's professions, I get a sense of what form of asset-protection discussions I should pursue. To make your life easier, Appendixes A and B include the estate planning questionnaires I send out (for married and single people).

By the end of the first 5 to 10 minutes or so of the meeting, this line of questioning gives me an overall perspective about what's important to you in terms of what you want to achieve with your estate plan. Now that I have a feeling for your goals, I turn to look at the other side of the equation: the assets.

What Are Your Assets?

As we move to the next stage of the meeting, I talk about how you build an estate plan from assets to goals. My conversation is something like this: "The structure of your estate plan has two main components: your assets and who you want to leave them to. The assets are actually the easy part, because assuming you want to minimize taxes, the amount and nature of your assets give structure to your estate plan. Think of this as the skeleton of the plan. Your goals, however, are what give your estate plan its body. How do you and your spouse or partner leave your assets to each other? How do you leave your assets to your kids? Who else do you want to benefit? Because the assets create the skeleton of the plan, I'd like to review your assets now."

If we're meeting in my office, I've asked you to complete a financial questionnaire. You can find it in Appendixes C and D (and I hope you completed it at the start of this book). My goal at this point is to get a snapshot of where you are today with your finances. In reviewing your finances, I examine the following components:

- *Total assets, liabilities, and net worth.* The total amount of assets drives the need for and type of discussion about estate tax planning.

- *Allocation of assets between spouses* (his name, her name, joint). In order to achieve tax-planning goals, we may need to reallocate the assets between spouses so each has probate assets in their own name.[1]

- *Retirement accounts.* These accounts can't be equalized between spouses, so I need to talk about them in terms of asset allocation. I also make a note to discuss income taxation and the importance of the beneficiary designation in coordinating the retirement plan with the estate plan objectives.

- *Life insurance.* If there's life insurance, I might discuss putting it into an ILIT if estate taxes are issued. Even if they're not,

---

[1] In Chapter 23, "Action Guide: Completing Your Plan," I go over the importance of how the assets are allocated in order to achieve your tax-savings goals.

we may need to talk about whether the insurance is sufficient given your assets and lifestyle, as well as the importance of coordinating the life insurance beneficiaries with the overall estate plan (for example, naming the trusts you created for your children as the contingent beneficiary, not the child outright).

- *Out-of-state real estate.* If real estate is owned in two juris-dictions, two separate probate proceedings will be required. This may lead to a discussion of using a revocable trust as the main estate planning vehicle or otherwise holding title to that out-of-state real estate in a non-probate fashion.

- *Probate avoidance and privacy.* If you're in a jurisdiction with expensive or lengthy probate proceedings, I talk about a using a revocable trust instead of a will as the centerpiece of your plan. We would have the same discussion if privacy seems to be of value to you in your estate plan.

- *Personal property.* Where there is significant personal property (jewelry, stuff, and so on), I make a note to have a discussion about how the property will be allocated among children or other beneficiaries.

Foundation Documents

I next turn to a picture of what the foundation document (be it a will or a revocable trust) should look like. I always start with a sketch of how the estate plan will look. I draw the structure of the plan as we're talking so the picture develops based on the give-and-take of our discussion. I'm not just being descriptive: I actually start with a blank piece of paper, draw a box at the top with the client's net worth, and add arrows and boxes as we discuss a family trust, marital trust, or lifetime trust for the kids. (Look at Figure 22-1.)

Real Stories from Around My Conference Table   Never underestimate the power of a picture. True story: I've had clients come back to see me seven or eight years after our first meeting, and despite all the documents, summaries, and printed-out flowcharts we've sent them, the thing they pull out is the piece of paper on which I sketched what their estate plan might look like. I think this is because I sit down with them and we draw the blueprint together. It's also important because the visual gives both me and my client a point of reference to come back to again and again as we discuss what different options associated with the plan might look like.

To echo this, I suggest you sketch your own flowchart of what should happen to your assets in the event of your death. I have even put up some videos at www.deirdrewheatleyliss.com sketching out some of the scenarios from Planning Guides part in this book to show you how this works.

Assets Create the Skeleton

The skeleton framework of the estate plan is driven by who needs to get what to achieve your necessary objectives.

For example, if you're married and you want to minimize taxes, the initial flowchart of your estate plan when the first spouse dies might look like Figure 22-1.

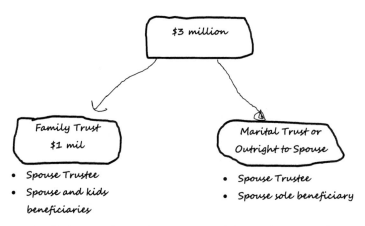

Figure 22-1. Hand sketch of the beginning skeleton of an estate plan

Next, I expand the skeletal structure to show what happens when the second spouse dies. This lets you see the no-tax side of the line, the tax savings achieved through the utilization of the family trust, and how taxes build up on the taxable side of the line. The net result is that the no-tax assets plus the taxable assets are what's available to be divided among your children or other beneficiaries.

Once I make sure you don't have any more questions about what happens when the spouse dies, I talk about how the beneficiaries inherit assets. I honestly tell every client that this is the most important part of planning. The assets and the structure necessary to reduce taxes or provide for your spouse are pretty straightforward; how you leave your assets to your loved ones makes your estate plan uniquely yours.

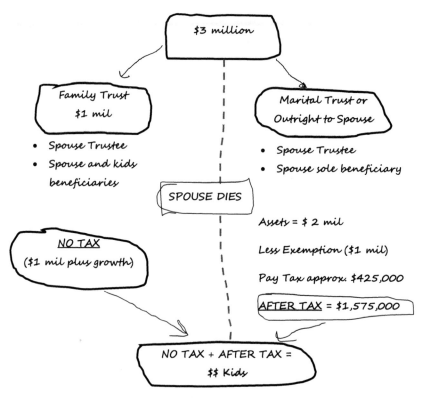

Figure 22-2. Sketch of the tax situation at the second death, highlighting the no-tax and after-tax assets

Here, I might illustrate how the assets are equally divided into trusts among the children. If you're single, this would be my starting point after demonstrating how the estate tax exemption amount would be applied to your assets, and how any taxes would be paid off the top before the assets are distributed among the kids or other beneficiaries.

Using this structure, I can talk about any questions that come up. Want to allocate assets differently between the children? Adjust the number on the flow of allocations to the children. Want to layer in a specific bequest? I put a box above the division of the assets to show who's getting what. Need to discuss generation-skipping planning? I divide each trust into a GST share to reflect the use of the GST exemption amount. Want to layer in an ILIT? I add a box representing the ILIT and the death benefit to Figure 22-2 on the No Tax side of the line. This is why I refer to the skeleton structure as the foundation. From here you can build anything.

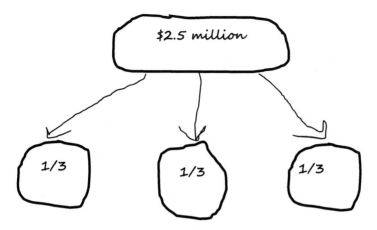

- Trust for life
- Child and g/children bene
- Child co-trustee at 25
- Child sole trustee at 30

Figure 22-3. Sketch of a possible distribution to the children

The Treatment of Family Creates the Body

The skeleton doesn't bring life to an estate plan. It needs to be fleshed out, I do that by talking about the details of each box, which represent how assets are being left to a beneficiary.

Before leaving each box, I go over the following elements of each distribution:

- *Is the distribution in trust or outright?* I talk about whether the distribution has to be in trust (such as a family trust) and the pros and cons of the distribution structure being in trust versus outright. How this discussion goes depends entirely on the family and their situation and needs. My goal is to (1) educate the clients about their options and (2) customize those options by asking lots of questions to make sure the result fits within the goals. All the items discussed in the Planning Guides part of this book represent the tools I might pull out of the bag to address any issues that come up during the meeting.

- *If you're holding the assets in trust, who will be the trustee?* If the beneficiary is acting as a trustee, I talk about the benefits and restrictions on that. We discuss the ability of the trustee to name a co-trustee, as well as who might be an appropriate successor trustee. At this point in the meeting, we're starting to identify the actual individuals who will participate as fiduciaries in the estate plan.

- *Will there be any specific bequests?* Now that we have the default distribution scheme down, should anything be carved out to provide specifically or differently for any person?

- *Who will carry all this out as the executor?* Because the trust is so important, I focus first on who will be the individual to carry out that long-term job. Before moving on to other documents, I need to understand whether the executors will be the same people or perhaps different people.

- *Who will be the guardian?* If you have minor children, this has to be in the will. I talk to you about the guardian's role and how you need to coordinate with the trustee to identify the right person to both act as guardian and be a successor guardian if necessary.

- *What haven't we talked about yet that you're still concerned about?* It could be that after all this discussion, there are still some points about the estate plan that you don't feel confident about. I want to make sure we circle back and get everybody on the exact same page before we move away from the will or revocable trust to the other documents.

Build From a Strong Foundation

I transition our meeting by saying, "OK. We're done talking about when you die. Now we get to talk about what happens if you become disabled." This is done with a smile on my face, because by this point in the meeting you might even be having—dare I say it—fun.

■ **Real Stories from Around My Conference Table**   If you do it right, estate planning can be fun. You're taking advantage of the laws to stick it to the government and make your own choices. You're imagining your family's future and how you can support their dreams and goals. True story: I have a Scottish client who at the end of our meeting said (imagine a Scottish accent here), "I don't know if I should be sayin' this or not, but Deirdre, yer deed funny!" We can all agree that the topics of death and taxes aren't fun, but there's no reason why meeting with your attorney can't be enjoyable.

The rest of the documents you need to round out your estate plan are (1) a general durable power of attorney and (2) a living will and health care power of attorney. I find out from you who should be the initial fiduciary under these documents, as well as their successors. I discuss the benefit of naming one person or multiple people, getting into the personalities, strengths, and weaknesses of the actual people we're discussing.

Finally, if time and attention span allow, I talk to you about advanced tax-saving techniques, if appropriate. I have to be honest; I usually hold off on this conversation until a future meeting simply because I think the initial focus needs be on getting the foundation documents in place. I may outline that at our next meeting we can discuss how a grantor retained annuity trust (GRAT), or qualified personal residence trust (QPRT), or transition of the family business, might fit into the overall plan. From my perspective, the advanced strategies are infinitely easier to draft once the foundation documents are in place because the questions about who the remainder beneficiaries will be and how they will receive the benefit are answered through this process.

What to Bring with You

Naturally, the more prepared you are for the meeting with your attorney (or the session at your computer if you're going the online route), the more you'll get out of it. Here is what I ask my clients to bring.

Family Information

Many attorneys will send you a questionnaire to complete before the first meeting. Even if they don't, bring with you a list of the complete legal names, ages, and addresses of you, your kids, any person you may be considering as a fiduciary, and any person you may be considering as a beneficiary (specific bequest or residuary), noting in each case the relationship of everybody to you. Just copying down biographical information will cut about half an hour from the meeting with the attorney. Not sure where to find the addresses? Look in your holiday card list.

If you're sent a questionnaire, it may be more or less extensive than the one in Appendixes A and B. Just fill it out to the best of your ability. If there's anything you don't know, leave it blank. Be sure to ask the attorney whether they want you to send it back before the meeting or bring it to the meeting (my preference).

Financial Information

The attorney needs to have an idea of your financial position in order to give you appropriate advice. Every once in a while, I get a call from the rare person who says, "I want an estate plan, but I don't want to divulge any financial information." I suggest they speak to another attorney.

You don't need a detailed financial statement listing every account down to the penny; as we discussed before, a snapshot categorized by type of asset and ownership will do. Again, even if the attorney doesn't ask you to bring this with you, I strongly suggest putting together a quick spreadsheet of what you own and owe. Feel free to use the one I've provided in Appendixes C and D.

If the attorney does provide a financial questionnaire, again, complete it to the best of your ability. If they ask for lots of detail, you may find it easier to photocopy your bank and investment statements rather than complete everything in the questionnaire. If it's likely you'll be using a revocable trust as the centerpiece of your estate plan, you'll need to fund the trust by transferring assets to it. From my perspective, because the attorney will want very detailed information to make sure all the assets are properly transferred, it's easier to photocopy the statements.

Who Will You Work With?

This is the $64,000 question (and no, that shouldn't be the fee). Do you work with an attorney, do something online, or go to your local office supply store? There is no absolute right or wrong answer to this question: you need to find a solution that works best for you.

Attorney

I'm going to be up front that I'm biased and think anyone who has a potentially taxable estate should work with an attorney. Although the computer programs may satisfy the estate tax structure, they can't have a give-and-take discussion with you about how taxes can affect you, how you might reduce them, and what things you should consider in the future. The value of the attorney relationship isn't the document you receive (although it's likely to be much more comprehensive if you're working with an experienced estate planning attorney). The value is the advice you get, the questions the attorney asks, and the way they customize their recommendations as you go through the conversation. Remember, if you don't get this right, you won't be here later to know about the problem or to fix it.

How to Find One?

If you're thinking about working with an attorney, the first step is to find one. I recommend that you look for an attorney who spends a significant portion of their practice focused on estate planning issues. One way to do that, of course, is to use the Internet. In doing a search, I would look for somebody who writes about estate planning issues—something beyond a blurb saying the law firm handles estate planning. Maybe the attorney has a blog or a more extensive article database you can look at.

Another way is to ask people who hang out with attorneys. No, there's not a special club, but accountants and financial advisors are likely to run across estate planning attorneys in their practice. Ask your accountant or financial advisor for their recommendation. They may give you the name of the one person who they think would be just right for you, or they might give you a list of three names to contact.

Once you've identified the attorney, I suggest you contact them and spend a few minutes on the phone getting a sense of their approach to the planning process. The purpose of this call is to see whether you like what they have to say. Don't expect the attorney to give you specific advice about your situation over the phone; that is what the consultation is for. And if you're asking for free advice, keep in mind that you tend to get exactly what you pay for. Instead, the attorney should be able to give you a sense of their methodology with people who are in a situation similar to yours, and their process when working with an estate planning client. For example, do they send out a questionnaire, provide a few dates for the first consultation, or tell you how long will the whole thing will take? And what about fees?

How to Pay for One?

Ah, yes. Fees. Sometimes people call me out of the blue and say, "How much do you charge for an estate plan?" I answer honestly: "It depends. I don't know what your needs are, so I can't give you an idea of what my fee would be." I then go on to explain to them that the purpose of the initial consultation is to determine their needs in part so I can set a fee. However, if we spend a few more minutes on the phone, I'm sometimes able to ballpark a typical fee for someone in their situation.

Some attorneys charge for estate planning services on an hourly basis. You're billed for whatever time they spend with you. Others charge on a flat fee basis and say a certain package of documents costs $X. (I'll let you in on a little secret here: the flat fee is based on the hourly rate. It's just that with a flat fee, the attorney is accepting the risk that the meetings and document preparation might not go according to plan.) Other attorneys take this approach: "It's a flat fee unless I let you know otherwise." This is really to say the attorney normally charges a flat fee, but every once in a while a client isn't well prepared, changes their mind often, is indecisive, or otherwise takes significantly more than the typical amount of time. In that case, the attorney is reserving the right to charge for their time. That's because the only commodity attorneys own and can rent out is time. From your initial call to the attorney, it would be fair to expect a ballpark figure as to what the documents might cost.

The attorney may or may not charge for an initial consultation. If they do charge, they may or may not apply that charge as a credit toward any eventual fee. Each attorney has their own method. I generally charge an initial consultation fee (which is a discount of my normal hourly rate) unless the client is referred to me by another professional whom I work closely with. If I choose not to charge a consultation fee in that instance, I do so as a courtesy to the professional who referred the client to me.

In selecting an estate planning attorney, I strongly suggest that cost not be your sole driving factor. This plan will be an investment. Done properly, it should last for years to come, with some minor tweaking. I suggest you try to find an attorney from whom you can get the most value. *Value* to me means looking at things such as their approach, your comfort level, and how good you feel about the relationship, as well as the fees.

What Should You Expect?

Once you've found an estate planning attorney you want to meet with, here is how you should expect the engagement to progress:

- You attend an initial consultation, during which you and the attorney agree on the elements of the estate plan. Depending on the attorney, this may take place in the office, over the phone, or as a video conference. Fees should be discussed at that meeting.

- The attorney sends a written engagement letter outlining what services they're providing, and details fees for their services. In order to avoid any nasty surprises, you should always make sure there is an engagement letter. The attorney will ask for a retainer, which is a certain amount of money to be applied toward the final bill.

- The attorney drafts documents for your review. You should have the opportunity to review them at your leisure. When I send out documents, I also include a summary of the documents as well as a flowchart to make it easier for clients to review them given their possible complex and archaic language.

- The attorney schedules a conference to review any questions or changes you may want made. Some people do this in person, but I prefer to do it as a conference call or over e-mail. Be aware that if you have a second meeting at this stage, it may increase the cost of planning. That's because many attorneys estimate two meetings (initial consultation and execution meeting) in the fees they set. At this conference, make sure you give the attorney any and all corrections, discuss any questions you may have, and essentially ensure that the documents are correct in terms of carrying out your wishes and goals as discussed in the consultation.

- An execution meeting is scheduled at the attorney's office. Estate planning documents are typically signed at the attorney's office because two witnesses and a notary must be present. The attorney may or may not supervise the execution meeting (presumably you went over all your questions during the prior conference).

- At the conclusion of the meeting, the original documents may be distributed to you, or you may agree with your attorney they will hold onto the originals and distribute a copy to you. In my practice, I typically retain the original documents, having dealt with a number of situations where clients have lost, misplaced, or, in one instance, had the original documents stolen. I provide my clients with both a booklet of all the document copies as well as a USB drive with an electronic copy so they can print out additional copies as needed.

- Asset retitling takes place following the document execution. The extent to which this is necessary depends on the type of assets you have, as well as the form of your estate plan.

Online Services

A number of online services can assist you in creating estate planning documents. Everyone should have an estate plan that they created and not rely on the one their state created for them. If meeting with an attorney doesn't work for you, perhaps because you don't see value in the investment at this time or even, quite frankly, because of a time crunch, these online services can prepare basic documents for you. Many services even customize the documents for your state's law.

I think these services work best for people in the following situations:

- Single parents who need documents that name guardians for their children and place all the assets in trust until a certain age

- Just-married couples who need a will that incorporates their relationship to each other, and a power of attorney and living will

- Young parents who don't have a taxable estate and similarly need documents that name guardians and hold assets in trust for their kids until a certain age

- College students who need to give authority to their parents over their financial assets and to make medical decisions

- Young adults who are starting to accumulate assets and are looking to leave them to a family member (maybe their siblings or parents)

There may certainly be other situations, but these are the ones that come to mind. I actually have people call me and say, "Do I need to see you, or can I do this online?" Depending on their situation, I'll suggest to them that they go one route versus the other.

■ **Caution**   When using an online service, be very careful about how you execute the documents. I've often seen perfectly acceptable documents in terms of what they said that were of no value whatsoever because they weren't executed properly in terms of witnesses and notarization. A will not properly executed is just a bunch of unenforceable wishes.

Fill-In Forms

OK: I have to say that I really don't like these. At least with the online services, when you answer a question in a specific way, there's intelligence in the computer programming that leads to the next logical question. In contrast, a fill-in form may or may not address your situation. I've personally been involved in a couple of very nasty estate litigations where fill-in forms were the issue. I honestly think they cause more problems than they solve and that you'd be far better served to use an online service or speak to an attorney with experience in estate planning.

Let's Get Real As much as I appreciate your taking the time to educate yourself with this book, both this book and your expenditure of time are useless if you don't take steps to put a plan in place. So go online, or call your accountant, or connect with me at www.deirdrewheatleyliss. com—but please do something to put your plan in place!

23

Action Guide: Completing Your Plan

Just creating a will or a trust isn't enough; you need to make sure your assets match your well-thought-out estate plan. This is where most estate plans fail. You thought hard about what you wanted, created a plan to turn your goals into action—but then didn't make sure your assets fit your plan. Don't drop the ball after all your hard work.

■ **Chapter Brief**   If you're looking to avoid probate, then assets must be titled to your revocable trust. Retirement plans, life insurance, joint accounts, and pay-on-death accounts need to be coordinated with your estate plan. Otherwise, they could destroy it.

Probate Assets: Part of the Plan

Quick refresher: Probate assets pass under your estate plan. When you die, whatever is owned by you in your sole name with no named beneficiary is distributed under your will. This is a good thing, because you've put a lot of thought into figuring out who gets what and how under your estate plan. Unless, of course, you have a revocable trust.

Assets Titled to Revocable Trust: Part of the Plan

In many states, a revocable trust, not a will, is the centerpiece of the estate plan. If assets are titled to (in the name of) the revocable trust when you die, they're non-probate and go to your beneficiaries in the manner you designed for your distribution scheme. This is a good thing. By funding your revocable trust, you avoid probate and make sure your assets are distributed in line with your goals and values.

If assets are *not* titled to the revocable trust, you do *not* avoid probate. This is where many a plan fails—you created a trust, was exhausted by the process, and never got around to funding the trust. Don't be a fail. Change the ownership of your assets to your revocable trust. If you're working with an attorney, there is likely a paralegal in the office who is in charge of helping you with funding your revocable trust.

I must warn you that sometimes pesky probate assets may throw a wrench in the works. For example, your car might be titled in your own name, or one bank account that you didn't want to put into the trust. As a workaround solution, consider identifying those outlier assets and putting them in joint name with somebody else. Doing so converts them to non-probate assets and avoids a lot of hassle with the probate court and title transfer upon your death. The outliers don't tend to have much value in comparison to your overall estate because you'll have retitled your larger assets into the revocable trust, but why go through the hassle of probate at all?

Non-Probate Assets: Not Part of the Plan

Some non-probate assets aren't just pesky; they could negate your entire estate plan. These assets need to be coordinated with the provisions of your overall estate plan so all your assets pass to your beneficiaries in the manner you designed.

Retirement Plan Beneficiary Designations

Alert! Alert! This is where most estate plans fail to come together.

Let's look at Samantha, who is a single mom with two young daughters, Hannah and Isabella. Samantha's biggest concern is making sure that if something happened to her, Hannah and Isabella would have every educational opportunity and the financial security to make a good start in life. Samantha agonizes over who the trustee should be and what distribution standards she should use. She creates a highly customized plan that truly reflects who she is as a parent and what she wants for her girls.

Seventy percent of Samantha's net worth is sitting in her IRA and retirement plan. When she opened the accounts, she was told she had to name a beneficiary, so she wrote down "Hannah and Isabella," just to get the account opened. She never gave it any further thought. When Samantha passes away, those retirement accounts will pass directly to Hannah and Isabella and will *not* be held in the trust Samantha so carefully designed. Instead, the funds will be managed by the court or court-appointed individual until the girls turn 18, at which time the balance will be distributed to them outright. This goes totally against Samantha's wishes and the design of the estate plan she worked so hard to bring to life. Whoops.

Let's look at another story. After a lot of fighting and huge legal fees, Paul and Tammy were divorced. To say they don't have a good relationship would be a vast understatement. Back when Paul was hired at a large company, he named Tammy as the beneficiary of his 401(k) plan. He never got around to changing it after they were divorced. Paul dies, and his estate plan leaves everything to his son, Ray. However, Ray is in for a nasty surprise. Because Paul never changed the beneficiary of his 401(k) plan, and because a 401(k) plan is governed by federal law, which trumps the state law that governs the will, Tammy is still the beneficiary of the 401(k) plan. This means all of Paul's hard-earned retirement dollars aren't going to Ray, as he clearly intended, but instead are being directed back toward the ex-wife, whom he loathed. Whoops.

Your attorney should counsel you about how your beneficiary designation needs to be structured to fit into your estate plan. This may be a question of whom you're naming as the beneficiary, or it could be how to name a trust as a beneficiary.

Further, when you change jobs or open a new retirement account, you need to make sure your new beneficiary designation continues to be coordinated with the estate plan. This is relevant whether you want the retirement plan to be distributed in the same manner as the rest of your estate plan, or if you're having it distributed to a separate person (such as a second spouse).

■ **Caution** Don't name your estate as the beneficiary of your retirement plan. Doing so can destroy the ability to defer income taxes over the beneficiary's life expectancy, thus diminishing the value of the retirement account. Name a human being or a trust designed to be the beneficiary of a retirement account.

Life Insurance

If you're not using an irrevocable life insurance trust (ILIT) to own your life insurance, then you need to make sure the beneficiary of the death benefit reflects your intentions and goals as described in your will or revocable trust. If your goal is to have the death benefit distributed in the same manner as your estate plan, then think about naming the same beneficiaries under similar terms. Consider these examples:

- *Your will names your spouse outright as the primary beneficiary and then to your children in trust.* Name your spouse as the primary beneficiary on the life insurance beneficiary designation form, and the trust for your children as the contingent beneficiary.

- *Your will says that your assets will pass to your descendants, per stirpes.* On your insurance beneficiary designation, identify the beneficiaries as the class of your children and indicate that it will pass *per stirpes* in the event one of them passes away.

- *Your will leaves your estate in equal shares to your then living nieces and nephews.* List each person with the appropriate percentage of interest on the life insurance beneficiary designation and indicate that a beneficiary must survive you to receive their share.

■ **Caution**   Don't name your estate as the beneficiary of your life insurance policy. In many states, life insurance is exempt from the claims of creditors upon death. However, that exemption is nullified if the death benefit is payable directly to the estate. Why take the risk? Name individuals or trusts as your beneficiary or contingent beneficiary.

Joint Accounts

Most married couples share the philosophy of "What's mine is yours, and what's yours is mine." As a result, many assets end up being owned in joint name. Although joint ownership with rights of survivorship avoids probate and makes it very easy for the spouse to gain control of the assets following death, it negates the ability to achieve any estate tax savings. Remember, in order to get estate tax savings, the assets of the *first* spouse to die must pass into the family trust. By doing this, when the second spouse passes away, fewer assets are included in the second spouse's taxable estate.

However, if everything is owned in joint name, then nothing is available to pass into the family trust. Everything goes straight to the surviving spouse, and the will is entirely useless because it doesn't govern anything. Whoops.

Married couples should consider dividing joint assets so each spouse has approximately half the assets, or at least an amount equal to the estate tax exemption amount, in their own name. This can be accomplished in different ways, depending on what the family finances look like:

- Change the form of ownership on investment and bank accounts from of joint tenants with rights of survivorship to tenants-in-common. With a tenants-in-common account, 50 percent of the account passes under the will of the first spouse to die.

- If one spouse has a large retirement account that can't be divided, consider transferring real estate or other assets to the other spouse to even out the ownership.

- Put the house into one spouse's name and the investment accounts into the other's.

If you don't retitle assets, your investment in your estate plan isn't entirely lost. The surviving spouse has the option to *disclaim* any assets passing to them as a result of your death. This disclaimer must be done within nine months of date of death and follow other technical rules. Your spouse could use this provision to disclaim the 50 percent of the joint assets that are passing to them. The disclaimer converts 50 percent of those joint assets into probate assets, which then pass under your will or revocable trusts. The cost of a disclaimer is that your spouse must give up any powers of appointment that they have to modify the family trust or marital trust going forward.

I've mentioned it before, but accounts held as joint tenants with rights of survivorship can give rise to the dreaded "convenience account" problem:

- Dad has a "you get nothing" prenuptial agreement with his second spouse. Dad and the young wife have a joint account. Did he mean for that account to go to her when he died, or was the survivorship aspect of the account an oversight?

- Mom has three daughters. One daughter helps with things, and mom adds her to the bank account "so she can write checks." Did mom intend that the daughter not only could write checks but also would receive the balance on death?

- An unmarried couple has a joint account that used to belong to only one of the partners. The account is used for joint living expenses. But did the partner intend that it would go to the other if they were no longer together because he died?

Murky questions like these can only be resolved by a *trier of fact*—aka a judge or jury. And who knows how they will decide? The better practice is to make a note in your will specifying whether you do or don't intend the account to pass to the joint owner in addition to what they might otherwise receive under your estate plan.

Pay-on-Death Accounts

Pay-on-death accounts are a great way to make specific bequests outside of your overall estate plan. The beneficiary receives the asset immediately, without having to deal with your executor or other beneficiaries. The issue with pay-on-death accounts is that their value in comparison to the balance of your estate will fluctuate over time. You need to make sure you continually revisit the balance of the pay-on-death account to see if the amount passing to the named beneficiary remains appropriate as your overall assets and situation change.

Let's Get Real It's so important that your assets are properly titled to reach your goals that when you think your planning is done, make this your last double-check. Go back to the list of assets you prepared at the start of this process. Update it to reflect any changes in title you might have made. Identify any beneficiaries or joint owners. Take out the flowchart you drew of your estate plan. List each asset and indicate where it will flow as part of your estate plan. Probate assets and revocable trust assets go into the box at the top (which branches off into the family trust, marital trust, or distributions for other beneficiaries). Other non-probate assets go directly to the beneficiary (put these in a separate spot on your flowchart). Add up the total passing to each beneficiary. Now, look at the dollar flow of who gets what. Are your goals being met? Is enough money available to fund the family trust? Are all your beneficiaries receiving the same amount? If the dollars don't match the plan, rearrange your assets until they do.

Action Guide: Reviewing What You Have

If you've already invested in an estate plan and wonder if it's working for you, or if you're coming back a year or so later to review your goals and make sure your plan still fits, here are the questions you need to ask.

▓ **Chapter Brief** A one-year review involves a refresher on what your documents say and how your assets are titled. A three-to-five year review should be more in depth and likely leads to a call to your attorney.

Annual Review

It's unlikely you'll have a fire, but you still change the batteries in your smoke detectors twice each year. It's unlikely you're going to die, but isn't your estate plan worth a look annually?

Documents

Here are the steps for an annual review. Remember where you stored your copies of the documents. Pull them out and read them, together with any summary letter or flowchart. Make sure the documents say what you remember them saying. Call your attorney if your recollection of what is in your documents and what you're reading don't gel.

That isn't so painful, is it? Maybe add it to your to-do list when daylight savings time ends and you get an extra hour.

Assets

When doing an annual checkup, make sure your non-probate assets continue to be coordinated with your estate plan. Have you opened any new accounts or named any new beneficiary designations in the past year? Are the assets still balanced between the spouses? Do the amounts of any specific bequests, or non-probate assets acting like specific bequests, continue to make sense?

In-Depth Review

Every three to five years, you should go a little deeper in reviewing your documents. After this timeframe, some tweaking or overhauling may be appropriate to make sure the documents reflect your assets and goals now, not what they were in the past (and let's face it, the 3 to 5 years might end up becoming 7 to 10 given the procrastination associated with estate planning). Here are the things you should look for in doing a deeper review of your estate plan. If some of these raise an issue for you, contact your estate planning attorney. If you don't want to deal with that attorney anymore, contact another one:

- Has the federal tax law changed? If you don't know, contact your attorney and say, "Hey, I'm reviewing my estate planning documents. Have there been any changes in law I should be aware of?"

- Have you moved to another state? If so, your estate plan could probably benefit from a look-see by an attorney in that state.

- Have you changed employers? If you did, ask your HR department for copies of beneficiary designations for any retirement accounts, pension, or life insurance. You probably filled out a bunch of forms at once, and you may not have had the time to closely examine them.

- Do you have a separate written personal property distribu-tion? Pull it out and look at it. Do you still have all the items that are listed on it? Do you still want those items to go to the people indicated? Are there any new items you should list? If you're making any changes, I suggest that you revise the list in its entirety; don't just insert things or cross them out.

- Have you made specific bequests? Does the thing or amount continue to be appropriate? What about how the beneficiaries are receiving the bequests? Are there any new specific bequests you would like to make?

- Have your assets grown or shrunk dramatically? Based on this, does the division of the assets between your beneficiaries continue to make sense? I suggest that you draw a quick flowchart of your estate plan with the new numbers to see how the amounts shake out.

- Have any beneficiaries passed away? If they have, how do you want to provide for their family, if at all? You might want to do a new trust for grandchildren or add your child's spouse as a beneficiary.

- Do the trust provisions that you had in place continue to make sense given where your beneficiaries are now in their lives? You might feel that a trust is no longer necessary. If a trust is still necessary, then the ages for distribution may need adjusting. (Contrary to popular belief, I find that the age for an outright distribution goes up as the beneficiaries get older, so you could be looking to make adjustments to hold assets in trust for a shorter or longer period.) Or, after reading this book, you may want assets to pass in trust with the beneficiary as the trustee instead of distributing the assets outright.

- Do any beneficiaries have special needs now that didn't exist when you last updated the documents? You may need to add a special-needs trust.

- Do the people or organizations you named as alternate beneficiaries if something were to happen to all of your main beneficiaries continue to make sense? You can change them through a quick codicil or amendment if they don't.

- Are your executors, trustees, guardians, attorneys-in-fact, and health care representatives still appropriate? Has your relationship with them changed, or have your beneficiaries reached the point that they can take over those roles?

Consider whether any co-fiduciary arrangement should be made or changed.

Location, Location, Location

Does somebody know where your estate-planning documents are? After all, it doesn't do you much good to read this book and put time, effort, energy, and money into your estate plan if nobody can find it when you die.

My last piece of advice: Even if you don't want anybody to know what's in your estate plan, let them know where it is (your attorney's office, your safe, the third drawer down in the dining room) or whom to contact to get it.

▓ **Let's Get Real** If you're investing in using an attorney to prepare your estate plan, you're investing in a relationship. That relationship should not end as soon as the documents are signed and the check is mailed. I send my clients a note every three years or so reminding them that it's time to for them look at their estate plan again. I use the same questions I posed to you in this chapter. I also communicate to my clients if there are any changes in the law that might make their documents no longer fit their goals (such as in 2010, when there was no estate tax). In meeting with your estate-planning attorney, ask them if and when they will contact you following the completion of your plan. If they don't have a process in place, then you might not be getting full value from your relationship with them. If that is the case, consider interviewing other attorneys. If they do have a process, and a need for changes is uncovered, be aware that they will charge to make those changes. Bear in mind that it's far less expensive to continue to invest in an estate plan with a solid foundation than to either create a new plan or have a plan that doesn't fit when you die.

Estate Analysis Checklist: Married

General Information

HUSBAND

Full Name _____ Name you go by _____

How do you sign your name? _____

Home Telephone # _____Work Telephone # _____

Social Security #_____

Mailing Address _____

Business Address _____

Business Telephone _____ Fax Telephone # _____

Date of Birth _____E-mail Address _____

Are you a U.S. citizen? _____ Yes _____ No If no, what country? _____

Occupation _____ Annual Income _____

State of Health _____ Insurable? _____

Armed Forces Serial Number _____Branch_____

Were you married previously? _____ Divorced/Widowed? _____

WIFE

Full Name _____ Name you go by _____

How do you sign your name? _____

Home Telephone # _____Work Telephone # _____

Social Security #_____ Covered Since _____

Mailing Address _____

Business Address _____

Business Telephone _____ Fax Telephone # _____

Date of Birth _____E-mail Address _____

Are you a U.S. citizen? _____ Yes _____ No If no, what country? _____

Occupation _____ Annual Income _____

State of Health _____ Insurable? _____

Armed Forces Serial Number _____Branch_____

Were you married previously? _____ Divorced/Widowed? _____

Children

Is there a physical possibility of more children? _____ Yes _____ No

Are any children adopted? ____Yes ____ No Who? _____

Are any children handicapped or in poor health? ____Yes ____No Who? _____

Child's Name _____

Address _____

Date of Birth _____ Social Security Number _____

Occupation _____ Annual Income _____ Net Worth _____

Child's Spouse's Name _____

Occupation _____ Annual Income _____

Child's Children (Grandchildren)

Name	Date of Birth	Social Security Number

Child's Name _____

Address _____

Date of Birth _____ Social Security Number _____

Occupation _____Annual Income _____Net Worth _____

Child's Spouse's Name _____

Occupation _____Annual Income _____

Child's Children (Grandchildren)

Name	Date of Birth	Social Security Number

Child's Name _____

Address _____

Date of Birth _____ Social Security Number _____

Occupation _____ Annual Income _____ Net Worth _____

Child's Spouse's Name _____

Occupation _____ Annual Income _____

Child's Children (Grandchildren)

Name	Date of Birth	Social Security Number

Child's Name _____

Address _____

Date of Birth _____ Social Security Number _____

Occupation _____Annual Income _____Net Worth _____

Child's Spouse's Name _____

Occupation _____Annual Income _____

Child's Children (Grandchildren)

Name	Date of Birth	Social Security Number

Extended Family

<u>PARENTS</u>

HUSBAND

Father _____   Mother _____

Living/Deceased _____   Living/Deceased _____

           If living: If living:

Address _____   Address _____

Date of Birth _____   Date of Birth _____

State of Health _____   State of Health _____

Financially Dependent? _____   Financially Dependent? _____

WIFE

Father _____   Mother _____

Living/Deceased _____   Living/Deceased _____

           If living: If living:

Address _____   Address _____

Date of Birth _____   Date of Birth _____

State of Health _____   State of Health _____

Financially Dependent? _____   Financially Dependent? _____

Do you have any special circumstances/concerns about your extended family? What types of concerns? _____

_____

_____

_____

_____

_____

_____

SIBLINGS

HUSBAND

Name _____ Living/Deceased _____

Age _____Marital Status _____Number of Children _____

Name _____ Living/Deceased _____

Age _____Marital Status _____Number of Children _____

Name _____ Living/Deceased _____

Age _____Marital Status _____Number of Children _____

Name _____ Living/Deceased _____

Age _____Marital Status _____Number of Children _____

WIFE

Name _____ Living/Deceased _____

Age _____Marital Status _____Number of Children _____

Name _____ Living/Deceased _____

Age _____Marital Status _____Number of Children _____

Name _____ Living/Deceased _____

Age _____Marital Status _____Number of Children _____

Name _____ Living/Deceased _____

Age _____Marital Status _____Number of Children _____

ANY EXPECTED INHERITANCES?

HUSBAND

From Whom? _____ Approximate Value _____

From Whom? _____ Approximate Value _____

WIFE

From Whom? _____ Approximate Value _____

From Whom? _____ Approximate Value _____

PROFESSIONAL ADVISORS

Name of Accountant _____

Address _____

Phone Number _____ Fax Number _____
Email _____ Website _____

Name of Financial Advisor _____

Address _____

Phone Number _____ Fax Number _____
Email _____ Website _____

Name of Insurance Agent _____

Address _____

Phone Number _____ Fax Number _____
Email _____ Website _____

Estate Analysis Checklist: Single

Appendix B | Estate Analysis Checklist: Single

General Information

Full Name _____ Name you go by _____

How do you sign your name? _____

Home Telephone # _____Work Telephone # _____

Social Security #_____

Mailing Address _____

Business Address _____

Business Telephone _____ Fax Telephone # _____

Date of Birth _____ E-mail Address _____

Are you a U.S. citizen? _____ Yes _____ No If no, what country? _____

Occupation _____ Annual Income _____

State of Health _____ Insurable? _____

Armed Forces Serial Number _____Branch_____

Were you married previously? _____ Divorced/Widowed? _____

Children

Is there a physical possibility of more children? _____Yes _____ No

Are any children adopted? _____Yes _____No

If so, list names:_____

Are any children handicapped or in poor health? _____Yes _____No

If so, list names: _____

CHILD #1

Child's Name _____

Address _____

Date of Birth _____ Social Security Number _____

Occupation _____Annual Income _____Net Worth _____

Child's Spouse's Name _____

Occupation _____Annual Income _____

Child's Children (Grandchildren)

Name	Date of Birth	Social Security Number

CHILD #2

Child's Name _____

Address _____

Date of Birth _____ Social Security Number _____

Occupation _____Annual Income _____Net Worth _____

Child's Spouse's Name _____

Occupation _____Annual Income _____

Child's Children (Grandchildren)

Name	Date of Birth	Social Security Number

CHILD #3

Child's Name _____

Address _____

Date of Birth _____ Social Security Number _____

Occupation _____Annual Income _____Net Worth _____

Child's Spouse's Name _____

Occupation _____Annual Income _____

Child's Children (Grandchildren)

Name	Date of Birth	Social Security Number

CHILD #4

Child's Name _____

Address _____

Date of Birth _____ Social Security Number _____

Occupation _____Annual Income _____Net Worth _____

Child's Spouse's Name _____

Occupation _____Annual Income _____

Child's Children (Grandchildren)

Name	Date of Birth	Social Security Number

Extended Family

PARENTS

Father _____   Mother _____

Living/Deceased _____   Living/Deceased _____

If living: If living:

Address _____   Address _____

Date of Birth _____   Date of Birth _____

State of Health _____   State of Health _____

Financially Dependent? _____   Financially Dependent? _____

SIBLINGS

Name _____ Living/Deceased _____

Age _____ Marital Status _____ Number of Children _____

Comments _____

Name _____ Living/Deceased _____

Age _____ Marital Status _____ Number of Children _____

Comments _____

Name _____ Living/Deceased _____

Age _____ Marital Status _____ Number of Children _____

Comments _____

Appendix B | Estate Analysis Checklist: Single

Name _____ Living/Deceased _____

Age _____ Marital Status _____ Number of Children _____

Comments _____

ANY EXPECTED INHERITANCES?

From Whom? _____ Approximate Value _____

From Whom? _____ Approximate Value _____

PROFESSIONAL ADVISORS

Name of Accountant _____

Address _____

Phone Number _____ Fax Number _____

Email _____ Website _____

Name of Financial Advisor _____

Address _____

Phone Number _____ Fax Number _____

Email _____ Website _____

Name of Insurance Agent _____

Address _____

Phone Number _____ Fax Number _____

Email _____ Website _____

Financial Worksheet: Married

Financial Worksheet - Married

Fill in with approximate values

ASSETS	JOINT TENANT	HUSBAND*	WIFE*
Real Estate			
Bank Accounts, CDs and Money Market Accounts			
IRA, 401(k), 403(b), etc.			
Brokerage			
Stocks			
Bonds			
Personal Property			
Car/Boat/Other Vehicles			
Business Interest			
Trademarks, Domain Names, Copyrights, Websites, etc.			
Loans/Mortgages/Notes (payable to you)			

* Identify if any assets are titled "Payable on Death" or "in Trust For"

Financial Worksheet - Married

LIABILITIES	JOINT TENANT	HUSBAND	WIFE
Mortgage			
Home Equity			
Outstanding Loans *(auto, student)*			
Other Debt *(credit card, bills, personal loans)*			

INSURANCE	JOINT	HUSBAND	WIFE
Carrier/Policy Number			
Death Benefit			
Group Term/Term/Whole Life/Variable			
Insured			
Owner			
Beneficiary			
Comments			

Financial Worksheet: Single

Financial Worksheet - Single

Fill in with approximate values

ASSETS*		LIABILITIES	
Real Estate		Mortgage	
Retirement Plan *(identify as IRA, 401(k), vested pension, Deferred Comp., or other)*		Home Equity	
Bank Accounts *(including money market accounts)*		Outstanding Loans *(auto, student)*	
CD		Other Debt *(credit cards, bills, personal loans)*	
Brokerage			
Stocks		**INSURANCE**	
		Carrier/Policy Number	
Bonds		Death Benefit	
Personal Property		Group Term/Term/Whole Life/Variable	
Car/Boat/Airplane/Other		Insured	
Business Interests		Owner	
Trademarks, Domain Names, Copyrights, Websites, etc.		Beneficiary	
Loans/Mortgages/Notes (payable to you)		Comments	

* *Identify if any assets are titled "Payable on Death" or "in Trust For"*

Glossary
Translating Legalese to English

I've compiled your personal Rosetta Stone, translating legalese to English. I find that the combination of both technical and old-fashioned language, with a bit of Latin thrown in, is a barrier to you totally understanding your estate planning documents. They're your documents, reflecting your assets, goals, and values. You should be able to read them and find yourself in them. Consider this glossary a public service.

▥ **Chapter Brief**   Legalese is a necessary evil. After all, attorneys and judges (who are attorneys) will be reading your documents when you're no longer here. However, just because it's legalese doesn't mean it's in a language you don't speak. Use this chapter as your Rosetta Stone to become smart about the law.

7520 Rate. A rate modified monthly to set the value of annuities, life estates, and remainder interests. It's equal to 120 percent of the then-published federal mid-term rate. It's used in the calculation of *Grantor Retained Annuity Trusts (GRATs)*, *Qualified Personal Residence Trusts (QPRTs)*, and other advanced tax-planning strategies.

A/B Trust Plan. An estate plan design for married couples in which a *Family Trust*, *Credit Shelter Trust*, or *Bypass Trust* is created (Trust B) and any balance passes to the spouse in a *Marital Trust* (Trust A).

Ademption. The failure of a *Specific Bequest* of property because the property no longer exists. This can be fixed by identifying in your will what happens to the bequest if the property is no longer owned by you.

Administrator/Administatrix. The person named to serve as the personal representative of an estate if the *Decedent* passes away intestate (without a will). After reading this book, needing one of these should be something that happens to other people, because you'll have your will or *Revocable Trust* in place!

Advance Directive. End-of-life care instructions. Also known as a *Living Will*.

Age-Restrictions Trust. A trust for the sole benefit of an individual that provides for distributions at a certain fixed age or ages, such as a single distribution at age 25, or distributions of half the principal at age 30 and the remaining principal at age 35. Commonly used for children and grandchildren, but a *Lifetime Trust* may be a better option.

Amendment. A change in or an addition to one or more sections of a trust. A *Revocable Trust* can be amended by the *Grantor* at any time. An irrevocable trust can only be amended in a very limited manner.

Ancillary Probate. A secondary *Probate* proceeding in a jurisdiction other than that in which the *Decedent* resided, normally due to ownership of real estate in that jurisdiction. This can be avoided through the use of a *Revocable Trust.*

Anti-Lapse Statute. Under common law, if a beneficiary predeceases the testator, a *Specific Bequest Lapses* or ceases to be in effect, and the assets subject to the bequest instead pass to the residuary estate. If the person was a residuary beneficiary, then the portion set aside for that person under the will passes through the intestate rules and not under the will. An Anti-Lapse Statute changes that rule to distribute the otherwise-lapsed assets to the issue of the deceased beneficiary or other classes of beneficiaries. Better yet, you should say in your documents who gets the asset if the beneficiary predeceases you.

Applicable Credit Amount. The *Estate Tax Exemption Amount* multiplied by the tax rate to determine its worth in taxes, not total dollars. Also called the *Unified Credit Amount.* If the Estate Tax Exemption Amount is $1 million, the Applicable Credit Amount will be $345,800.

Applicable Exemption Amount. Referred to in this book as the *Estate Tax Exemption Amount*, this is the amount of dollars excluded from estate tax. This amount was $5,120,000 in 2012 and is scheduled to be reduced to $1 million in 2013.

Attorney-in-Fact. The person named to act as a *Fiduciary* under a *Power of Attorney* to make financial decisions for you if you can't.

Beneficiary. The person for whose benefit a trust is established. A trust can have one or more beneficiaries.

Beneficiary Trust. A category of trusts for the benefit of a younger generation. These include the *Age-Restrictions Trust, Lifetime Trust, Common-Pot Trust,* and *Generation-Skipping Trust.*

Bypass Trust. A trust created at the death of the first spouse to die, containing an amount of dollars up to the federal *Estate Tax Exemption Amount.* The trust is for the benefit of the surviving spouse (and possibly children). The purpose is for the balance of the Bypass Trust to pass estate-tax-free on the death of the surviving spouse. It's also referred to as a *Family Trust, Credit Shelter Trust,* or *Trust B* of an *A/B Trust Plan* in the context of estate tax planning.

Charitable Lead Trust (CLT). A split-interest trust between a charity and individual beneficiaries where the charity receives a percentage of the assets of the trust for a fixed time period and the remainder is distributed to the individual beneficiaries at the end of that term. A contribution to a CLT creates a deduction for income tax, gift tax, and estate tax purposes.

Charitable Remainder Trust (CRT). A split-interest trust between a charity and individual beneficiaries where the individual(s) receives a percentage of the assets of the trust for a fixed time period and the remainder is distributed to the charity at the end of the term. Like a *Charitable Lead Trust (CLT),* a CRT creates a deduction for income tax, gift tax, and estate tax purposes.

Codicil. An amendment to a will that modifies or adds one or more sections of the original will. The original will, together with all of its codicils, makes up the collective document that governs the distribution of your assets upon death.

Common-Pot Trust. A *Sprinkle Trust* where the trustee has the discretion to distribute assets among the beneficiaries without regard to any prior distributions made. The trust is typically created for group of children until the youngest child reaches a threshold age or life event, at which point it's separated into individual trusts for each beneficiary.

Community Property. A form of joint property ownership between spouses in certain states in which each spouse is deemed to own 50 percent of any assets acquired during the marriage.

Contingent Beneficiary. A beneficiary who receives an interest under a will or trust only in the event that an occurrence comes to pass. That occurrence is typically the death of another beneficiary, but it may be another standard set by the person creating the will or trust.

Credit Shelter Trust. A trust funded at the death of the first spouse to die with an amount of dollars up the federal *Estate Tax Exemption Amount.* The trust is for the benefit of the surviving spouse (and possibly children) and is designed to pass estate-tax-free on the death of the surviving spouse. It's also referred to as a *Family Trust, Bypass Trust,* or *Trust B* in the context of tax planning.

Cy-Près Doctrine. A power held by the court to amend a charitable trust or bequest to correct it to be as near as possible to the testator's intent. It's applied to prevent a charitable bequest from failing if the organization isn't then in existence by distributing the assets to another organization.

Decedent. The formal name referring to the person who died. Much more respectful than "the dead guy."

Durable Power Of Attorney. A *Power of Attorney* that continues to be effective following the disability of the person making it. Any Power of Attorney that is part of your estate plan needs to contain this provision.

Dynasty Trust. A *Generation-Skipping or -Sharing Trust* designed to pass assets from generation to generation in trust in perpetuity (forever) without being included in the taxable estate of successive generations.

EGGTRA. The *Economic Growth and Tax Relief Reconciliation Act* of 2001 (aka the "Bush Tax Cuts"), which radically modified the tax code through massive tax reductions, including changes to the gift and estate tax laws.

Equivalent Exemption Amount. Referred to in this book as the *Estate Tax Exemption Amount* but technically named the *Applicable Exemption Amount, Unified Credit Amount,* or Equivalent Exemption Amount. The amount of dollars excluded from estate tax. This amount was $5,120,000 in 2012 but is scheduled to be reduced to $1 million in 2013.

Estate Tax Exemption Amount. With the technical name *Applicable Exemption Amount, Unified Credit Amount* or *Equivalent Exemption Amount,* this is the amount of dollars excluded from estate tax. This amount is $5,120,000 in 2012 but is scheduled to be reduced to $1 million in 2013.

Executor/Executrix. A person who is nominated in a will to be in charge of the *Decedent's Probate* assets at death. This person is in charge of carrying out the instructions in the will after payment of all debts, expenses, and taxes. They're akin to the president of the business that is your estate. Also known in some states as the *Personal Representative.*

Fair Market Value. The value of an item for tax purposes. The shorthand formula is the price for which a willing seller and willing buyer in possession of all the facts would transact the item.

Family Trust. The name I use to refer to a trust for the benefit of the surviving spouse (and possibly children), designed to pass estate-tax-free on the death of the surviving spouse. The Family Trust is created with an amount of dollars up to the federal *Estate Tax Exemption Amount* of the first spouse to die. It's also referred to as a *Credit Shelter Trust, Bypass Trust,* or Trust B in the context of tax planning. A Family Trust can be more generally used to describe a *Sprinkle Trust* for a person and their children (such as your sister and nieces and nephews).

Fiduciary. A person acting in a position of trust for the benefit of other individuals. This would include an *Executor, Trustee, Guardian, Attorney-in-Fact,* or *Health Care Representative.*

Form 1040. Income tax form for individuals.

Form 1041. Income tax form for trusts and estates.

Form 706. Estate tax return.

Form 709. Gift tax return.

General Bequest. Also called a *Residuary Bequest.* Identifies the beneficiaries of all your remaining assets in your will or *Revocable Trust* after payment of debts, expense, taxes, and any *Specific Bequests.* It should identify primary and *Contingent Beneficiaries* in case someone passes away before you.

General Durable Power of Attorney. Document granting your *Attorney-in-Fact* financial control over all your assets. Because it's durable, it continues in effect if you become incompetent in the future. This is the preferred form of *Power of Attorney* for estate planning purposes.

Generation-Skipping Tax (GST Tax). A tax levied on any amount of dollars in excess of your exemption from Generation-Skipping Taxes on any assets passing from your estate to a member of a skip generation (grandchildren or relations 37.5 years younger). The GST Tax rate is currently 55 percent.

Generation-Skipping Tax Exemption Amount (GST Exemption Amount). An amount of dollars that can pass to members of a skip generation (grandchildren or relations 37.5 years younger) GST-tax-free. The exemption can be applied to transfers during life (*Inter-Vivos*) or at death. The GST Exemption Amount is $5,120,000 in 2012 and is scheduled to be reduced to $1 million in 2013.

Generation-Skipping Trust (GST Trust). A trust designed to pass tax-free upon the death of one generation (your children) to the next generation (your grandchildren). It can be funded during life (*Inter-Vivos*) or at death (*Testamentary*) with an amount up to your exclusion from *Generation-Skipping Taxes.* If the trust is designed also to pass estate-tax-free in your grandchildren's estates to their descendants and so on, it might also be called a Generation-Sharing Trust *or Dynasty Trust.*

Grantor. A person who creates a trust. Also called the *Trustor* or *Settlor.*

Grantor Retained Annuity Trust (GRAT). An advanced tax-strategy trust designed to allow a person to pass assets to beneficiaries at little or no gift-tax cost by investing in assets with a rate of return in excess of the *7520 Rate.*

Gross Taxable Estate. The total value of all the assets in your taxable estate before any deductions.

Guardian. *Fiduciary* in charge of a minor person (under age 18).

Health Care Proxy. Document naming a *Health Care Representative* to make medical decisions for you if you're unable to make them yourself. Also known as a *Medical Power of Attorney.*

Health Care Representative. *Fiduciary* named to make medical decisions if you're unable to do so for yourself.

Holographic Will. A will entirely in the handwriting of the *Testator.*

Inforce Illustration. A projection of the continued viability of an insurance policy based on assumptions based on the current economic conditions.

Inter-Vivos. An action taken during lifetime. This applies to the creation of a trust or the exercise of a power of appointment, for example.

Intestacy. A distribution of assets by state statute when a person dies without a will or *Revocable Trust.* Don't let this happen to you—make a will!

Irrevocable Life Insurance Trust (ILIT). A trust designed to be both the owner and beneficiary of one or more life insurance policies so they aren't included in your taxable estate upon death.

Joint Tenants with Right of Survivorship (JTWROS). Form of ownership where one or more people own an asset together and the surviving owner(s) gets all of the asset at the death of one owner.

Lapse. The failure of a *Specific* or *Residuary Bequest* because the identified beneficiary predeceased the *Testator.*

Lifetime Trust. A trust created within a will or other trust document (revocable or irrevocable) that lasts for a term defined by the life of one of the beneficiaries. This is commonly used as a trust for a child and their issue, where the trust lasts for the child's lifetime.

Limited Power of Attorney. A document in which you give another person the ability to make financial decisions for you under very limited circumstances, such as the purchase or sale of real estate. Not useful in an estate plan.

Living Trust. A document that distributes your assets at death as a will substitute. By funding the trust with your assets during life, you can potentially avoid *Probate* upon your death. Also called a *Revocable Trust.*

Living Will. End-of-life care instructions. Also known as an *Advance Directive*.

Marital Trust. A trust for the sole benefit of the spouse designed to qualify for the unlimited marital deduction from gift and estate taxes. The spouse can be the only beneficiary and must get all of the income generated by the trust each year. Also known as a *Qualified Terminable Interest Trust (QTIP)* or *Trust A* in an *A/B Trust Plan,*

Medical Power of Attorney. Document naming a *Health Care Representative* to make medical decisions for you if you're unable to make them yourself. Also known as a *Health Care Proxy.*

Net Taxable Estate. The gross taxable estate minus debts, expenses, and deductions. The estate tax rate is applied to this amount to determine the *Tentative Estate Tax.* The *Applicable Credit Amount* (the *Estate Tax Exemption Amount* multiplied by the estate tax rate) is subtracted from the *Tentative Estate Tax* to arrive at the estate tax due.

Non-Probate. Assets held as Joint Tenants with Right of Survivorship or are *Payable on Death* to a named beneficiary and thereby avoid the *Probate* process because they pass to the beneficiary by *Operation of Law* and outside of a will. Also includes assets owned by a *Revocable Trust.*

Operation of Law. Distribution of assets at death due to their titling as *Joint Tenants with Right of Survivorship* or *Payable on Death* to a named beneficiary. Assets that pass by Operation of Law avoid *Probate.*

Payable on Death. Assets that by the terms of the contract governing them are directed to a named beneficiary and avoid *Probate* upon the death of the owner. Also called *Transfer on Death.*

Pecuniary Bequest. A bequest of a specific amount of money.

Per Capita. A distribution scheme whereby the assets are left to a group of people, and if one the beneficiaries dies before the *Testator*, the deceased beneficiary's share is divided among the other then-living beneficiaries in the group. For example, if you have four siblings and one dies, each of the remaining three receives one third of your estate.

Per Stirpes. A distribution scheme whereby the assets are left to a group of people, and if one the beneficiaries dies before the *Testator*, the deceased beneficiary's share is distributed to their then-living descendants. If you have four siblings and one dies, survived by two children, each sibling receives one quarter of your estate and the deceased sibling's children each receive one eighth.

Personal Representative. A person who is nominated in a will to be in charge of the *Decedent's Probate* assets at death. The person is in charge of carrying out the instructions in the will or following the state *Intestacy* statutes if there is no will (gasp!), after payment of all debts, expenses, and taxes. Also known in some states as the *Executor* or *Administrator*.

Power of Appointment. A right given to a person to alter the distribution of a trust by reallocating the trust to another person or person.

Power of Attorney. Document granting your *Attorney-in-Fact* financial control over all your assets.

Probate. The process of transferring legal title from a deceased person to their beneficiaries, following satisfaction of all creditors of the *Decedent*.

Qualified Domestic Trust (QDOT). A marital trust created for the benefit of a noncitizen spouse to allow estate taxes on the assets funding the trust to be deferred until the earlier of (1) the distribution of principal of the trust for reasons other than hardship or (2) the death of the surviving spouse.

Qualified Personal Residence Trust (QPRT). A split-interest trust in which the *Grantor* gives away a remainder interest in residential real property and maintains the right to live in the property for a term of years. If the Grantor survives the term of years, then the residence is transferred to the remainder beneficiaries for a reduced gift tax value.

Qualified Terminable Interest Trust (QTIP). A trust that qualifies for the unlimited marital deduction from estate taxes. The trust must provide that the surviving spouse receives all the income at least annually and that there are no other beneficiaries of the trust during the surviving spouse's lifetime. The *Executor* of the estate of the first spouse to die must elect for the trust to qualify for the marital deduction, and by that election agrees that any balance of the QTIP trust will be included in the taxable estate of the second spouse to die.

Remainder. The amount passing to a beneficiary after the completion of a certain condition. Example: If the trust is "For Stacy during her lifetime, and then to Mike," Mike will be the beneficiary of the Remainder after Stacy passes away.

Residuary Bequest. Identifies the beneficiaries of all your remaining assets in your will or *Revocable Trust* after payment of debts, expenses, taxes, and any *Specific Bequests*. Also called a *General Bequest*.

Restatement. A complete and total amendment of a *Revocable Trust* so that the new document (the restated trust) is the effective document and all prior versions of the Revocable Trust or any amendments are deemed null and void and of no further effect.

Revocable Trust. A possible centerpiece of your estate plan. This document distributes your assets at death as a will substitute. By funding the trust with your assets during life, you can potentially avoid *Probate* upon your death. Also known as a *Living Trust.*

Right of Representation. A method of determining the proportion of inheritance among the group of beneficiaries that provides that each beneficiary of the oldest generation, plus any children of a member of that generation who has passed away, share an inheritance equally. If a person had three children, and one child has passed away and is survived by two children, then each of the two children and the two grandchildren receives one quarter of the residuary estate.

Rule Against Perpetuities. A common-law concept prohibiting a trust from staying in existence indefinitely by mandating an outright distribution to its beneficiaries at some future point in time. This has been repealed in some jurisdictions, allowing for a *Dynasty Trust* to be created.

Settlor. A person who creates a trust. Also called the *Grantor* or *Trustor.*

Special-Needs Trust (SNT). A trust designed for the benefit of a person who may need to qualify for public benefits (Medicaid, SSI, and so on) at some point in the future. The assets held in the trust are not deemed available assets for purposes of determining financial eligibility for such public benefits.

Specific Bequest. A distribution upon death of a specific asset or sum of money. This is paid before any *Residuary Bequest* is satisfied.

Spendthrift Provision. A restriction in a trust preventing the beneficiary from having any power to sell, distribute, pledge, or otherwise transfer the assets in the trust. The existence of this provision creates asset protection for the beneficiary against any creditor.

Springing Power of Attorney. A *Power of Attorney* that becomes effective only upon the occurrence of certain events, such as a physician's diagnosis of mental incompetence.

Sprinkle Trust. A trust that permits the trustee to make discretionary distributions to one or more of the beneficiaries based on each beneficiary's needs.

State Estate Tax. A tax on assets levied by a state as a result of a person's death. It's separate from any federal estate tax.

Tax-Allocation Clause. Direction to your *Executor* or *Personal Representative* about who should pay taxes. The payment normally comes from the residuary but can be allocated among people based on how much of your assets they receive.

Tenants by the Entireties. A form of joint property ownership between spouses where each spouse is treated as owning 100 percent of the asset. It provides asset protection because the assets can't be used to satisfy a claim against only one spouse.

Tenants in Common. A form of joint property ownership where each owner has a specified percentage of the asset in their name, which will pass pursuant to that owner's estate plan and not to the co-owner(s).

Tentative Estate Tax. The *Net Taxable Estate* multiplied by the estate tax rate. The *Applicable Credit Amount* (the *Estate Tax Exemption Amount* multiplied by the estate tax rate) is subtracted from the Tentative Estate Tax to arrive at the estate tax due.

Testamentary. Something that happens under a will or is created under a will, as opposed to an *Inter-Vivos* action, which takes place during your lifetime.

Testate. To die with a will.

Testator/Testatrix. The person making a will. (As with *Executor/Executrix*, "or" designates a male and "-ix" designates a female.)

Transfer on Death. Assets that by terms of the contract governing them are directed to a named beneficiary and avoid *Probate* upon the death of the owner. Also called *Payable on Death*.

Trust Protector. A person or group of people charged with the limited role of removing and/or replacing a *Trustee* of an irrevocable trust.

Trustee. The person in charge of any type of trust. This person exercises all control over the investments in the trust and the distributions from the trust.

Trustor. A person who creates a trust. Also called the *Grantor* or *Settlor*.

Unified Credit Amount. The *Estate Tax Exemption Amount* multiplied by the tax rate to determine its worth in taxes, not total dollars. Also called the *Applicable Credit Amount*. If the Estate Tax Exemption Amount is $1 million, the Applicable Credit Amount is $345,800.

Index

I

N

Needs-based benefits, of SNT, 266
Network. *See* Storage and network
New York, trustee compensation in, 166
No-contest clause, 218
Noncitizens, planning guide for, 253
  annual and lifetime gifts, 255
  noncitizen spouse, estate-tax exemption
    to, 254
  planning alternatives, 256
    gifting, 257
    ILIT, 256
    illiquid assets, 257
    unitrust, 257
    US citizen, 257
  QDOT, 254
  tax treaties, 256
Noncitizen spouse, estate-tax exemption to,
  254
Non-probate assets, 40, 183, 288
  joint accounts, 290
  life insurance, 290
  pay-on-death accounts, 292
  retirement plan beneficiary designations,
    288
Non-probate assets
  annual review of, 294
  in estate plan, 223
    joint tenants, with rights of
      survivorship, 223
    pay-on-death accounts, 224
    retirement accounts, 224

O

Online services, for estate planning, 283
Open group, 17
Organ donation, 101
Out-of-state real estate, 274
Outright gift, 127

P

Parents, planning guide for, 259
  financing long-term care, 261

  leaving assets, 262
  legal obligations, 261
  shifting care relationship, 260
  tax burden, 259
  tax considerations, 262
Partner-owned life insurance, 244
Pay-on-death (POD) accounts, 65, 224, 292
Perpetuities, rule against, 52
Peripheral interface standards. *See* Advanced
    Technology Attachment (ATA)
Permanent insurance, 134
Personal property, 27, 274
  and will, 42
Personal share, of assets, 26
POD account. *See* Pay-on-death (POD)
  account
Portability, 207
Pourover will, 69
Power of attorney. *See* Attorney, power of
Practical authority, on family business, 245
Predators, 19, 80
Prenuptial agreement, 237
Primary beneficiaries, 17
Private debt, 37
Probate
  assets, 40, 287
  avoidance, 59
  avoidance and privacy, 274
  process, 58
Public standards organizations. *See*
    Standards-developing organization
    (SDO)
Pull the plug authorization, 99

Q

QDOT. *See* Qualified domestic trust
  (QDOT)
QPRT. *See*Qualified personal residence trust
  (QPRT)
QTIP trust. *See* Qualified terminable interest
  property (QTIP) trust
Qualified domestic trust (QDOT), 254
Qualified interest, 144
Qualified personal residence trust (QPRT),
  144, 145, 279

CPSIA information can be obtained at www.ICGtesting.com
Printed in the USA
LVOW06s1401071015

457313LV00002BA/248/P